SONG
WITHOUT
WORDS

SONG
WITHOUT
WORDS

Discovering My Deafness
Halfway through Life

GERALD SHEA

A Merloyd Lawrence Book
DA CAPO PRESS
A Member of the Perseus Books Group

All translations of works quoted from the French are by the author.

Library of Congress Cataloging-in-Publication Data
Shea, Gerald, 1942–
Song without words : discovering my deafness
halfway through life / Gerald Shea.
pages cm
"A Merloyd Lawrence Book."
Includes index.
ISBN 978-0-306-82193-6 (hardcover)—
ISBN 978-0-306-82194-3 (e-book)
1. Shea, Gerald, 1942– 2. Deaf—United States—Biography.
3. Deaf lawyers—United States—Biography. I. Title.
HV2534.S.S54A3 2013
362.4'2092—dc23
[B]
2012042840

Published as a Merloyd Lawrence Book by Da Capo Press
A Member of the Perseus Books Group
www.dacapopress.com

Da Capo Press books are available at special discounts for bulk
purchases in the U.S. by corporations, institutions, and other organizations. For
more information, please contact the Special Markets Department at the Perseus
Books Group, 2300 Chestnut Street, Suite 200, Philadelphia, PA 19103, or call
(800) 810-4145, ext. 5000, or e-mail special.markets@perseusbooks.com.

10 9 8 7 6 5 4 3 2 1

FOR CLAIRE

*"Je ne marche pas seul . . . et la route est
moins longue en la faisant à deux."*

—FERDINAND BERTHIER

The most beautiful privilege of man is undoubtedly his ability to communicate his thoughts and feelings. This precious faculty forms the gentlest knot of society, enabling souls to touch and hearts to mingle. Our joys would soon decay and die within us if we could no longer convey to the bosom of a friend the emotions that stir within our own. A pleasure shared is sweeter, a sorrow lighter. Tears of compassion flow through the heart of the unfortunate like a balm that heals its wounds, just as they soothe the cares of those who shed them. This commerce of souls is for all of us more than a simple pleasure; it is a necessity. Sever the links that bind man to man, and his life is no longer a gift from heaven; it becomes an almost unbearable burden. Without memory, without hope, his existence is linked neither to past nor to future, and comes to a standstill with the needs of each moment, filled with anxiety and sorrow.

—Roch-Ambroise Auguste Bébian,
In Praise of the Abbé de l'Épée, 1819

A light breeze sprang up and set the reeds and bulrushes rustling. Rat, who was in the stern of the boat while Mole sculled, sat up suddenly and listened with passionate intentness. "It's gone! So beautiful and strange and new! Since it was to end so soon, I almost wish I had never heard it. For it has roused a longing in me that is pain, and nothing seems worthwhile but just to hear that sound once more and go on listening to it forever. No! There it is again! O, Mole, the beauty of it! The merry bubble and joy, the thin, clear happy call of the distant piping! Such music I never dreamed of, and the call in it is stronger even than the music is sweet! Row on, Mole, row! For the music and the call must be for us."

—Kenneth Grahame,
The Wind in the Willows, 1908

By ordering me to spare my hearing as much as possible, my intelligent doctor almost fell in with my own present frame of mind, though sometimes I ran counter to it by yielding to my desire for companionship. But what a humiliation for me when someone standing next to me heard a flute in the distance and I heard nothing, or someone heard a shepherd singing and again I heard nothing. Such incidents drove me almost to despair; a little more of that and I would have ended my life—it was only my art that held me back.

—Ludwig von Beethoven, age thirty-one,
Heiligenstadt Testament, 1802

CONTENTS

SONG
WITHOUT
WORDS

For Armin and
Barbara, who
have done so much
for so many,

With
admiration,

Gerry

March 16, 2013

CHAPTER 1

THE INVISIBLE CURTAIN

IN THE BEGINNING I HEARD THEIR VOICES WITH clarity. The days of my early childhood are distant now, but the comfort of the words of those I loved is engraved in my memory. We had just bought a large house on top of a hill in Riverdale, north of Manhattan. I remember the singing in the garden, so many birds, music instead of the early morning horns and sirens that had breached the walls and windows of our apartment in the city. I heard the birds that morning too, outside my window, urging me to stay home from school and listen all day. I was six years old. I woke up tired and, in spite of the music, did not want to venture out nor to make the long walk down the hill. I pretended to be sick. The family doctor came and announced that "the boy has the chicken pox"—I'd fooled him! He returned a day later and said, "The boy has scarlet fever."

In fact, I had both, and the next fourteen days were a battleground of fever and infection, along with an erupting mass of rashes and poxes, mostly red, periodically puffing into large white boils. Every other morning a nurse came, took a needle out of her small black bag, and lanced the latest litter. I was separated from my three brothers and lived in my parents' bedroom, while they took the guest room beside it. I still remember the approaching footsteps of Mrs. Pearce, and I imagine her today as the attractive, unassuming nurse who cuts off the thumbs of Willem Dafoe in *The English Patient—doh cuh be doh tuh don't cut me.* The boils were afraid of her, too, and showed it in a throbbing crescendo as she approached the top step.

My first day up, when I looked in the mirror, the face I saw seemed someone else's; I had to strain to distinguish the eyes, the nose, and the mouth from all the other holes around them, as if the dots were there to be connected to find them. When I went downstairs to breakfast, my father, who had delayed going to work until I appeared, gave me an enormous hug and a kiss on each pitted cheek.

"Jack—" said Mother.

"I can't go back to school, Daddy," I said. "I don't ever want to go back to school."

Up to that point in my life, my father had been a distant authority, like a judge you had to please for his regard or, if you had broken a window or locked your baby brother in his room, to make a reasoned or at least contrite appeal if you wanted to escape confinement to your bedroom. But to my astonishment he said, smiling, that I would never have to go back to school unless I wanted to. It was the last time he would take me in his arms.

By the end of four more weeks the scars had faded, and I decided to return to school, my father never having raised the question again. What none of us knew was that the real battle had been a covert one, waged in the cochlea, the most complex, sensitive, and vulnerable component of the ear. I had in fact won part of the battle against scarlet fever, for a number of epithelial cells (hair cells) in the cochlea of both of my ears emerged relatively intact. Many other people have lost the fight, recovering only to find themselves profoundly deaf, including Alexander Graham Bell's mother; his wife, Mabel; his celebrated protégée, Helen Keller; and her precursor in Boston, Laura Bridgman. Illnesses left virtually all of their epithelial cells dead or moribund.

My epithelial cells for some reason managed to remain alive and unaffected in the cochlea's winding upper paths, which give us low-frequency sounds. But most consonants and some vowels (*ee*, *ih*, *ah*) gradually faded to softness, as the epithelial cells in the lower part of the cochlea declined. While Mrs. Pearce was popping the boils, the fever was permanently wilting these cells in my ears. Unlike certain regenerative or self-repairing parts of the human body, like fingernails, bones, and the liver, when these cells wilt, they never grow back.

Prior to my illness the sounds of crickets, birds, and water were unmistakably clear and distinguishable, and like the early voices of those I loved, they are fixed in my memory. But as the pockmarks faded, my young life was transformed into a mysterious play in reverse, shaped by the slow descent of an invisible curtain creating a quieter world—and isolating me within it. The following summer, on the North Shore of Massachusetts, at my grandfather's house at Marblehead's Main Harbor, birdsongs were thinning out and the sounds of crickets growing dim, though they, the wind, and the waves were also acquiring new voices for me. As the absence of consonants in my playmates' words turned them into mysteries, those voices of nature were my new acquaintances, short-lived but graced with a fading, irresolvable beauty.

Along with the ephemeral voices of wind and wave come the *lyricals* produced by speech. These are what I call the transitional words, wrong words, and often nonwords that, in lieu of those

actually spoken, register in the minds of the partially deaf. Lyricals
show us the way to the right ones. When I finally returned to
school, I wasn't conscious of any change, just increasingly tentative
about what people were trying to say. I slid gradually into a particular world, though I thought it one that everyone else experienced
exactly as I did.

"Gerry, you have nothing to work with. Come get a *plaa
bencer*."

"What—?" *bencer pencer*

"Up here, on the table beside the *maa more*." The box near the
maa more, the *blackboard*, was full of *pencers pencils*. I took a blue
one.

"No. *Paa*."

"Ba."

"*Blaa*."

"Bla."

"*Black*!"

"Sorry, sorry. Black."

For me, spoken words were a riddle I assumed everyone had to
figure out, an exercise we all had to practice in order to understand
the spoken language of others. I was to live with this assumption,
to believe in it, for almost three decades. I am sure that my
mother's words when I was a child were magically clear, spoken in
close intimacy. In later life I could always hear women in proximity, facing me, in the light, speaking softly. But the words of most
people—teachers and professors in classrooms, children in a
courtyard, characters on a stage, actors in a movie, and lawyers and
bankers sitting around a table—were all puzzles to be solved. I
believed others had to solve them too but were simply better at it
than I.

As a child I remained happy in the halfway world that scarlet
fever created, though I knew not "factor" from "tractor" from

"actor" from "sacked her," and so on, except by context and lips and the sounds of most vowels. But this sheltered happiness was short-lived. My father, who had been so concerned about my own health, would die of a rheumatic heart less than a year later. Mother bustled us into St. Elizabeth's Hospital, where we saw him for the last time, pale and thin and lying in an oxygen tent. I don't recall his saying anything—just his smile. I can't imagine today what he was thinking as he looked through his own invisible curtain at Mother and at us, his four children—Patrick, George, myself, and John, ages two, four, six, and eight—and contemplated our future without him.

CHAPTER 2

HOUSE OF MYSTERIES

I LOVE MY LANGUAGE OF LYRICALS, MY SECOND TONGUE. When others speak, I, and millions of others like me, hear only the contours of an elusive language to which, in the rapid course of conversation, we endeavor to give meaning. The words of our language, its lyricals, are formed by the stream of high-pitched vowels that must be translated back into the words that were actually spoken. The transitions stir the imagination with nonexistent places and people, like the *Doubtful Asphodels* not found on any library shelves of Nabokov's prose. Though lyricals usually show the way to the commonplace expressions of other voices, their path can also take an uncharted course where the spoken "what'll happen after Nora leaves" becomes the lyrical *water happens after coral reefs*, and "her way of speaking gently" yields *arrays of seas he lent me.*

I don't remember grammar school as being academically difficult, in spite of my confusion over what people were saying. Writing and arithmetic were not complicated, and I could do both rather well even if questions and answers passed me by in the classroom. I could still hear most vowels (low-frequency sounds) and a few consonants (high-frequency). My lyricals were born of the sounds that were left. Lipreading, with varying degrees of proficiency, is a talent naturally acquired by partially deaf children and those who become partially deaf years or decades later, provided they retain useful residual hearing, as I have. The speech we do hear, the lips we see, and the context we discern give us a mix of words and lyricals that lead us, gradually, as our minds race through them, to the speaker's words and thus to his ideas.

There is an immense linguistic distance between children born profoundly or severely deaf, to whom spoken language is out of reach at all frequencies, and those who, like me, lose only part of their hearing after they have acquired fluent speech. If a child is able to hear half-words, or half of the words, he will turn naturally to lyricals. If not, he will rely just as naturally on his eyes and his hands—on sign language. If you cannot hear at all, it is extremely difficult, if not impossible, to learn to speak well, for the ear is in effect an organ of speech as well as of hearing.

Everyone needs—it is a universal need—to be able to use his own language, the one in which he can most effectively express himself and understand others. Very few prelingually deaf people are able to speak with any degree of clarity, and even they arrive at that point only after painstaking effort and years and years of dedicated help from parents, speech therapists, and others. They are able to make themselves understood by the hearing only with difficulty and not at all by the deaf, whether those who sign or those who read lips. The deaf child thus naturally turns to sign, in which he can express his own thoughts and understand the ideas of others as immediately as the hearing do when they speak and listen.

When I heard new words for the first time after returning to school, I would listen carefully and focus on the blackboard and the word lists in a grammar book ("opaque," "prism") or labels on a map ("Caribbean," "Hebrides"). If there was a general silence, I could still guess at the consonants when spoken, and I could sometimes read them on the teacher's lips if there was a good light. I knew how the consonants were pronounced, and, of course, I could say them myself since I had been speaking for five years. When that didn't occur, I'd let the new word go and try to find out what it was later, though of course the word was then used in lyrical-studded sentences in which whole phrases could be missing.

The meter of our tongue can be helpful too, and I'm sure I used its clues as a child time and again. For example, the triple spondee of vowels *euh oh ay* is all confusion. But the dactylic expression *be airful washing the trees* rather easily becomes "be careful crossing the street." If that phrase has been spoken immediately following *euh oh ay*, the longer phrase's lyricals, born largely of its meter, readily transform the spondee into "look both ways!"

For children like me, blackboards and other visual aids are critical instruments of learning, as are books accompanying speech, cards around the upper walls of the classroom with letters and words, reading primers, a seat in the front of the room. But above all the problem needs to be *identified*, as mine was not. Along with the other students entering the first grade in Riverdale, I was given a hearing test; this was a few months before I contracted scarlet fever. I remember the very large earphones, made for the enormous heads of grown-ups, put on my head, and I recall pressing a button at the sounds of beeps and bells. But whether as a result of neglect or inattention or custom, it was the only test I would have until, almost by chance, I finally had another one at age thirty-three.

I welcomed many of the classroom visual aids in grammar school, though my silent world remained invisible. I learned to laugh often, to sing (musical notes in the lower ranges are far more audible than consonants and do not carry a precise message), to speak as often and as long as I could, to enjoy the clarity of my own voice (you always know what you're saying), and to puzzle through the obscurity of others. My own spoken and singing voice and the lyricals of others thus became my language, as they are today. Elocution helped, too. I *loved* our elocution teacher in the second grade, Mrs. Moroni, spelled like the legendary Mormon angel. Her voice appeared to emanate from her enormous bosom, which, when showing us how to recite poetry, she thrust forth with each beat to punctuate her trumpeted dactyls and spondees. She would bounce them (the spondees) off the blackboards: "I'M an a-MERican, YES SIR REE, and it's a WONderful PRIVilege DAD TELLS ME!" and "ABu ben AD-hem aWOKE ONE NIGHT [unsurprisingly] from a DEEP DREAM of PEACE!"

Music was always present in clear, lovely lows. The winter after my father died, we were shown a movie at school about a whale who sang opera—a miracle, really, because whales have no larynx and breathe through an aperture at the top of their head. Undaunted, this whale managed to sing a number of arias throughout the film, though I remember only one, "Figaro," which I thought was his name. He would sing above water, dive under, breach, spray, turn over on his back, and keep on singing, enchanting the Italian sailors, who, ordered by their captain to harpoon him, danced instead to *lu lu la Figaro, ha ho ha he he ho, ha ah oh Figaro, la lo la dee dee doe, tortela dee dee doe, tortela be be doe, tortela dee dee doe, oh ta ta ta*—my version of "*ah bravo Figaro, bravo bravissimo, ah bravo Figaro, bravo bravissimo, fortunatissimo, fortunatissimo, fortunatissimo per verità!*"

The film was a fantasy created by music-loving animators at the Disney studios during World War II to keep themselves occupied while not working on propaganda films. It was a heavenly production, an enchanting dream until, at the end, poor Figaro was finally harpooned and sent to heaven. The image of the whale stays with me still: his happiness and the way music, even without violins, high winds, and overtones, can take you over, hold your attention, stay in your head, and keep you smiling—long after your return to the mumbled mysteries of the classroom—and singing even as you come home and as you put your head on the pillow at night.

My father's last present to me was a radio in the shape of a house. I kept it for years and loved it both for its origin and for the mysteries that emerged from its peaked red roof, white walls, and green shutters, all made of wood. I never understood my house's offerings of plots or words, but I recognized all the programs and the principals' voices (Sky King, the Green Hornet, Sergeant Preston, Jack Benny, Fred Allen, and others). I could pick their respective vowels out in a split second, but the words were generally not there, other than stock phrases like "You're under arrest in the name of the queen!"

The Lone Ranger, too, appeared in my house of mysteries and then on television: the man who wore the black mask over his eyes and shot silver bullets. I never understood what the Lone Ranger was doing, but he looked terrific on TV, and his opponents were clearly up to no good. It was reassuring to see him, unlike the hapless Figaro, prevailing over his enemies week after week. But for me the real message of *The Lone Ranger*, what I waited for each week and throughout the program's mumbling images of heroes and villains, was the *end*, when he rode to the blaring winds, booming basses, and beating drums of an orchestra playing "The William Tell Overture." This was the part to look forward to every time, the part I could understand, as it showed how well and how fast he could ride to the music of the just. He was the second of my two Rossini heroes: the one with the mask and the snow-white horse, who lived in wide-open spaces.

It is hard to say whether my hearing was better in grade school than in high school or college, or whether I had to use lyricals increasingly as time went by. My unnamed lyricals were a natural part of my life, and I never took their measure. I had several sensitive teachers, yet all I remember from our personal encounters are degrees of puzzlement. In the sixth grade I wrote a poem about the beauty of something—of mayflowers or the Virgin or both—I don't recall. It was ungrammatical, but I thought it worked. Two nuns puzzled over it and asked me to come up and discuss the words with them. They spoke in confusing sentences that were more complex than the poem itself: "*Where to you be here*, Gerry, 'so near as beautiful'—*clearly* as beautiful?" *clearly nearly—where do you be here what do you be you mean?* Another teacher took me aside one day into an adjacent, empty classroom because, she said, I seemed to be drifting, lost somewhere: "*To you wah do dah about it?*" *Do you want to talk about it?* She wasn't concerned about academics but about where my mind was at these times. I imagine I was trying to figure words out, or taking a break from doing so, or going back over them—I don't know. But I was surprised by the interview, which left me in tears.

People at a distance were always impossible to understand. On Sunday mornings the prayers of the congregation, said collectively aloud, were to me a mumbling, over and over again, throughout the church, of what sounded like *pissa pissa tumity* (*blessed is the fruit of thy—?*). After a time, I began to recite it aloud in order to talk like the rest of the faithful, until an angry lady with a black-dotted veil attached to her dowdy dark beret turned around and told me to stop. Perhaps, I thought, I was too young to pray. Priests' sermons were always streams of piously intoned unfathomables, but I would listen to the nonsense and search for enlightenment in the timbre of their voices.

The mysteries pervaded lay assemblies too. The year after my father died, toward the end of summer camp in Wolfeboro, New Hampshire, the director, William Bentley, stood on a stage outside with a campfire blazing and told us all a story about a golden arm. His narrative was a parade of meaningless words. Near the end of the story he held the golden arm in his own. Where the arm came from, whose it was, what it signified, whether it had once been a real arm or was a prosthetic arm that had been found somewhere in the camp, perhaps by Mr. Bentley himself, whether in some remote part of the world people had golden arms and this was a specimen, and why Mr. Bentley was telling us this crazy story in the first place, I had no idea, though I jumped along with everyone else when, for some reason, he let it drop at the end, and it bounced on the stage with an 80-decibel *BAM Klump Klump*!

On the afternoon of the next day I was nervously poised as a base runner, with a lead off third. It was the final inning of the final game of the year for the camp's Blues against our opponents, the Grays, so designated I suppose in a nod to the Civil War. (*Get ready for the next war, boys!*) Our Blues batter hit a long fly ball to the outfield. I was seven years old and unsure of the rules, though I knew it became complicated when such fly balls were hit. I had no idea what to do. My teammates jumped off the bench and ran toward me, pointing in both directions shouting *kah saa! kah saa!* I could run fast, and I was all legs (but no experience), so I may even have been put on that base for that reason.

But I was more or less stuck in place, my feet doing a rapid tap dance as I pondered the meaning of *kah saa!*, not knowing which way to go, wondering whether the other boys were shouting at me in some unknown language—a special, secret Blues' baseball vocabulary, perhaps, or even the tribal language (how did they know it?) of the far-off men with the golden arms. Alas, I was tagged out before I could decipher their words—"Tag up!" The event ended the game, but I was among the younger campers, and it became the baseball play we all laughed about in the waning days of the summer.

The power of gesture was always there, in one form or another. One cabinmate in Wolfeboro wet the bed, and dawn after dawn he had to sit outside the cabin alone to play sentry to his soggy mattress for half an hour or so as it dried. I couldn't bear to see him there, finally wet my own bed, and joined him. At school a boy just in front of me constantly fainted while we were standing in class, pledging allegiance or hailing Mary or something or other, and it became my responsibility, if he started to fall, to catch him. I promptly started fainting myself on my own separate schedule. These were considered laudable (or at least empathetic) acts by camp counselors and teachers alike.

But these efforts, I think, were no more than alternative, subconscious ways of communication, of making good friends. At the end of the summer, in front of the whole camp Mr. Bentley held his *real* arms over my head, as he did over the heads of two other finalists, calling for applause in a popularity contest. I won—and was happy but genuinely surprised. My relationships with everyone were shrouded in mystery, and so, I imagined, were theirs with me. But my efforts to cement them exhibited a certain guileless innocence that everyone recognized and, to my astonishment, helped me to win their hearts. I became dependent on the hearing, unknowingly and affectionately, and they loved me for it.

Still, deafness is an invisible affliction, partial deafness even more so. Thus no one—not Mother, not my brothers, nor I myself—had any idea that I could not hear well. My struggles with lyricals remained private not because I thought them a secret but because I was sure that that was the way *the whirl quirks the girl shirks the world works.* To add to the confusion, my ephemeral friends—the clouds, the wind, and the waves—were competing with preternatural sounds of locusts—a buzzing and ringing in my ears that came out of nowhere. The locusts were immortal, buzzing day and night in the summer, fall, winter, and spring.

The sound of real locusts is so overwhelming that a theory of their origin can be found in Greek mythology. Socrates tells Phaedrus how locusts came to exist. Certain men were so seduced by the Muses they decided to take up singing themselves all the time; they were so entranced that they failed to remember to eat or drink and died of their forgetfulness. Their descendants, the locusts, sing from birth to death in need of little else. The dissonant locusts of my inner ears need no sustenance other than my heartbeat. But they are sounds, not creatures, and born of infection. They are of no evolutionary transitional value, and they are here to stay.

The English-speaking world onomatopoetically calls these sounds "tinnitus" (usually pronounced "TIN-a-tiss"). The French call it *bourdonnement*, the Italians *ronzio*: both meaning "buzzing in the ears." The Germans call tinnitus *orhenklingen*, "ringing in the ears." Characterizing his bad health as an "evil demon," Beethoven complained as a young man that his ears "buzz and ring day and night." Emmanuelle Laborit, the deaf French actress who won the Prix Molière for the French version of the play *Children of a Lesser God*, says that she hears a high-pitched hissing or whistling (*sifflements*). "I think," she writes, "they come from elsewhere, from outside of me, but no, these are my sounds, it is only I who hear them. I am noise within and silence without." Tinnitus is anything but musical; Socrates must have confused his locusts with their seducers.

Tinnitus can afflict both the profoundly deaf and the hearing impaired, and those without hearing loss as well. Approximately fifty million Americans have tinnitus to some degree. Sixteen million of us have tinnitus severe enough to seek medical attention for it; about two million are so seriously affected that they are unable to function effectively on a day-to-day basis. Some think tinnitus is produced by the efferent fibers of the acoustic nerve, which in healthy ears supplement sound by carrying signals in reverse, from the brain to the ear. I don't remember exactly when these dissonant sounds came into my world, though beginning with the post-scarlet summers of my childhood at Marblehead's Main Harbor, they were to me the sounds of dragonflies, visible and invisible; in the fall in Riverdale they were the wind; in the winter the falling snow; in the spring the rustling of new leaves. They are the sounds of silence, most audible when all else is quiet.

As I began to understand that the clouds, the wind, and the waves were voiceless, I found other companions, spoke to them, listened to them carefully, and had no need for lyricals. I would let no earthly being interfere with them, for they were angels and saints. On the way back from school I would listen to my guardian angels. I had several, and they seemed to work shifts. Like policemen, they had no names; they were there to see me home. I talked to them, and they made their thoughts known to me— about the day, a class, a teacher, a friend, where my father was, where Figaro was. In the morning and evening my interlocutors were saints. The Virgin if I had lost something. Theresa of Lisieux if I were at Mass, particularly in Main Harbor, where Our Lady Star of the Sea Church was graced with her statue. I whispered to her during the three quiet hours of the Good Friday service, when I would sit or kneel before her, silent but for the rustling spring leaves in my head.

My saints and angels didn't really speak to me but uttered their thoughts voicelessly, and I in turn would reply. John Locke wrote that without spoken words—what he called the "signs" of our ideas—our thoughts lay trapped within us, hidden from others. But the silent thoughts of angels and saints were not hidden from me. Look here for the baseball glove; cross the street there. When I would pray in the evening to the statue of the Infant of Prague in my bedroom, I would whisper to him, another child, and listen to what he had to say. My mother's parents had died not long after my father—death seemed to be everywhere—and it was this thirty-inch statue that I chose from among my grand-parents' affairs and clung to. I shared the room with my older brother, John. He would mock these quiet sessions, as I tried to disregard his laughter. Finally, I would give up and laugh along with him. But the saints and angels were always there, circling, teaching me about the world—my faithful, voiceless, spiritual friends.

CHAPTER 3

VOICES IN THE AIR

THE VOICE OF CARUSO, A FLUTE IN THE DISTANCE, the wind in the willows, these and the infinite numbers and types of oscillations of our physical world produce vibrations in the air, which we call sound. Air is the medium through which those of us who hear express our thoughts to others and they to us, enabling our souls to touch and our hearts to mingle. Even if we could somehow live and not breathe, without air we would hear nothing, and our screams, our tears, our laughter, our music, would be silent, our words nonexistent. From birth to death we breathe in and out, conscious every moment of our waking lives that we can't live without air. But we are less aware that air is also our means of communication with other hearing beings, and the rest of the world around us.

A Whisper of Physics

Air is elastic, and the vibrations of objects temporarily alter its form. The vibrations don't move the air from one point to another;

its molecules move back and forth about an average resting place, like the vibrating object itself. When Caruso's vocal cords or the reeds of a flute or a willow oscillate, they cause the adjacent air molecules to vibrate in the same fashion, creating a zone of compression and rarefaction (expansion) as the molecules push together and then draw apart. The pattern is repeated as successive adjacent air particles are nudged by their predecessors. Not to hear the pattern can be devastating. To hear it, as Kenneth Grahame's Rat put it—"O, Mole! The beauty of it! The merry bubble and joy"—can be the measure of one's happiness.

We call these vibrations in the air sound "waves." They are usually depicted as transverse waves, like waves in the sea, curves traveling over (compression) and under (expansion) a horizontal line representing normal atmospheric pressure, to show the sound's alteration of the air. The amplitude of these waves—the height and depth of their peaks and valleys—illustrates the intensity or loudness of the sound produced by the vibrating object. What we call the "pitch" of a sound, that is, how high or low it is, depends on how quickly the sound wave vibrates—that is, how frequently the cycle of one compression and expansion repeats itself. The lofty sound of a piccolo, for example, plays the Green Hornet's "Flight of the Bumble Bee" with a frequency of about 4,500 cycles per second. It is thousands of cycles higher than the *da da da DUM* of a bass fiddle giving us the first four notes of Beethoven's Fifth Symphony at fewer than 60 cycles a second. A single cycle in a single second is called one Hertz (Hz). The average human ear can hear sounds as low as 20 cycles a second, or 20 Hz (a low rumbling sound), and as high as 20,000 cycles a second or 20 kilohertz (a high-pitched squeak).

We speak as we breathe. To make voiced sounds we draw our vocal cords together with the muscles of our larynx, making them touch. The vocal cords vibrate when we breathe out. The sounds they produce, the lower frequencies of our speech, all of the vowels and the voiced consonants, are then further shaped by our mouths and noses. When we produce unvoiced sounds (such as *f*, *p*, or *s*), we leave our vocal cords open as we breathe out. When we raise the pitch or frequency of our voices—for example, from the sound of *oh* to *ee* (as in "go see") or to sing the first few notes of "If I Loved You"—we are flexing muscles in our throat to tighten the vocal cords, causing them to vibrate at a higher frequency. The frequency of normal speech generally ranges from 250 to 8,000 Hz, although many speech sounds are much higher.

Unvoiced consonants are the highest-pitched sounds or phones of speech, principally in the 1,000 to 8,000 Hz range. Vowels and several voiced consonants generally occupy the lower, from 250 to 750 Hz. Speech is readily available to those who hear well. Those of us who are severely and profoundly deaf, with critical loss at all frequencies, hear virtually no vowels or consonants and thus no meaningful speech. Since childhood I have been severely deaf in the higher ranges of speech, moderately so in the lower. I hear a number of vowels and voiced consonants, at least in a quiet space, but do not hear most consonants and some vowels. The toxins that cause scarlet fever permanently damaged the cells in the cochlea that receive the signals of speech above 500 Hz. It is these sounds that I remember hearing as a young child, not so much the sounds of those vowels and consonants as the natural high-frequency sounds in the world around us, ranging from insects to birds to the sprinkles and splashes of water.

The higher frequency sounds are critically important, for consonants are an indispensable key to understanding speech. They serve both as our markers within words and signals that mark the separation between one word and another. It is usually possible, for example, to figure out a sentence or phrase even if the vowels are deleted. Compare the following:

_a_e _ _ e _a_ a_a_!

with

T_k_ th_ c_t _w_y!

The consonants tell us the cat's being banished. Vowels, on the other hand, while they convey little meaning in and of themselves, are helpful to the partially deaf listener, indeed to all of us, in measuring the general attitude or intention of the speaker. If you heard only the vowels in the above example, you would at least know, from the tone of voice, that the speaker was telling someone to do something. Malcolm Gladwell illustrates the point in *Blink* when he cites an experiment in which people chosen at random were able to predict which patients would end up suing their doctors. They listened to recorded conversations between surgeon and patient in which the consonants had been deleted, leaving a linguistic garble. But the vowels yielded the speakers' intonation, pitch, and rhythm—giving the listeners the key to whether or not the relationship was headed for trouble. But the problem of missing consonants for the deaf is that we need not only to perceive the temperament of the speakers but also, of course, to know what they're saying.

Hearing and interpreting speech will depend on who is speaking—a man, a woman, or a child; a nasal, whispered, or timid voice; in noise or in quiet; two feet away or at the opposite or distant side of a table or room. Whether voices can be understood by imperfect ears depends not only on the voices' frequencies and volume but also on the environment, the alertness or fatigue of the listener, and a host of other factors. Almost any spoken word can be beyond the comprehension of an ear that receives a number of frequencies poorly but others ostensibly well, with or without hearing aids.

The average ear is able to hear sounds with an extraordinary range of intensity, so great that it is measured on a logarithmic scale. The basic unit of measurement was originally the bel, named for Alexander Graham Bell a year after his death in 1922 by engineers at Bell Telephone. Zero bels is the level of sound at the threshold of hearing. One bel is 10 times that level, two bels is 10 × 10 or 100 times the threshold, and so forth. Today the standard unit of measurement is the decibel (dB), adopted to denote the tenfold increases in energy from each bel to the next. Ten decibels are thus 1 bel, 20 decibels are 2 bels, and so forth.

The loudest sounds we can hear without injuring our ears are at about 140 decibels, equivalent, for example, to the sound of an accelerating jet engine a hundred yards away. This means that the jet engine's sound-pressure level is 10^{14} (10 × 10 × 10 . . . 14 times in all) relative to that produced by the faint whisper we hear at our hearing threshold at just above atmospheric pressure. In other words, the loudest sounds we hear contain one hundred trillion times more energy than the faintest. And yet both the loudest and the softest sounds involve almost an infinitesimal displacement of air molecules and of the eardrum—about one-seventh the thickness of this page for the most intense sounds and one-tenth the radius of an atom for the softest.

The intensity of sound diminishes dramatically as it travels away from its source. A sound wave moves in rapidly expanding spheres, dispersing its energy over an ever broadening area. A nail can cut into wood because the blunt force of the hammer is transferred to the nail, giving the blow on impact far greater intensity at the nail's tiny point than at the broad hammerhead. Our voices traveling over distance are like the nail in reverse, for the energy released by our vocal cords rapidly diminishes as it moves away from us, much the way the expanding surface of a balloon grows rapidly thinner until it pops (though the sound waves end with a whimper). The area of a sphere is equal to $4\pi r^2$ and is thus directly proportional to the square of its radius, or the square of the distance of the expanding sound wave from the vibrating source of sound at its center. The intensity of a sound, like that of the nail, is its force per unit area, and it therefore diminishes by a factor equal to the square of the distance of the listener from the speaker. A sound two feet away is four times less intense than the sound at one foot; a sound four feet away is sixteen times weaker, etc.

All the above elementary points of physics are a defining aspect of my life and of the lives of all partially deaf people. The inverse square relationship between sound and distance and the quietness and inaccessibility of the key markers of speech are our ineluctable enemies. This was the source of Beethoven's early anguish, as to both music and speech: "From a distance I do not hear the high notes of the instruments and the singers' voices. . . . Sometimes too I hardly hear people who speak softly. The sound [i.e., the vowels] I can hear it is true, but not the words." Two years later, at age thirty-one, Beethoven was devastated when he discovered that he couldn't hear *any* sound from a flute he was told was being played "in the distance," what Rat calls "the thin, clear happy call of the distant piping." If the flute was fifty yards away, it was a faint, high-pitched sound, and its fragile melody contained 2,500 times less energy than the notes Beethoven would at that time in his life have heard at the podium or the piano ("I have to get very close to the orchestra"). The distant flute was too faint for his own ears but not for those of the person beside him, who brought him close to despair by saying there was music in the air. "It was only thanks to my art," he wrote, "that I did not end my life by suicide."

The Ear: A Mortal Trinity

How does the healthy ear manage to hear? How do the hearing identify and distinguish a flute, a harp, a drum, a robin, a snake, a Domingo, a Callas? How do the ears, as a mechanical and physical matter, collect and process spoken language and other sounds and transmit them to the brain? Why do the profoundly deaf hear virtually nothing at all? Why do my lyricals exist?

The ear is a wonder of nature, a work of art, a mortal trinity. To many of us it is just the ear we see. But its most critical components lie inside the head. The visible ear, the auricle, gathers sound waves and channels them into the ear canal. The canal funnels them to our eardrum, a thin membrane separating the outer from the middle ear. The eardrum vibrates back and forth between them at the same frequencies, and with the same intensity, as those of the arriving sound waves. If the incoming sound wave cycles are shorter, the eardrum oscillates faster. When a higher-intensity sound wave arrives, there is a larger displacement of the eardrum from its resting position.

The second part of the trinity, the middle ear, contains three tiny bones (ossicles) called the hammer, the anvil, and (named for its shape) the stirrup. They are the smallest bones in our body. The arm of the hammer is attached to the inside of the eardrum and vibrates with it, sending the vibrations inward to the anvil, which conveys them to the stirrup. The stirrup's "footplate" slips into the membrane of an oval-shaped "window," the outer boundary of our inner ear and the entry to the liquid-filled cochlea. The stirrup sends the vibrations passed to it by the eardrum into the oval window.

The cochlea is tiny, about the size of a small fingernail. Its snail-like shell coils upward in diminishing diameter, with two and a half turns from its base to the top or apex. It is the innermost part of our auditory trinity. When the stirrup's footplate strikes the oval window, it generates a pressure wave that moves in a spiral through the liquids of the cochlea. The liquid wave moves the tips of the cochlea's fifteen thousand epithelial cells (hair cells) that float in it.

The motion of the cochlear hair cells results in the release of an electrical charge. The current mirrors both the frequency and the intensity of the mechanical input signal of the sound wave, relayed by the hair cells. The electrical charge is in turn transmitted to nerve threads and to the central auditory nerve. Successive neurons in the auditory nerve then set the charge's path from neuron to neuron through to the brain stem. The neural charges follow labyrinthine patterns to the auditory cortex of the brain, where the sound is interpreted and understood.

The cochlea is the inner sanctum of our language, our music, all that we hear. No human-made system can equal its performance. Hearing loss caused by cochlear damage is the most common form of deafness and partial deafness in the world. It affects more than thirty million people in the United States alone. Cochlear structures are vulnerable to disease (in my case scarlet fever), to damage by certain antibiotics and other drugs, to infection and allergy, and to genetic disorder. They also deteriorate with age.

Often the cause of cochlear damage is not known and cannot reliably be determined. There are, to be sure, many other forms of hearing loss. A conductive loss is caused by defects in the transmission of sound through the middle ear, caused by damage to the eardrum or ossicles or by the presence of fluid in the middle ear as a result of infection. Mechanical problems of the middle ear can often be corrected by surgery, and middle-ear infections are usually treatable by medication. For most people with hearing loss, however, the incapacitating damage has been done to the cochlea. Its cells and membranes are inaccessible, irreparable, and irreplaceable.

What do these fundamentals of physics and biology signify to the deaf? They define our situation and how we participate, or endeavor to participate, in the commerce of souls. Our way of life seems to us on the surface a straightforward matter of *difference*, almost an emotional or spiritual concern—of lost oral messages, vacant eyes, the locusts within us. But the deeper structure of our existence is far more complex. Our surest path to engagement with others, however, is not necessarily a scientific one—not necessarily one that should be traced by trying to replicate what has been lost.

The Prelingually Deaf

It is critical for all of us to have and to use the language we need. A healthy child learning to speak hears not only the people around him but also his own voice, which is tuned, checked, adjusted, and modified in a constant, real-time exercise in self-training of the voice and ear together. For the child who is deaf before learning to speak, virtually all spoken language has prematurely died in the cochlea, including his own speech. He is helped neither by the physics of sound nor by his inner ear, and he is unable to engage in the listening and speaking exercises that a hearing child performs instinctively.

But such a child will learn to "speak" just as quickly in his own language, for a baby born profoundly deaf turns immediately to sign. At first he will use his own home signs—in their early form an equivalent of the babbling of hearing children. And as soon as he is exposed to it, he will rapidly acquire the sophisticated sign language of his peers. Even Alexander Graham Bell, an elocution teacher, a eugenicist, and an enemy of sign (though less well remembered for these distinctions), conceded that sign language was the quickest way to reach the mind of a profoundly deaf child. The child will soon be able to communicate effortlessly and to understand, fully and immediately, the ideas expressed by those around him, whether addressed to him or not, in any environment.

More than 95 percent of children deaf from birth, however, are born of hearing parents. And while the parents immediately engage with their child in the home signs they develop together, they almost invariably want him or her to be able to speak and to listen, and to live in their own larger hearing world. In the past, the attempted solution had been lipreading and hearing aids, but the former is virtually impossible without meaningful residual hearing, and the latter bring no interpretable sound to a child's cochlear cells, if they are dead or moribund at all frequencies. Those attempts thus fail. Today, the solution proposed by doctors and generally accepted by these parents is the cochlear implant. If my illness had struck me as a child today, and had been more effective in destroying my cochlear cells, I might well have been implanted myself.

The cochlear implant is a device whose components are worn outside and just inside the skull of the child. It sends electrical signals derived from speech and other sounds directly to the auditory-nerve fibers in the center of the cochlea. The signals bypass the inactive cochlear hair cells. It is generally conceded that even after implantation these children remain severely deaf at all frequencies; the problem is not so much the detection of the electrical signals as their lack of clarity and the inability of the brain readily to interpret them. The implanted child has only eighteen channels, one for each of the eighteen electrodes implanted in the cochlea—more than these have proved to be of little or no additional help. Those channels provide nowhere near the clarity that the fifteen thousand epithelial cells in the cochlea provide to hearing children. The implanted children therefore have great difficulty functioning in normal (nonhermetic) environments because of ambient and other noise. They require extensive training with the implant, wholly dedicated parents, and years of speech and lipreading therapists, with no room or time left over for sign language. In school, supplementary FM radio systems are required, in which the teacher speaks into a microphone (worn around his neck) that is electronically connected to the implant.

Hearing parents are understandably reluctant to surrender their children to the world of the deaf and of sign language, to the potential control of others, to a language the parents do not know, to a world of no speech at all, to a life of silence. And yet it is a language that the parents can learn, albeit perhaps with difficulty, for they have the faculties (eyes, hands, facial expressions) necessary to practice it. And that world is not as grim as they might think. Hundreds of thousands of Americans communicate in sign language, and their world includes scholars, businesspeople, teachers, intellectuals, artists, writers, tradespeople, laborers, and others— all fully functioning and communicative human beings. To deny a deaf child that world, I fear, threatens leaving him not just without his first language but without any effective language at all.

The Postlingually Deaf

For those profoundly deafened after they have learned to speak, science tells us that their cochlea are no longer sending any signals to the brain. The sound waves die in the nerve center of the cochlea, among the withered cells, untuned to their respective optimal frequencies, or to any other. Sign language is generally not an alternative, for the late-deafened are usually too far along in life to learn it with any proficiency. Their first language is speech; they still speak like their hearing peers, and cochlear implants can afford some help.

As noted by the Massachusetts Eye and Ear Infirmary, implants provide aid in lipreading, in the perception of environmental sounds, and in monitoring one's own voice. Nevertheless, for these individuals as well, years of hard work and training with therapists is required. The signals sent to the auditory nerve can be sufficient to enable them to hear, to the extent their brains are able to relate and convert the signals they receive to the speech they still utter and remember hearing before they were deafened. These late deafened individuals will not have the language they need, but they will at least be able to hear some recognizable speech, and they have the benefit of a memory that will help them carry on as best they can in what was and remains their first language.

The Partially Deaf

For the millions of us who are partially deaf or hard of hearing, a familiarity with the physics of sound and with how our ears function is a key to our self-understanding. We are given incomplete signals from the surviving cells. The brain strives to assemble the message by racing through the possible alternatives, tossing life rafts as we drown in oceans of signals. We can call on no other anatomical organ or structure to do so. Our cerebral neurons explore the choices by plunging into our acquired treasury of language. We hear too well to benefit from an implant. Hearing aids can be of some help, but ultimately the message may remain obscure.

In my case, scarlet fever permanently obscured not only the consonants and vowels in the higher frequencies of speech but also the merry bubble and joy of crickets, birds, wind, and water, and the higher tones and instruments of music. The lower frequencies were left mostly alone, giving me the illusion, for almost thirty years, that I heard as others did and that the intellectual efforts to fill in the gaps, my translations of lyricals, were a normal practice exercised by all. Today, as I say, I have a particular affection for them. And I now know what they are.

CHAPTER 4

A SCHOOLBOY'S LYRICALS

Y OU HAVE NEVER HEARD OF LYRICALS BEFORE; I
have given them their name. For years, for generations,
for centuries, they have been an unknown language. Whether
or not you can hear well, you will find that learning about lyricals, imagining them, letting them take you along with them,
can be like reading or writing poetry. If you are partially deaf,
they are a defining element of your life, as they are of mine.
They are the thread that binds us to the commerce of souls, the
clues that let us in, albeit through a dark, narrow, winding, and
uncertain hallway. As an adolescent I lived with them, explored
them, struggled with them. I didn't know what they were, and I
had no name for them, for they were not of my conscious cre-
ation. But I did believe that they were the gateway, for everyone,
to understanding.

Meanwhile, in my first year of high school, I discovered that I
could run faster over short distances than just about everybody else,
having started when I was eleven by winning some local July 4

running races in Massachusetts (where we had moved a few years after my father died). Perhaps it was the shock of the starting gun bursting into my veiled world. But I continued to win, and one happy Sunday in May my picture appeared on the front sports page of the *Boston Herald* winning the state track meet when I was fifteen. An uncle who had seen the picture offered to take me up to Andover for an interview. We had no money.

Phillips Academy and its admissions officer, Joshua Miner, liked my grades, more or less, but he *loved* my times at the age of fifteen. "*So your tie are teh at at twenty-two fla.*" *your tie twenty-two flat your times are ten flat for the 100-yard dash, twenty-two flat for the 220*

"Yes, sir."

"And you have a 95 *adge* at St. John's. Good." *adge edge average*

"Yes, but I guess here it would be—lower."

"Perhaps, Gerry. Few get 90s at Andover, that's true, and you might be prepared for that."

"We don't have any money."

"That's not an issue. Admissions are *knee bligh*—everyone who is admitted can come to Andover."

"Knee bligh, what's that?"

"Regardless of need. Need blind."

This man, a physics teacher, seemed genuinely interested in me—he knew I was terrified—and was trying to make me feel at home. My slow and confused responses probably seemed to him a result of my nervousness. In any event, they did not hurt, and I was admitted.

Mother took me up to Andover, only a fifty-minute drive from Salem, in early September 1958. We attended the opening assembly, to which new boys (Andover was then an all-boys school) and parents were invited. John Kemper, the headmaster, addressed us all, saying in his introduction that we would be proud to *doe that you Arthur Dobbs super sense of the country*. "Aren't you proud?" said my mother,

  to doe
   to know
    arthur dobbs
     are the dopps
      are the top—

"Very," I said, still half-wondering who Arthur Dobbs was and what he had to do with us.

"The top 2 percent!" she added.

I was sad when she left, but there was too much else to do to worry about it. On about the third evening, as I was climbing the stairs toward my room on the third floor of the dormitory, I ran into a stocky, short, athletic-looking, well-dressed boy who did not seem particularly happy to see me. "And who are *you*?" he asked, meaning something like "please explain your insignificance."

"I'm a new student." I was wearing a white shirt with a pocket you could see through my open jacket, with three pens in it (your shirts should not have pockets at Andover), ugly dark shoes pretending to be loafers, an undershirt (you do not wear undershirts), short dark socks (you always wear long ones), and a badly cut "tweed" suit (with red threads running through a vague grayish-brown herringbone) from the Empire Clothing Store just on the other side of the A&P warehouse beside our apartment in Salem.

"You look it, wimp. Where on earth did they *fine you*?" *fine you fine you find you*

"I transferred—"

"*Locatid*?"

"Sorry?"

"You from around here? You a *kownie*?" *kownie brownie townie local local kid townie*

"I'm from Salem."

"Even worse." He disappeared into a friend's room with a sneer. I remember that encounter well. His was an attitude that made Andover a tough place for new boys whose personalities or looks varied from the norm, who were not—cool.

Two nights later, four other boys in our house, Johnson Hall, and I stayed up relatively late, until eleven o'clock or so, and wound up talking about religion. In spite of the gradual ascendance of girls—or at least their appeal—over my angels and saints, the latter were still lurking about, and I defended them with vigor, as I did the divinity and resurrection of Christ (*so what was the metazinit? metazinit mechanism*), the virginity of his mother (*how exactly did she become pregnant? what did tea aid'll too? aid'll too aid'll angel tea ange the angel what did the angel do?*), the immortality of the soul, and the infallibility of the pope.

It wasn't really a conversation but an exploration of my views, and I was happy to tell them—to spread the Word to all the Protestants (there were few Jewish students at Andover at that time and not that many Catholics). They were astonished by my beliefs, insisted on evidence, and asked how I could go through life believing in *dairy dales dairy fales fairy dales fairy tales*. I fell back on the mysteries of faith and, on the whole, was a miserable *defensor fidei*—my lingering saints were not happy.

I had been playing for the first two days with the junior varsity-1 football team (the first of the five JV football teams at Andover). I played without hip pads because I was so skinny they had to order some, which made it very easy for me as a running halfback to slip through the line. I was sent up to the varsity two days later and introduced to everyone by the head coach. I ran a couple of plays, saw some daylight, and raced through the defense, stopped only by the safeties. That evening, as I crossed the campus's west quadrangle, going back to my room again, wearing a sport jacket and sneakers this time, and feeling more relaxed, I met the well-dressed jock who, it turned out, was a linebacker on the varsity though I hadn't recognized him on the field.

"Hey, Gerry! Sid Albright! How's it going? How'd you *Ed Ashby*?" *Ed Ashby no not Ashby—get past me*

"Well, it was the offensive linemen, Sid, not me. And how are you?"

"I'm just great. Look, if you need anything at all—to be *tow the rolls" tow the rolls shown the ropes* "just let me know!"

I was feeling much better. But as I got back to Johnson Hall after dinner, still delighted by my new friend Sid's change of heart, and I started up that staircase, all the radios on the first floor went on at the same time. I heard a voice I had known since we first started coming to Massachusetts for the summers. It was Richard Cardinal Cushing, Archbishop of Boston. And here he was again, saying the Holy Rosary, brought to you by Beacon Wax at six forty-five every night, and that night to Johnson Hall.

As I got to the first landing, I heard the inevitable *blessed is the froot 'o thy womb, Jeeezuz*. At the second flight the radios on the second floor joined in, *Glooorrrry be to the faahther an' to the Son and to the Hohly Spihr-it*, and then onto the third, where a mighty chorus of all the radios in the house gave us, *Holy Michael Aachangel, drive inta hell Satan an' all the othah evil speerits, who wanda thru tha world seeking the ruin o' souls!* It could have been devastating, but I was still aglow about Sid. As all those Protestant heads peered out of their doorways, I laughed along with them. Cushing's voice was always kind of a joke anyway; I could imitate it, and often did.

Nothing was sacred at Andover: not a president, not a queen or a statesman, not a politician, actor, or rich alumnus, no one, unless and until they proved themselves in some tangible way to the students—such as Humphrey Bogart, an alumnus, for being one of the coolest men on earth; George Marshall for helping to rebuild Europe; John Thomas, who came out from Rindge Tech in Boston a few times to compete with us, for setting the world high jump record. Slowly, subtly, my world was becoming less mysterious. It was still a world of puzzling lyricals but a practical, less spiritual world in which, if you could somehow prove yourself—and as we matured, it came not to matter how you did it— you were an equal.

On Saturday nights much of the student body would go to a movie in George Washington Hall. Movies have always been incomprehensible to me. Until the advent of infrared and FM transmitters plugged into television sets and their earphone-receivers, with the voice of each speaker literally in the ear canals, I have never been able to figure out what was going on. Movies I saw as a child, to which I was first introduced, happily, by Rossini, were composed not so much of words as of a series of actions, of not much more than Jean-Luc Godard's "a girl and a gun" without the embellishments—people saying something, tears, an embrace, a shooting, arrests, smiles, kisses, a lion roaring, The End. The quality of the script doesn't matter—the words of *Rocky* can be just as difficult to understand as the labyrinths of David Lynch's *Mulholland Drive*.

Bad Day at Black Rock, which I saw one Saturday night at GW, was a thicket of mysteries. The film has an exceptional script and cast—including Spencer Tracy (who won the Palme d'Or at Cannes for his performance as best actor), Robert Ryan, Lee Marvin, Ernest Borgnine, and Walter Brennan. A few years ago I bought a DVD of the film, played it, segment by segment, listened to it, sometimes with the hearing aids I've worn now for decades, sometimes without—and I wrote down the words I heard. Hearing aids are of little help for me with movies because they amplify original soundtracks that are themselves amplified and insufficiently clear.

The result of my effort was not any revelation of the plot but a festival of lyricals, showing how it is so easy for the partially deaf to get lost in everyday conversation:

What I Wrote Down	**The Script**
TRACY Not use in a grobiddy yet. What stops do?	I don't seem to be going any place. What stopped you?
RYAN Dezible. Wouldn't take me. Bunny after Pearl, I was the first man in line in the murdy gurdy at standstill. They wouldn't take me.	Physical. Wouldn't take me. Morning after Pearl, I was the first man in line in marine recruiting at Sand City. They wouldn't take me.
TRACY Tough.	Tough.
RYAN [Laughs]	[Laughs]
TRACY What makes you bad, Mr. Smith?	What makes you mad, Mr. Smith?
RYAN Me? Nothing is so insular.	Me? Nothing in particular.
TRACY The Japanese make you bad, huh?	The Japanese make you mad, huh?
RYAN Some do, and a come around smokin'.	Some do. When they come around snooping.
TRACY Whistle sign up.	Snooping for what?
RYAN I don't know, I side it's, somebody's lookin' for something.	I don't know. Outsiders coming around, lookin' for something.
TRACY Looking for what?	Looking for what?
RYAN I don't know! Somebody's always looking for someone in this market for wet. In this song, it's nowhere to the backrocker, it's the "Wild West." The same as man, it's the "Undeveloped West." They're all filling in hodder books, we are. We	I don't know! Somebody's always looking for something in this part of the West. To the historian, it's the "Old West." To the book writers, it's the "Wild West." To the businessmen, it's the "Undeveloped West." They all say we're backward and

don't even have enough rudder. Look this place, to us, is our ways. And I just wish they'd leave us alone.

poor, and I guess we are. We don't even have enough water. But this place, to us, is our West. And I just wish they'd leave us alone.

TRACY Leave you alone to do what?

Leave you alone to do what?

RYAN I own all to you mean.

I don't know what you mean.

TRACY What happened to Kamoko?

What happened to Kamoko?

RYAN He went away, I told you. Sorting out to west a king's way out there and burst the place out. That's how it was—you know how kids are.

He went away, like I told you. Shortly after he left, some kids went out there and burned the place down. That's how it was—you know how kids are.

RYAN Radio can figure it out.

Maybe you can figure it out.

I would come away from *Black Rock* and other films with a flight of mysterious ideas, as I assumed everyone did—when would things be of use in a *grobiddy*, the significance of *dezibles*, the advantage of being first in line at the *murdy gurdy at standstill*. As a child, and at Andover, and indeed until I began wearing hearing aids, I was unaware that my lyricals were particular to *me*.

Grobiddies and *dezibles* are, of course, the offspring of the laws of physics and the ear's disjointed cellular life. When people speak, they signal differences in meaning by changing, substituting, mixing the phones, the vowels and consonants, the basic elements of our speech. We can have "ball" versus "hall" versus "call" (a consonant switch), or "lack" versus "luck" versus "lock" (vowels), or "lad" versus "lug" versus "log" (consonants again). When the words don't come through to the partially deaf, we search for meaning in the sounds we do hear. They are all arbitrary sounds, born of custom. As John Locke writes,

Man['s] . . . thoughts . . . [lie] within his own breast, invisible and hidden from others. . . . [To make them known,] nothing was so fit, either for plenty or quickness, as those articulate sounds, which with so much ease and variety he found himself able to make.

Thus . . . men came to use words . . . as the signs of their ideas; not by any natural connexion that there is between particular articulate sounds and certain ideas, for then there would be but one language amongst all men; but by a voluntary imposition, whereby such a word is made arbitrarily the mark of such an idea.

Our search for these sounds is a search for the speaker's idea, as we try to resolve the meaning of a *grobiddy yet* (going any place), a *dezible* (a physical), or a *murdy gurdy at standstill* (marine recruiting at Sand City). Our eyes and ears explore alternative meaning and syntax, looking for noun, verb, object, and they often fail. It's a hunt for what has stayed hidden in the breasts of others.

NOTWITHSTANDING INCIDENTS LIKE MY FIRST UNHAPPY encounter with Sid Albright, Andover was, and remains, a fundamentally egalitarian institution. They took me and paid for me, and I was in general as welcome in that community as any Dulles or Bass or Olivetti or Du Pont, all classmates. I managed fairly well with my constant search for words and hours of reading, though a number of my courses were difficult. Andover's history classes, for example, offered no easy surveys and required no mastering of dates or memorization of lines of kings. We had to read the writings of complex statesmen, pompous courts, and (it seemed to me) obscure political theorists, and in class we answered what appeared to me to be elliptical questions about them.

French was taught using the direct method: our teachers were usually French, and no English was spoken beginning with the very first *bonjour*. In a sense this was an advantage for me, for we were all struggling with meaning, and I was focusing on lips, gestures, eyes, expressions, which served me fairly well as the others wrestled with the words. While I could never read lips in French, I could imitate the accent and manner when I spoke it, and of course eventually I could read it. There were occasional moments of confusion, as when I stayed up until four in the morning the night after a class to study the next five chapters of the book, a daunting forty pages, instead of the assigned first five pages of Chapter 6.

Physics was especially difficult. It was taught with a college textbook and in a large classroom with about thirty of us. My seat was toward the back of the leftmost row, as the teacher, Tom Hankins, addressed us from his podium and the blackboard in the front of the room and to the right. I had little aptitude and almost no idea what he was saying. After a few weeks, he generously offered me a second, private class, just the two of us, four hours a week, all year long, immediately following the regular class, and the unfamiliar words worked their way into my visual lexicon. In those private sessions, his words were spoken closely, the two of us sitting opposite each other, our knees touching and our heads leaning forward over the coffee table. Slowly the classroom's *errant* was transformed to *current*, *drag nets* to *magnets*, *a tensile L-I-G* to *potential energy*, *a celebration* to *acceleration*, and so on.

The translation of my physics lyricals was immediate, utilitarian, and result-oriented, and I was seldom tired, even though we'd just been through the formal class. At times, when a partially deaf person is tired or distracted, or the hearing environment is difficult, or he has been deciphering lyricals for hours, or he is simply in a dreamy mood, lyricals can lead in many different directions. If I let them, they conjure up shifting images from my life—a song, a poem, a love, a fear, a memory, a saint—or from nowhere—images, like *grobiddies* and *dezibles*, I had never seen before and may never encounter again, all measured in seconds or, more commonly, fractions of a second.

English class was an awakening for all of us. We were only nine students (the physics class was unusually large). Our English teacher, Dudley Fitts, was a distinguished poet and classicist. He was wheelchair-bound for life with a chronic illness, and we could not imagine why he wanted to spend the time he had left teaching us. He spoke precisely but quietly, as if inviting each of us to pay careful attention to what he had to say or, rather, to what he was asking us about. But his soft words led me in wonderful lyrical directions. "*Water happens after coral reefs?* Gerry?"

> *water happen*
> *water*
> *water*
> *happens*
> *what er hap,*
> *what'll happen*
> *after coral reefs*

"Are you with us, Mr. Shea?"

"Yes, sir, um—"

> *cora nora Nora reefs—*
> *Nora sees*
> *Nora*
> *leaves at the end,*
> *she leaves—what'll happen!*

"—when Nora leaves her husband, Mr. Fitts, that's the end of *A Doll's House!*"

"That's certainly true, Gerry, but *ooh dee see she's golfer good?*" *ooh dee see ooh to you do you dee see think do you think she's gone for good*— "*After* the play, if you will? Could she *huh paa*" *huh paa huh paa back huh back kuh back come back* "through the door in a year, a *muh*, the very next day? Are you suggesting she'll *never* come back?"

On the football field, as a right halfback I proved to be far less talented than my friend Sid, who had the courage of a bullfighter. In fact, I was terrified and no threat unless I could see a large gap in the defensive line, which I seldom did. Our team beat everybody, including all of our secondary school rivals as well as respectable college freshmen teams like Bowdoin and Tufts. I rarely got off the bench—our line average was 206 pounds and I weighed 137 (160 in the printed football program). If I didn't see any light, I would run for the sidelines. Play calls in the huddle were a problem at first (I had to know what to do before running away from everybody), but eventually a *splissis* was a *split six* (right halfback over tackle), and *Whit's YTD* was a *quick 93* (a short pass to the right halfback).

In my senior year I did manage to become cocaptain of the track team, which also beat most of its rivals, including the Brown and Harvard freshmen. But running is a grueling sport and takes its toll when you start as young as I did (age thirteen). I began to sing as well in the chorus, in the octet, and finally in the spring musical, *Finian's Rainbow*, in which I played Og, the leprechaun who turns into a mortal during the production. We did the play with the school's orchestra and, in the female leads, young women from the New England Conservatory of Music. Og sings E. Y. Harburg's amorous lyric, "When I'm not near the girl I love, I love the girl I'm near," and falls in love with practically every woman he sees.

The unworldly luxury of knowing the words these musical girls would never change or fail to sing—"thou art sweet thou'rt sort of grandish thou outlandish cavalier"—and what I would answer—"I'm so *cherchez la femme*"—created some of my happiest moments. When the opening curtain was raised, my invisible one was too, and I became an ordinary mortal: myself, on stage, home at last. The performance brought praise on Monday morning even from our redoubtable history teacher, Leonard James, the chair of the department:

"*Jay!*" said James. The boy behind me tapped my shoulder. *Jay Jay Shea!*

"Didn't know you had *a sinew*" *a sin it sin it in—had it in you.* "Not from your *icelets* here." *Icelets iceland silence*

Off the stage, girls were generally affectionate but often a source of confusion, despite the proximity. Intimacies developed a certain protocol, refined in the spring during Sunday afternoon visits to the Cochran Bird Sanctuary with girls from nearby Abbot Academy. We would meet in the woods on clement days, pursuant to appointments made through elementary lipreading in the Andover chapel on Sunday mornings—*two o'clock; three thirty*. At the appointed times we would kiss and play in the grass until the five o'clock chapel bell tolled us home.

The summer following my senior year at Andover, I met Elizabeth Adams—Beth— a soft-spoken, dark-haired, extraordinarily beautiful girl from Salem. When we were speaking to each other, she would often laugh, holding her dark-eyed glance as her head turned away as if to say, *Gerry, your eyes and your mind are traveling separate wa*ys. Then her eyes would look away. She'd come back, full face, with smiling, then laughing lips, saying on one occasion, "You are a *lurioscopy.*" *lurioscopy god a medical device a—*

"What's a 'lurioscopy,' Beth?"

"Curiosity, Gerry."

"Is that a compliment?"

"Of course. You are many things, and yet a curiosity too. That's what makes you so *into things*."

into things

into these

foolish things

intrutings

interesting

I took Beth one night to a beach movie, animated this time, Walt Disney's *Lady and the Tramp*. Movies of this sort remind me of what psychologists call the McGurk Effect. If you show a silent video of a speaker pronouncing one syllable (say "map"), but you provide a different spoken syllable on the audio ("tap"), most listeners will come up with "nap," which, of course, is a lyrical for one or the other. Confusions of this kind are particularly apparent in dubbed movies, which, for the partially deaf, are an otherworldly experience—what you might call the Magoo Effect—since for two hours or so you never see what you are trying to hear, and there are no lyricals at all, just a mess.

Lady and the Tramp produced what you might call a modified Magoo Effect. It presented an even greater challenge than, say, *Rocky* or *Batman* because there are no lips at all but just jaws that open and close in synchrony with the human soundtrack, like a puppet's. The plot of *Lady* is clear enough from the actions of the animal characters: the mutual affection of Lady and Tramp, the nasty Siamese cats, Tramp's rescue of a sleeping baby from a rat, the wicked aunt, the dogcatcher, the happy ending. But the characters, while making all the sounds of speech, were never, I thought, saying anything *comprehensible* to each other.

"What are they saying, Beth?"

"Who?"

"Well, I don't know, *all* of them."

"You want to know what all the *cows are a saying*?" *cows are a saying*

"There *weren't* any cows."

"Gerry! What cows? What's wrong with you, for heaven's sake!? I never said there were cows."

"What's wrong—"

"You're always—adrift, it seems to me, thinking of things—beside the point!" *cows-are-a—char-ac-ters*

"Sorry. You meant what all the characters are saying. Yes. What were they saying?"

"I didn't mean it, Gerry—I said it! It's a cartoon, for Pete's sake."

I changed the subject, and Beth let it go, as we drove to a hidden lane leading to the sea, where her vowel-filled sighs set our pitch, intensity, and rhythm. But today, thinking back, I wish we'd talked it through, at least at some point, for Beth came closest to figuring things out or to helping me do it or to our doing it together. We might have gotten to the root of the problem. Beth suspected something, to the extent she could see it in my drifting eyes, what I call my *regard du sourd*, my "look of a deaf man," as I try to decipher the words. But I never let her explore the matter further—I suppose out of pride or mostly fear—until twenty years later. Fear of those who always seemed to understand everything more quickly, of the better lyricists, or whatever I called them, or thought of them as, then—fear even of the girls to whom I was becoming so close, fear of the world rushing past me.

I REALIZE TODAY THAT LYRICALS ARE NOT A NORMAL part of everyone's speech, but instead my way of getting to words that others have already heard and understood. I have also learned that other partially deaf people have long struggled with lyricals and written about them—about their own transitions—without naming them or being wholly aware of their nature or origin, in some cases even of their existence. In *Deaf Sentence* (2008), at times a hilarious novel, David Lodge's principal character suffers the difficulties posed by Lodge's own partial deafness. Lodge resolves lyricals in the book not by replicating his character's inner codes but by translating them in speakers' (requested) repetitions. Thus, the speaker reveals *the pastime of the dance went to pot* as *the last time we went to France it was hot*, and *we seared our asses on bits of plate* gets repeated as *we were near Carcassonne, a pretty place*—illustrating with a wink the loss of a number of vowels and consonants at various frequencies and the mind's incorrect substitutions. Georges Knaebel (*Brouhaha*, 2001) writes of Mozart as a lyrical in a conversation on music he thought to be about food: Is it mimoza, or something like *orza, coza, poza, loza, roza*?

To Josh Swiller (*the unheard*, 2007), voices amplified by hearing aids aren't saying words so much as the idea of words. With guesswork, "your brain has to turn the ideas into words," as in his *this place is going to rah*, searching for *this place is Gommorah*. The effort fails in Swiller's thoroughly unresolved lyricals (at a Yale lecture), *rub-a-rub-a errgh rugga wub*. Michael Chorost in *Rebuilt* (2006) progresses from *the ates physician* to *the Bates physician* to *the Gates physician* to *the Gates Foundation*. The title of Henry Kisor's book (*What's That Pig Outdoors?*, 1990) is itself a lyrical for *What's That Big Loud Noise?* (it was a fart), the correction of four consonants and a vowel at between 250 and 1,200 Hz. Kisor writes, "Often we never catch up, falling further and further behind as our minds slowly make sense of what we are seeing."

Kisor's title and Lodge's variation on "near Carcassonne" bring to mind the more comical stories about misunderstood phrases and song lyrics, sometimes called "mondegreens," and the coffee-table books that feature them. The mistakes are often homophonic, as in the original *Lady Mondegreen*, mistaken for *laid him on de' green*. One book writes of listeners hearing *I'm your penis* for *I'm your Venus*, *the cross-eyed baby* for *the cross I bear*, *you shaved my wife* for *you saved my life*, and so on. The absent-minded Professor Calculus in Hergé's *Tintin* is a walking lyrical himself (in his case a result of partial deafness) and constantly misunderstands what others are saying.

One work on mondegreens holds that "just because you've misheard a song's lyrics, that doesn't mean you need to get your ears checked. . . . The brain's neurons can misfire for many reasons when you listen to music." But if one looks carefully at the mistakes, it is almost universally misheard *consonants*, softer than vowels, that are obscured by the music or the acoustics. The brain's neurons are not misfiring but receiving inadequate signals from the listener's cochlear hearing cells. Thus, though the confusion can often be amusing, it is an illustration of what, for millions of us, is a way of life. The mondegreens play with the misheard phrases and accompany them with illustrations (a cross-eyed baby, a bald wife), but we struggle with them, whether sung or spoken, in noise or in quiet, amusing or not.

Lyricals are not just the child of damaged cochlear cells but also the product of the lipreading we, the partially deaf, practice in order to understand the world around us. For the profoundly deaf, however, those who hear very little speech or none at all, lipreading is an extraordinarily difficult, if not an impossible, task. In sixteenth-century Spain, Juan Pablo Bonet undertook the task of teaching profoundly deaf children how to speak. He met with little success, although his task was often to get just a handful of words out of the child so that he could inherit. The deaf "and dumb" had generally been forbidden inheritance in Europe since the Roman era. But even Bonet, who touted his own skills as a speech teacher (all you had to do was "press on the right frets"), knew that lipreading didn't work. Too many critical markers of our speech (half of our consonants) are hidden in the mouth (*d, g, h, k, s, t*) or visually indistinguishable (*p, b, m; f, v*).

In trying to read lips the profoundly deaf are not receiving any idea but being forced to observe obscure lip movements in order to guess sounds they can't hear so that they might infer the other sounds the lips fail to show at all—a kind of mental torture of the Dark Ages. Auguste Bébian, the preeminent French teacher of the deaf, wrote in the early nineteenth century: "If the deaf student is brought to a standstill to begin with by the singular difficulty of pronouncing sounds of which the signs fixed on paper [words] lie stationary before his eyes—how is he going to understand the rapid signs that slip through the lips?" For Emmanuelle Laborit, the deaf actress who was deprived of sign until she was eight years old, the "choice" first imposed on her by her doctors and teachers was speech: for her, a combination of no sound and no language, just the lipreading crumbs—as many crumbs as she could muster, of course, but crumbs nonetheless—of what those professionals considered the only real tongue. It mattered not to them if they sent individuals with virtually silent ears, and a pitiful handful of sounds, out into a world of unreadable lips to fend for themselves.

But for the partially deaf, the hard of hearing, people like myself—talking to Sid, sitting with Hankins, swimming through Dudley Fitts's coral reefs, listening to Beth—lipreading works hand in hand with our imperfect ears in both the making and the unraveling of our lyricals. Where the line of feasibility might be drawn—how much you have to be able to hear to make lipreading an effective tool—is a difficult question. David Wright, a South African poet, was deafened by scarlet fever at the age of seven and retained only slight residual hearing. He observes in his book *Deafness* that "lipreading is 90% guesswork . . . It may take a lipreader a few seconds to make the choice while he runs the various possibilities through his mind. All the while, the lipreader's eye is engaged in taking the next sentence or two, and at the same time he is working out a reply or rejoinder to keep his end of the conversation going."

Wright at times praises his own lipreading skills with the very little hearing he retained. But in less guarded moments in the book, he concedes that he has always had great difficulty understanding people he doesn't know. Even those he does know are difficult to understand, in noise or in quiet, including the poets Sidney Keyes ("as I never learned to lipread him our conversations took place on paper") and David Gascoyne ("he talked, or rather wrote in his elaborately rococo script, for I could not lip-read him"), half of the people he meets ("I find about half mostly unintelligible . . . [and] there are [friends] I still cannot lipread, after twenty years"), and probably everyone else ("I have never reached a high standard of lipreading").

But I hear more than Wright did, and lipreading today gives me, and I think partially deaf people generally, sufficient information to decode lyricals. It is a complex exercise. The lyricals are relentless, insistent, clamoring for our constant use, attention, and respect. But they are the link between our two worlds. Oliver Sacks calls his book on the deaf and sign language *Seeing Voices*, meaning of course that the profoundly deaf are able to see the voices (hands, expressions, eyes) of their language with their eyes. An important European teacher of the deaf in the early nineteenth century, Jean Massieu, himself profoundly deaf, conversely described the hearing as having "auricular sight"—the capacity to see voices with their ears. One might at first think Massieu's term simply a synesthetic formulation, a mixing of the senses, as in giving a color a smell or a taste. But it is more than that. He was emphasizing that for all of us it is the *mind* in search of the other's ideas and that our paths to understanding, whether ears or eyes or both, are equal means to the same end.

CHAPTER 5

GAUDEAMUS

COLLEGE WAS FOR ME A TIME FOR FRIENDSHIPS AND songs without words, like the marvelous Mendelssohn melodies. Words I had first heard sung inevitably became a bundle of surprises when I read them. *You are the tear two ties of a keeper of incoming loot* would suddenly appear on paper as "you have the clear cool eyes of a seeker of wisdom and truth," and Cole Porter's *the bliss of mocking* was, of course, just "a glimpse of stocking."

With friends I would always try to keep talking myself or, when I couldn't, patiently assume that they were speaking for themselves, not really trying to make their thoughts known. But some uncertainty—or insecurity—began to creep in. The minds of teachers at the lectern weren't muddled—just too complicated for me. At my early academic lectures in one of the great halls at Yale, with over two hundred students in attendance, I was alarmed by the ability of my classmates to take notes on what the lecturers were saying. Occasionally I would catch a phrase or two and write down a piece of it, quiz a neighbor, or copy from the notes they would tilt in my direction. I thought he (or they—this happened many times, with different people—you sat anywhere) thought I was simply slow, and I was grateful for the kindness. I didn't do it too often, though, because it was embarrassing.

A centerpiece of the introductory course in modern European history was a lecture by Charles Garside, a dazzling young associate professor, on the emperor Charles V. I would hear patches of it, something like:

> Charles indebited the minstrel stills of this automatic million, and from the inheritance of his full grandparents was named a fir cedar of what dry dip abodes a two knighted stirrup. . . . He retired as a monster leaving his possessions to another Ferdinand, and torsion filled as a second in spades.

When in fact his words were:

> Charles inherited the administrative skills of his grandfather Maximilian and from the inheritance of his four grandparents became the first leader of what might have foretold a united Europe. . . . He retired to a monastery, leaving his possessions to his brother Ferdinand and to his son, Philip II of Spain.

Garside's talk was given with great theatre and a tragic sense of the emperor's effort and failure to unite Europe, but despite his acting and an illuminating phrase or two, the lecture to me was nonsense. I stopped listening, preferring just to behold the magnificent Garside, a Charles himself, and looked for learning in the gestures that accompanied his spectacular delivery. Many members of the history department and other faculties attended the lecture each year, and all proclaimed, teachers and students alike, that Charles Garside's talk was the very model of what Yale teaching was all about.

French classes at Yale were smaller affairs, though because they were given wholly in French, as at Andover, following the line of discussion was difficult. I understood the texts themselves, if not the teachers' views of them—a potentially serious limitation because they were all stars and keenly aware of it. One written technique that worked well was the *explication de texte*, a written analysis of a single paragraph in a work, in which you could explore how individual words fit into the narrative and philosophy of the book as a whole. I used it again and again and, though they found few of their own ideas in my *explications*, the teachers loved it because the technique was, in effect, a celebration of their language.

In one course we read plays that ranged from Corneille and Molière in the seventeenth century to Sartre, Genet, and Giraudoux in the twentieth. The small class was as lively as the plays, because we discussed specific pieces of dialogue—indeed recited them, as our teacher, Jacques Guicharnaud, asked us to do in order to taste the full flavor of his language. He helped us with pronunciation, tonality, and the subtleties you could derive from each playwright by the way you delivered his words, much as you can best understand Pinter by reading (or pausing) him aloud. Many of the lyricals in class were thus already translated for me, the answer right there on the page, and I did the usual *explication de texte* working with ideas now much appreciated by Guicharnaud.

In larger classes like Garside's, however, distance and the lack of time for transitional language were formidable challenges, and at the end of each lecture my notebooks would show but a scattering of commonplaces. Though I could more or less catch up by reading, the lecture hall and even the seminar room, easier but still difficult, should have given me hints of the reason for my separate, quieter world. But I attributed the problem to a slower intellect, and I considered myself lucky to be at a great university, with a lurking suspicion that I didn't belong there.

Economics was particularly difficult. Our teacher, leading a class of about twenty, had an obscure, muffled voice, and the ideas were complex and new to me. I immediately thought of Tom Hankins at Andover, but this man, Stephen Saunders, seemed likely to be less sympathetic. And in any event, college students were expected to be able to get along on their own. I managed to corner him after an early February class and started asking him questions about the production of guns and butter, elasticity of demand, the Samuelson text—along with some unusual ones.

"Why does the government have the right to print money whenever it wants?," I asked. "Why do people accept it? How do people and institutions accumulate it? What underpins their right to do so? Why doesn't my mother have any money?" The last question drew a wide-eyed look, but in fact Saunders proved to be as much of a softy as Tom, and we met right after class three times a week, as he went through things a second time for me, indulging my repeated questions with the patience and grace—*we're in the money*—of Mr. Chips. The course became a breeze, an exercise in thinking about the tangible world, another blow to my vanishing saints.

English literature was an easier matter. There were fifteen of us in the class, and I had a seat in the first row. Our teacher, Robin Seligman, was a visiting lecturer from Berkeley. He sat on his desk, literally, legs folded, all through the class every day, as we discussed our readings of Chaucer, Milton, and Dante in translation. I loved reading and hearing from Seligman that Satan was little more than a wily character in *Paradise Lost*: not a devil, folks, just one of us. Seligman was a delight, and I understood him—not so much his words as his lips, his lyricals, and his demeanor. A look at the text and a look back at him gave me the gist of what he was saying.

In the spring of my sophomore year I met Mary Choate, who had eyes that would change color right before you, over the ridges of her olive cheekbones, from a calm pale blue to a bright green that seemed to depend not on the light, as with many chameleon eyes, but on her mood. I imagine Locke would agree that there are ways other than words to make your thoughts known to those who are falling in love with you. I had met Mary at a party on the North Shore. "You are definitely my favorite *sodomite*, Gerry Shea," *well! no no sodomite mite emite demite lemite Salemite!* Mary said, still smiling, as she took a sip of champagne. Everything about her seemed perfect, from her pearl necklace to her well-shaped calves, legs crossed, her long dress floating around her knees. It wasn't so much Mary's words that counted. It was the way she moved, the timbre of her voice, the changing color of her eyes.

After relatively happy academic experiences the spring of my second year, I decided to devote myself almost exclusively to what I loved as a child and still loved, and still love today: singing—in a small group, in the Glee Club, and finally two years later in the Whiffenpoofs. Founded over a century ago, in 1909, the Whiffs are the oldest a cappella group in America. Cole Porter was a member from the class of 1913, and indeed he wrote the music and lyrics of many of our songs, found in the *Whiff Blue Book* passed on every year. The Whiffs are a short-lived experience, for members are all seniors and thus together for only one year. There are no auditions. On a chilly night in April each year, as the cherry blossoms and hyacinths are starting to bloom, the existing group appears at your doorstep, hauls you out of your room, fills you with Green Cup (the traditional drink at Mory's, where they sing), and you are in.

So I was sung in, and academics were permanently out, at least as a current goal, and I was overjoyed. I would sing—do nothing but sing—for the coming year. As one of our songs goes, "Phi beta kappa, not them goofs, I'll take my orders from the—Whiffenpoofs." We all felt that way, but I, I suppose, in a special way. If you sing together two or three hours a day and on weekends, and on Monday nights at Mory's Temple Bar, and words are a riddle for you but musical notes are not, the music makes you free. You have your song without words: you don't need to listen to the words of others. The voices singing beside me were clear enough, and we would serenade the world, "while life and voice shall last!," and we did, and we do.

In my senior year Mary came down to New Haven every weekend the Whiffs stayed in town. She would be with us when we sang at Mory's on Saturdays after the football game and later at concerts on the campus. She learned the words to "Shenandoah" and "Mavourneen" and the "Crucifixus" of Palestrina, "*etiam pro nobis, sub Pontio Pilato*," lovely written lyricals in no need of translation. At times during our courtship she would tell me that I failed to listen to others, that I was escaping from the tedium of "just listening to people, Gerry." But we were young, and in a world of reading, friendship, and song, it mattered little. "*Juvenes dum sumus*," we would sing, "*Gaudeamus!*"

I managed to schedule a weekend free in February, and Mary asked me to come to her grandfather's weekend place in Petersham, in western Massachusetts. Many friends were there, as well as one of Mary's aunts, and we were unable, or so we thought, to sleep in the same room. On Sunday morning we took a walk in the snow, deep snow, in the broad fields—more like plains really—that stretch out from the house to the Worcester Hills to the southeast. All was quiet except for the call of my locusts *in the winter the fallen snow.*

"Did you have fun last night, Gerry?"

"Wonderful."

"I loved your singing."

"Al was great." I had asked Al Rossiter, the "pitchpipe" or musical director of our group, to come too, and we had sung together.

"Do you know something?"

"What?"

"You're *always* singing—or speaking, and I love *two kittens*" *two kittens kissin to kissen lissen to listen* "to you. But you seldom seem to—*listen*. Very often you seem to be preparing your *own* thoughts when other people are talking. I—I'm reminded of that cartoon in *Look* magazine, where a woman is in her Park Avenue apartment or somewhere, talking to a friend. Her husband is in a chair nearby, well dressed, smiling, with blond hair and glasses, looking like you. With a bit of an absent look. 'You know,' she says to her friend, '*some tie*'" *some tie! sometimes* "'I think he understands everything we're saying.'"

"Come *on*."

"Well, not really—because you follow the drift, I don't know, then break in with your own thoughts or suddenly sing a goddam song—well, not a *goddam* song. A wonderful song. But there's often no—no continuity! You're not a—is there an adjective—not a—a *continuous* person!"

"Well, I'm not very good at it, at listening, and I've lots to say! But when I listen, I, uh, get confused. It's a quirk. People's thoughts get changed, and I have to change them back."

"Does anyone else notice that you don't listen?"

"No. Just you. I'm sure I'll get better. In fact I've never talked about how I—change words—before. But the problem is there, I guess. It's there all the time."

Mary's eyes were changing color, and I could see she was suddenly elsewhere—in the future, perhaps thinking, *What to say? What to say? That listening is important, in graduate school, in professional life, perhaps in our life together?* She finally said, "Well, I'm here to *have you to it.*" *have you help you through it*

"That would be wonderful, Mary. But I think I can manage it. I just have to learn to concentrate."

"In any event, one thing is very clear."

"And that is—?"

She gave me a kiss, a great big smack on the lips as she put her arms around me, and then ran farther into the field, her boots threading the snow. She fell, and I picked her up and turned her around. We looked at each other in silence, in an instant of recognition, one of those moments when no arbitrary signs are needed to unlock the heart.

CHAPTER 6

LAW SCHOOL MYSTERIES

AFTER YALE, I WENT TO COLUMBIA LAW SCHOOL IN New York City. I found my world unbridled, and one way to try to take the reins was to study the law (from *lex, legere*: to read) and thus perhaps to impose a certain order on things—or so I thought when I was twenty-one. With a friend from college I shared an apartment on 120th Street, between Morningside and Amsterdam, and took a job doing research at the law school for Julius Goebel, the country's preeminent legal historian, to help pay the rent.

The law school's building is an odd and somber structure, which then and now has been said, correctly, to look like a toaster. The protrusion on the south side of the rectangular building looks like a lever waiting to be bashed down by some gargantuan breakfaster standing in Morningside Park. But the large lecture halls inside—four quadrants with floors descending gradually toward the lectern, holding about 250 students each— were not badly designed, and the acoustics were somewhat better than those of the high-ceilinged New Haven halls. I was unsettled, however, to learn that all of my courses would be in these large rooms, for I thought that great numbers of people made it difficult to concentrate. Alas, there would be much more to the law than simply reading it.

Because "Shea" is toward the end of the alphabet, I sat in my assigned place more than halfway back in the large quadrant. On the first day my neighbors were again recording the proceedings with smoothly flowing pens, while I searched for lyrical rescues. We were learning a new vocabulary, and teachers were asking us unanswerable questions designed to make us think: "*While thus protory is topical require sections in appliance?*"

> *while thus*
> > *why thus*
> > > *why does*
> > > > *promontory is topical*
> > > > *promissory estoppel*
> > > > > *require*
> > > > > > *sections*
> > > > > > > *actions*
> > > > > > > > *why does promissory estoppel*
> > > > > > > > *require action in reliance?*

By the time I got the message, the discussion had gone beyond where I was, and I would look around at the smooth, silent scribblings of my classmates. At night I would glance at my sparse notes and then read the cases assigned for the next day intently, trying to find in the judges' opinions the answers to the next day's garbled riddles. I did passably well, for I could read, at least, and write, and intermittently get things straight. Law school classes were more intense than those at college, and I was generally quiet, tense, and terrified. When I juggled lyricals, the teacher and other students—or so I believe—had the impression I was just another first-year student trying to come to grips with how a lawyer should think about things.

But it might have been better had I not gone to class and skipped the private humiliation. The law school has its ghosts, including justices John Jay, Charles Evans Hughes, Harlan Fiske Stone, Benjamin Cardozo, William O. Douglas, and others of the Supreme Court; Paul Robeson; both Roosevelts; and a lyricist too: Oscar Hammerstein (*I've a one-two Japan, oh so alight, I compete and differ and type—I'm a one woman man, home-lovin' type, all complete with slippers and pipe*). And I was letting them all down. I could see that Professor Goebel was disappointed in my grades as well, and I was terrified that I would never find a suitable job, let alone a place anywhere near the law school's lingering spirits.

My confusion in law school reminds me today of a misguided teacher of the profoundly deaf in the nineteenth century, the abbé Sicard, who taught his students written words without enabling them to form the simplest judgments about the world around them. He would draw the word "ball" in solid capitals with "thing" in lower case between the letters to show that a ball was an object— t *B* h *A* i *L* n *L* g—and an animal a being—*A* b *N* e *I* i *M* n *A* g *L*. Sicard failed to explore the differences between the two words by giving extensive examples, because of his limited knowledge of sign language. So he stitched two words together in writing, producing something less useful than babble for the hearing, bearing no resemblance even to an obscure lyrical, and more meaningless even than spoken words for the deaf. My new law school lyricals were not as obscure as Sicard's tbhailnlg and abneiimnagl, but they were dizzying. To what extent, after all, were *promontories* and *appliances* pivotal parts of enforceable promises?

Mary, meanwhile, had transferred to Cornell Nursing School at New York Hospital in the city. I saw her only infrequently, and I was too proud to tell her more about the words that floated by.

When we were together, she said I failed to listen to her, that I was still drifting, now to some unreachable place. She wanted to help, as she had said at Petersham, but I wasn't letting her. It was true; I never even asked her to stay with me. She saw my apartment only once. I was ashamed of it, not because of its uninhabitable state, but because I felt it showed how hard I worked with such little success—my desk, the coffee stains, the empty notebooks with half-phrases half-crossed out, the worn pages of the casebooks.

At the nurses' residence on Seventieth Street, one of our last times together, Mary guided me over to a dark corner and leaned backward into it. She pulled me to her, kissed me. "Listen, Gerry," she said, moving her lips to my right ear. "I love you, and I don't want to lose you. Do you love me?"

"I do, Mary, I do, I just—"

"*Just* what, Gerry?"

"I just need to, to, master what I—"

"You don't have to choose, you know. You *callambo*." *callambo ambo habo have both you can have both* "I don't care how well you do or don't. You never used to care. But now it's the *all*. And I seem to have no place in your life."

"Soon it will be different, Mary. I don't want to lead you down a path to—"

"Are you afraid of poverty? Well, I'm not. I don't care what you do. We'll manage."

"I'll never love anyone else," I finally said.

"But you have to *tow* it, Gerry, to *tow* it to me like you used to. *Gaudeamus*, you would sing, Oh, let's rejoice! You wouldn't listen often, but you would *sing*, you would *sing* to me, and *speak* to me, and *spend time* with me. Well, *clearasil sung*, Gerry," *clearasil sung juvenes dum—young we are still young* "and I don't know where this stiffness, distance" *you're always adrift, said Beth, adrift adrift adrift* "and sadness has come from, and, and, I can only think, on your part it's, Gerry, just—I don't know, *hear" fear* "or just plain . . . indifference."

"Mr. Shea."

"Yes, sir."

"Tell us about the *Gulliver race*."

race race case Gulliver is Sullivan, the Sullivan case, New York Times v. Sullivan "The court held that a public figure can't recover for libel even for false statements about him, unless the false statements are published with knowledge that they were false."

"Why, *Tom, Ed*, why this rule? Shouldn't a newspaper *bay tooritite*?"

> *Tom Ed*
> > *why*
> > > *tomed*
> > > *why*
> > > > *tomedge*
> > > > *knowledge*

"Mr. Shea?"

> *bay tooritite*
> *be sure it's*
> > *right*
> > *a newspaper*
> > > *make sure it's right—*

"It should, but the issue is whether liability for being simply incorrect, wrong, without more, would chill free speech, at least as to public figures—restrict free and open public and political discourse."

"So I just *doeneck and trouble shit*." *doneck trouble shit?! publish it, doeneck doeneck?*

"Sorry, sir?"

"So I just go ahead and publish it."

"Well, then, if you know it's incorrect—"

"That's just the point! I don't know. I *dinteck*."

"Didn't check?"

"Precisely. I'm waiting. Would you like some help? *Misbegones* over there is *sighing* to have a word." *misbegones begones buttons miss buttons sighing dying trying to have a word beautiful brilliant Miss Frances Buttons—*

"Well, said Fanny, "that sounds like recklessness—that is, you just don't *eck don't check* so you don't *owe owe owe know don't know*—that won't work either. Seems you do know, or you *doe dare*." *doe dare don't dare don't care*

"Sounds right, Miss Buttons. Do you like the rule, Shea?"

"The knowledge rule, yes. But it's a tough rule for a politician. My skin wouldn't be thick enough to survive all that."

"Ah, Shea, thin skin! Yes, Miss Buttons?"

"Open discussion is *misbetorpant*" *misbe—more important* "than Gerry's skin," said Fanny (she is now a celebrated litigator), turning her eyes to me—truth in those blue eyes, but all pallor in winter.

Mary flew to Labrador for the summer to work in a makeshift hospital in the backwoods, while I spent it reading eighteenth-century manuscripts and newspapers for Professor Goebel at the law school and the New-York Historical Society on Central Park West. I loved turning the rolls of microfilm in a dark, quiet room in the library, trying to solve the silent riddles of the past. I learned a great deal about the formative history of the Bill of Rights and the Judiciary Act of 1789, which set up our federal courts, but nothing about my own mysteries.

CHAPTER 7

LANGUAGE IN AIR,
LANGUAGE IN LIGHT

MARY CAME BACK TO NEW YORK HOSPITAL IN THE fall, resolved to shape her own life. I was beginning my second year of law school and determined to try to make sense of mine. It was during the coming year that I would invent a private solution to the problem of my strange words. It was only a partial, palliative solution—my discovery of the real problem would be far away.

When I arrived at my first class, I found I could sit where I wanted, so I darted to the first row, to a seat near the nose of the large quadrant, opposite the teacher. It was this day, the first of my second year, that I discovered my new way of learning. I decided never to speak unless called on, to say as little as possible even then, and to focus on my own private text. By the time the day was complete I had a notebook full of three hours of classes written in a tongue, I thought as I glanced over them, that I might never understand. But it was the fullest book in my own hand I had ever had, not two pages but ten. As I headed back to my dark room, I was worried that these new written words would be as difficult as the spoken ones. I sat down and looked at the first five lines:

> Sequest his way for the privilege is the client's for a lawyer didn't it? Toss a purple of pre-ex collusion very cool—to keep these communications now of the tortful? To protect lawyers or two courage confidentiality? Where is the dying wave? Can the lawyer's bill pay it? What? Ah Misbegones lest he bite if the client's a lawyer, took and fair at tiring the other. Fairies choosing, Misbegones.

I read and worked through them line by line. *Lex, lego, legere!* "Misbegones"—Miss Buttons—was a given, of course; with a little effort "Where is the dying wave?" became "What if the client waives?" "Can the lawyer's bill pay it?" showed itself to be "Can the lawyer still raise it?" "Tortful" was "courtroom" with a little thought, and "Toss a purple of pre-ex collusion very cool" is a lyrical for "What's the purpose of the exclusionary rule?" The result was a revelation:

> The question is whether the privilege is the client's or the lawyer's, isn't it? What's the purpose of the exclusionary rule—to keep these communications out of the courtroom? To protect lawyers or to encourage confidentiality? What if the client waives? Can the lawyer still raise it? What? Ah, Miss Buttons says he might if the client's a lawyer, too, and they're advising each other! Very amusing, Miss Buttons!

I looked at the microfilm projector and wondered whether my summer in the eighteenth century had taught me something about understanding obscure words. If you gather as many fragments as you can, even to the point of jotting down nonsense, and piece them together with patience and time, and refer back to a related written text, if there is one, you can find the speaker's ideas. In Alexander Hamilton's letters and briefs the text was there: to be studied on film for as long as it took to decipher his handwriting. In my case the text was also there but needed to be decoded in a different way. From context, from the judges' written opinions, and using my general familiarity with lyricals, I could transpose and substitute letters and words to find the intended meaning. I figured that this was how everyone does it, only, in my case, it took more time. I was getting warm, but this convoluted path, as coiled as the cochlea, was unlikely to work in everyday life. It was not the language I needed.

This method of decoding my lyricals, I would learn later in life, was not unlike the way William Stokoe (pronounced "Stokie") of Gallaudet College (now University), the eminent American Sign Language scholar, took up the study of sign language in the 1960s. He and his colleagues, using a small movie camera powered by an electric-train transformer, filmed individuals conversing in sign language in order to compile and analyze its linguistic components. Stokoe studied the films frame by frame. I was studying sounds—vibrations in the air—syllable by syllable; he was unraveling extraordinarily fast, often almost invisible movements in light. He was looking for a language; I was seeking meaning in my own. His studies would lead to a modern understanding of the morphology of sign; mine would tell me no more than what I was looking for—what had gone on during the day.

But writing down lyricals was an answer to my immediate academic problem. I was engaged in what Auguste Bébian called the "fixing" of the "signs" of our ideas on paper—in my case transitional signs—recording them as they slipped through the lips of my law teachers. The constituent elements or configurations of our speech, our language in air, are the sounds we make when we place, shape, and move our tongues, mouths, and vocal cords. These configurations exist not to be seen but to rearrange air molecules so that they will carry the speaker's ideas, with uncanny precision, to the listener's eardrums and cochlea. The ideas I was writing down were muddled by missing or confused phonemes (consonants and vowels), carried in the air from the teacher to my seat in the front row. But I could hear enough of the configurations to record my lyricals. And working into the night, I could make sense of them.

When I think today about my difficulty, and my clumsy though instinctive effort to find a solution, I can't help but admire the language Stokoe was studying—what I call the language of light. It is a stunning solution to the dilemma of the profoundly deaf—their inability to hear, or to shape effectively with their own voices, the configurations of our language in air. Alphonse de Lamartine describes the role of light in a few lines he wrote to the deaf poet Pierre Pélissier in 1844:

> It is through the senses
> that light descends upon us.
> But I see in the accents of your verse
> in your captive heart it enters first,
> thwarting nature
> and making sense of itself.

The airborne constituents of speech reach the ears of the deaf, of course, but there they die unheard. Their eyes might look to the lips for the speaker's idea, but there its configurations are obscure or hidden, and it is a search in the wrong medium. Thus the profoundly deaf, for thousands of years, have signed and made sense of the world, shaping light into a sixth sense of their own. Their hands, expressions, eyes, all have their own constituent elements—place, shape, and motion—that convey their ideas to the listener's eyes in a language endowed with a syntax, vocabulary, and meaning that is every bit as sophisticated as that of any spoken tongue.

My language of lyricals is an uncertain one, but sign language is crystal clear. The deaf who sign would not, and could not, exchange their language for mine, nor would I forsake the language I speak and imperfectly hear. Nevertheless, for centuries the profoundly deaf have been forced to turn to the impossible configurations of the language of the hearing. In the Middle Ages, the principal goal was to teach them to speak. Juan Pablo Bonet never understood sign language, but he wrote that if you "place two deaf mutes in each other's presence, meeting for the first time, they can communicate because they use the same signs." The important thing for Bonet, however, was "never to let the mute use it." His pupils would spend all their time learning how to speak a few words they couldn't hear and would barely understand.

The ideas of the Middle Ages were to be revived in the mid-nineteenth century, and they remain with us today. It is a kind of Hundred Years War that has been waged in various forms since 1880. At a teachers' congress held in Italy that year, sign language was effectively banished, throughout Europe and the United States, from virtually all deaf teaching institutions. The Congress of Milan—a gathering of hearing, speaking educators with little or no knowledge of sign—proudly proclaimed "the incontestable superiority of speech over signs." Schools were to teach only by "the pure oral method," in order "to restore the deaf to society and to give them a more perfect knowledge of language." After Milan, signing played virtually no role in deaf education for a century, until Stokoe revived it. Milan had committed the gravest of human offenses: language is the core of who we are. I lost a part of mine by chance; Milan's willful objective was to deprive the deaf of their language entirely.

But the deaf had, for a time, thrived in an age of reason. The late eighteenth and early nineteenth centuries were an extraordinary time for them—an age that was and remains a source of enlightenment for all of us, deaf and hearing alike. Auguste Bébian and his Parisian coadjutors learned sign language and, in that language, taught the deaf to read and write. Central to Bébian's approach was Locke's notion that words, and signs, are the expression of ideas. But Bébian put emphasis on the fact that an idea (whether material or abstract) necessarily preexists the spoken word or given sign that interprets it. The idea must give the word or sign meaning before the word or sign can, in turn, become an effective interpreter of the idea, or what John Locke interestingly (referring to the word alone) called the "sign" of the idea.

The idea and the spoken word or given sign it generates merge when they are expressed or understood, in what Bébian calls a "simultaneity of circumstance." Those of us who hear enough sound convey our thoughts ordinarily by speaking and by writing down words made of letters that stand for the sounds we make with our voices—what Bébian called the "painting" of our speech. Because speech is the conventional sign of our ideas, in the Dark Ages people were led to believe that speech was indispensable to the exercise of thought. The deaf were therefore regarded as "almost a being of a different species."

Bébian proved this to be utter nonsense. He mastered sign, deciphered and analyzed its morphology and syntax, taught it to perfection, and used it to teach his deaf students how to read and write "painted speech." His methods were adopted throughout the Western world, where hearing teachers learned the signs of the deaf in their respective countries—for the deaf, like the hearing, have their own national or regional languages, each as different from the other as are spoken tongues. Bébian's students, and those of his successors, entered the professions in great numbers; they worked in lawyers' offices, schools, banks, trading companies, shipping firms, railroads, government ministries, and manufacturing. Some became painters, writers, and poets.

The key to their success was Bébian's recognition that we all carry the same "timeless and limitless" principle within us—that of our first language, the language to which we are first exposed and thus learn. It gives immediate expression to our thoughts. It is not a translation of any other tongue. It expresses directly, without difficulty or hesitation, our intimate connection with ideas: "The deaf student must be able to write the word in order to read it, and to be able to read it he has to understand it; and he'll be able to understand it only if he understands the whole sentence. . . . To do that, his instruction must begin in sign." Speech cannot be the first language of a child born profoundly deaf, because he cannot be directly exposed to it; he cannot hear it, and he is remote from any semblance of simultaneity. Sign is his first language. That is why the medieval speech teacher Bonet and his oralist successors, even today, have thought it important "not to let the mute use it"—for the child would soon forsake our language in air for his own. But letting the "mute" use it *was* important, for it became not only his own tongue but his gateway to reading and writing.

Bébian recognized that, in order to converse and learn, the deaf, like the hearing, need not only to merge their ideas and words into one but also to "understand the whole sentence," to appreciate the relative value of words, that is, "the influence they have over each other." And here lies a lesson for those of us who hear poorly and those who want to understand our predicament. A misheard word or unknown or displaced sign cannot, of course, be given its relative meaning if it conveys no idea at all. For both those who hear well and the signing deaf, there is a direct progression from the idea of the speaker or signer, to the relative meaning of his words or signs, to the ears or eyes of his interlocutor, and to his brain, where the idea is firmly planted:

SPEAKER OR SIGNER   INTERLOCUTOR

idea ⟶ words ⟶ ears ⟶ brain ⟶ idea!

idea ⟶ signs ⟶ eyes ⟶ brain ⟶ idea!

But for the partially deaf, the sequence is indirect:

SPEAKER   LISTENER

idea ⟶ words ⟶ ears+eyes ⟶ brain ⟶ lyrical 1

⟶ lyrical 2 ⟶ lyrical 3 ⟶ idea!

or ⟶ wrong idea

or ⟶ no idea

Our lyricals are thus but the journey, through what might be called the wrong ideas of words, usually but often not to the right ones, that is, to the preexisting idea of the speaker. We are left without the simultaneity enjoyed by both the hearing and the signing deaf; ours is a staccato-like comprehension (when it comes), as with lightning speed we hunt for syntax and meaning in a jumble of sounds and lips.

⌣

"HOW ARE *TINGS ON*?" ASKED JULIUS GOEBEL WHEN HE saw me in the hall the second day of school.

tings on "Sorry?"

"How are things going, Gerry?"

"Oh, very well, sir, very well."

"You can stop *talking beezer*, I'm not *sat cold*, and you're not that *'un*."

"No, I guess I'm not." The rugless, uncurtained, windowless, reverberant toaster lobby swallowed the sound. I moved closer to him.

"Why not bring Mary to lunch a week from Sunday?"

"I'd love to, sir."

"Gerry, I said you needn't call me 'sir.'" *stop talking beezer calling me sir I'm not that old and you're not that young you can stop calling me sir*

"Oh, sorry. I'll call her. We haven't spoken for a while, but—"

"Don't lose her, Gerry. She's the best you'll ever get. The law's not everything, you know. It's not what's going to make you happy."

"I guess not. But I want to succeed first—here—it comes first, and then—"

"Well, get her over to *our base. Doe the parchment eyes* your life." *our base our place the parchment compartment eyes compartmentize don't compartmentalize your life.*

I nodded.

"By the way, I've got you in *toxitacon*, you know." *toxitacon con on toxic coccyx consicks conflicts conflicts of laws* "You'll love it."

"Yes, I'm looking forward to it. I'll be able to reach Mary at six."

"You may know her schedule, Gerry, but that's not enough." He turned toward the elevator, waved, and repeated himself as he walked away, "That's not enough!"

CHAPTER 8

THE SOUNDS OF SILENCE

MARY WAS THERE AT SIX. WHEN I ASKED HER TO come to the Goebels' house for lunch she said Sunday was a working day for her, and she would have only half an hour. In fact, the entire fall would be very busy for her, as she was sure it would be for me. "Well, Mary, it will be. But when it's over, I think I've found the solution—that it's going to be all right. I'll be able to do what I want."

"I'm happy for you, Gerry. *Cats rarely can choose.*" *Cats? God. Cats?*

"Cats?"

"That's very good news, I said."

"And then, I thought we—we—"

"We'll speak again."

"I need to tell you something—"

"Oh, Gerry, it's—we'll talk again soon."

"Very soon."

Rosalind Rose was the dean's guardian at the gate. If you paid Roz a visit, and courted her a bit, she would tell you your grades before they were formally given. This I did one sunny day in late January on the dean's floor of the toaster building. Roz was all smiles, radiant at forty-eight, with broad and pliant lips, the sun full in her face.

"You want your grades, Gerry Shea, or you want me?"

"You!"

"Promise?"

"Absolutely."

"Tonight, *atlas herdy* in the gym, the small room with the wading pool. It's humid down there in and out of the *hallowed* water."

tonight atlas herdy six thirty hallowed sallow—humid in and out of the shallow water "Miss Rose, you're too much for me!"

"Too young, Gerry? OK. Another day. Let me see. . . . Want them now, or shall I write them down?"

I smiled and gestured with my right hand, as if writing. She folded the paper and gave it to me, her own smile little changed.

"Are they OK?"

"You'll see."

I carried them around in my pocket all afternoon trying to interpret Roz's smiles, and finally, down in my dark room in the library, I sat in front of a stack of typed translated notes, the progeny of piles of notebooks of nonsense and stationary lyricals, and unfolded the paper. I took a deep breath as I saw constitutional law, evidence, antitrust, and commercial transactions all afloat, each of the As looking like a sailboat setting out to sea, the mast, in Roz's delightful hand, standing well over the nose of the gaff, soaring off to starboard. A fleet of As. I looked at the paper again and again, in disbelief. A trivial matter. But I was, if not first in the class, very close to first; I had unlocked my troubled mind and could now join one of the great firms and marry whenever I wanted.

Though I didn't know it, I had not found my first language, and I never would. I had simply broken a code in an exercise that was anything but immediate. Freezing the lyricals in writing and figuring them out over time was unlikely to be practicable in the working world. Still, I had achieved my immediate objective, and it was time to make sense of my own life, of all the *gulliver's races* and *plaa bencers*, *grobiddies* and *coral reefs*. I would have Mary to share the beauty of my mysteries, helping me through them with her sparkling, parchment eyes. *Gaudeamus igitur, juvenes dum sumus etiam.*

"May I see you?"

"Yes. *I'm a spee* to you." *spee speak I must speak to you*

"I'm sorry it's been so long."

"Can you come over *to write* for dinner?" *to write too tight too to—night for dinner*

"Sure."

"We'll go to Hallows. *First Aztec at entity's word.*" *first Aztec First Avenue at Seventy-Third* "I'll *beat* you there." *beat you defeat you, meet you.*

We had dinner at Hallows. It was a time for tears, the final time. She was to marry George Hutchins, a doctor, a surgeon and savior of men. "Forget me, Gerry."

"But you have to understand. My world has opened up; I now understand it. I'll be a good lawyer—together, we—"

"Listen to me! There is no together! Not for us. I'm living with George. We went to *hell his fairly an ill toy* last week. Gerry, it's—"

"His fairly—"

"His family, Gerry, to tell his family, in Illinois. Listen to me!"

"I've no chance—you waited until now!?"

"It happened quickly. Daddy suggested *my whale to*" *my I whale hail wait 'til* "you finished your exams. And he was right. Besides, I believed, I still believe, you want something else. Not me."

"That's not true."

"That is not how it seemed."

"I was working . . . so hard, Mary! But now . . . "

"Now is too late. Now, for us, is never. I belong to him. I love him."

"You—"

"Love him."

"Listen to me, Mary. Listen. Remember—two years ago at your grandfather's house in Petersham? It was snowing in the meadow. Lots of snow. And last spring, right across the street, right there, at Docs' Deli, you said we now lived in a kind of mirror, a mirror of four images, our own of ourselves, yours of me, and mine of you. That's what you said. Right there at Docs' Deli, not far from us now, here, at Hallows. And you said the first pair of images were being wondrously transformed by the second. That's what you said."

"I was *attled* by them then."

> *attled attled*
>> *dazzled by them*
>>> *then*

"But listen to me. The image dearest to me is now someone else's. I'm sorry. I'm so sorry. You have to put that mirror away—with all its images. Don't break it—just tuck it away, in the back of your mind. And some day—"

"There's no room there for anyone else. It's unimaginable."

Mary put her head in her hands. There were many eyes on our proceedings, mostly the sympathetic eyes of the elderly Hungarians who frequented Hallows. The head waiter came over to ask whether the food was all right, and we both laughed, an old *Gaudeamus* laugh. Mary shook her head and dried her eyes. I had never seen her blue eyes become so green so quickly. They looked squarely into mine, piercing them. "Gerry, I did love you, once. But it's over."

We left our platesful of Hallows specials on the table, and I walked her over to the medical school library. When we got to the reading room, Mary stopped, pressed my hand, and stepped away without looking back, her light brown hair slightly curled, falling just below her neck and resting on her broad shoulders.

In the taxi on the way back to Columbia—mourningside, I now thought, I couldn't bear returning to the little dark room with stacks of mysterious papers, to my *misbetorpant promontories*. The price of my victory over them was all too clear. I went directly to my apartment on 120th Street, put on a tape, lay in the dark, and listened to the sounds—of silence.

CHAPTER 9

A VOICE UNTOUCHED

WHATEVER THE DEGREE OF MY SENSE OF ISOLATION with my half-language, the burden lightens when I think about a person who was doubly separated from the world: Helen Keller. Deprived by scarlet fever of both hearing and sight when she was nineteen months old, Helen could neither hear language in air nor see it in light. Helen's story is a telling illustration of the effects of being denied her own first language and being taken over by others. Her birthright was sold for what a contemporary blind writer, Thomas Cutsforth, called "a mess of verbiage." This brought her fame, and benefited others, but lost Helen her identity.

As a child, Helen had developed a vocabulary of many dozens of home signs that were seen and understood by the Keller family. Helen could neither hear voices nor see signs. She could, however, express and receive ideas through her sole remaining communicative resource—her sense of touch. Her parents and siblings signed into her hands, and she understood and responded. This was a wholly natural solution. By means of that sense she was fully capable of understanding and expressing herself in the language of the deaf.

Helen signed "bread" by simulating the cutting of slices and buttering them. To sign "ice cream," she would move her hands and arms as if opening the ice box and then shiver. To announce that the family dog had just had puppies, she pointed excitedly to the fingers of one hand and suckled each fingertip. To tell Helen that something was small, her mother would pinch the thin layer of skin on the back of Helen's hand. To sign big, Helen would spread her hands apart, bring them toward each other, and stop halfway, as if she were holding a large ball. She had signs for where to go, what to get, men and women, likes and dislikes, aunts and uncles, and many other concrete and abstract ideas.

In fact, Helen was developing the rudiments of the formal language of the deaf who are also blind, tactile sign language, which alters or supplements conventional sign in a number of respects to accommodate blindness. In conventional sign language, a question is indicated, for example, by a lifting of the eyebrows. In tactile sign it is signaled by a mark on the hand. The medium of this language is neither light nor air, but the touching hands of the conversants. It can be as efficient, sophisticated, and rapid as speech and conventional sign language, and those who use it can converse with ease even, of course, if both people are deaf and blind.

But when Helen was six years old, her father brought her to Alexander Graham Bell, already noted for his efforts to teach the deaf to speak. Bell recommended Helen to the Perkins Institute for the Blind in Boston, which found a teacher for Helen: Anne Sullivan, a young (hearing) Perkins graduate who had impaired vision as a child but had regained much of her sight through surgery. Consistent with Bell's views and Perkins's practices, Anne forbade Helen from using her signs, and her own language was permanently silenced. In its place, Anne taught Helen how to fingerspell into the hand, using the manual alphabet first formalized by St. Bonaventure in the thirteenth century for monks who had taken the vow of silence.

Fingerspelling is unworkably cumbersome. The deaf use it to spell exotic proper names (Kuala Lumpur) and for personal names or new ideas. But it is not a part of their formal language. Imagine trying to talk with someone solely by spelling the words out loud. Throughout her life, as one of her later companions wrote, Helen was "dismal at conversation." As Bébian stressed, it is the idea that gives a word meaning before the word can, in turn, become an effective interpreter of the idea. The word has to become part of the fabric of the idea. Written and fingerspelled characters, for the deaf, are far more complex than their painting of sounds for the hearing. Those characters are too far removed from the idea to become, like sign language, an effective way to speak and listen.

When Helen fingerspelled her thoughts, the ideas were generally a repetition of ideas given to her (usually by her teacher) rather than the expression of her own. She was nevertheless extraordinary. Helen graduated from Radcliffe in 1904 at the age of twenty-four, with Anne as her medium in the classroom and study hall, fingerspelling lectures and books not available in Braille into her hand. During her lifetime Helen wrote several books, the most acclaimed of which was *The Story of My Life*, published in 1903 and written while she was at Radcliffe. She dedicated the book to "Alexander Graham Bell, who has taught the deaf to speak"—an enterprise, unlike the telephone, at which he was a thorough failure. Helen also wrote several articles and had an extensive published correspondence. She was presented to the public as a phenomenon.

Bell himself claimed that Helen could speak and could read lips by putting fingers and thumb on the noses, lips, and larynxes of her interlocutor. For as long as he lived, he claimed Helen as a stunning example of what the deaf could accomplish. If deaf and blind Helen could do it, he argued, then why not the deaf who can see? Helen was not congenitally deaf and thus not a part of what Bell called the undesirable "deaf variety" of our species— and thus, given her success and popularity, an ideal subject for Bell to promote. But contrary to the general impression he had helped to engender, Helen never developed intelligible speech and could not, of course, read lips by touching them without her teacher's ever-present hand touching her own and spelling out the words letter by letter. Helen was in an important sense not one person but two, as Anne became Helen's almost exclusive intermediary throughout her life—her eyes, her ears, and her voice. They remained inseparable until Anne died at the age of seventy in 1936, when Helen was fifty-six.

Helen's intimate relationship with Anne, the nature of Helen's instruction and writing, the loss of her natural language, and other circumstances raise the question whether, or to what extent, Helen's celebrated work was her own. As the historian Roger Shattuck has gently put it, "one has reason to wonder if to any degree" Helen's work was ghostwritten. When Helen was eleven years old, Anne presented as Helen's a children's story that greatly impressed the Perkins school, who decided to have it published. It created a national sensation. The story is resplendent in its descriptions of sounds and colors.

Yet Helen had no memory of sound or of light and virtually no conception of what either was. In fact, Anne had plagiarized the story, almost verbatim, from one that had been written fifteen years earlier by an American writer, Margaret Canby, and was no longer in print. Below is an extract from the story in Canby's hand, marked to show the changes made by Anne:

> They plainly heard the tinkling of many drops falling like rain through the forest, and sliding from leaf to leaf until they reached the ~~bramble~~ little bushes ~~beside them~~ by their side, when, to their ~~great dismay~~ astonishment, they ~~found~~ discovered that the rain drops were melted rubies, which hardened on the leaves, and turned them to ~~bright~~ crimson and gold in a moment. Then, looking around more closely ~~at the trees around~~, they saw that much of the treasure was ~~all melting away~~ already melted, ~~and that much of it was already, spread over the leaves of~~ for the oaks ~~trees~~ and maples, ~~which~~ were ~~shining with their~~ arrayed in gorgeous dresses of gold and ~~bronze,~~ crimson and emerald.

Anne falsely claimed that she had never heard of Canby's story, as did Helen, who had no choice. Perkins lost all confidence in Anne, and in Helen as well, and permanently broke off contact with them, oblivious to the fact that the inadequacy of their own teaching methods was partly to blame for the dissimulation.

The problem continued throughout Helen's life, in the broader sense that she wrote not for herself but to please the sighted and the hearing. She often set out rich descriptions of sounds and colors for their benefit, as to which, because of her predicament, she was never able to formulate any clear idea at all. They were images borrowed from Anne or from works that she encouraged Helen to replicate in her own writing. As Cutsforth tells us, the blind (and deafblind), when writing in their *own* words, would describe, for example, not a "snow-white, innocent, gamboling, [bleating] lamb," but a "kinky, woolly, bony, wiggly one."

Helen wrote in her autobiography of a girl "with long golden curls and childish prattle," "everything that could hum, or buzz, or sing," "noisy-throated frogs who made the summer nights musical with their quaint love songs," "crickets . . . trilling their reedy notes," the "luminous shadows of trees and the blue heavens," "a tree shimmering in the soft light," "crowds of laughing negroes," horses "with bridles ringing and whips cracking," the "charging hunters with hark and whip and wild halloo." In 1930, when she was fifty, Helen wrote the following of Scotland:

> I love it all—the moorland peace and hills of beauty. I love the mountains when they are cloud-capped or when soft veils of mist, spun of wind and dew and flame, are drawn around their shoulders. . . . If I am ever born again, I know I shall be a Scot.

She was even more entranced with Ireland:

> The bluest sky you have ever been under—white, crimson, scarlet, pink, buff, yellow and every shade God has painted on leaf and flower! . . . As if this was not beauty enough, you come out of a mountain pass and gaze, breathless and trembling, upon "purple peaks that out of ancient woods arise," and there, in the gorge below, are silver lakes reflecting as in a row of mirrors all the glory that surrounds them!

Helen could not have understood these words, for trilling crickets, ringing bridles, and cracking whips were all silence to her, and she was blind both to Ireland's silver lakes and to Scotland's sunlit mists. Her predicament with language, throughout her life, was that even when the words were her own, they were not.

I have lost a part of my language, as I have said, and I feel further diminished when I see others losing theirs. Helen wrote that, even before Anne's arrival, she had noticed that others "did not use signs as I did when they wanted anything done, but talked with their mouths." She was taught to reject those signs: "I do not like the sign-language," she wrote when she was twenty-three, "and I do not think it would be of much use to the deaf-blind." But if Helen had been given a teacher fluent in sign (something neither Bell nor the Perkins School would have provided), she could rapidly have developed and kept her own ideas. She would have become a writer with her own voice and perspective and a consummate speaker and listener, through touch, in her own language.

Other deaf children deprived of their language at an early age, or from birth, have managed to find it again when they were still young. It's not easy, despite the fact that the language they want is the one they need, because their struggle is an institutional one. A remarkable case in point is Emmanuelle Laborit, who was born deaf. When she was a very young child, her speech therapists insisted that she be allowed neither to sign nor to meet children or adults who did. She was sent to an oral school in Paris, where she felt the vibrating throats of her speech teachers and, for hours, formed the lip movements of the same word, over and over again "like a little monkey."

But in 1979, when Emmanuelle was seven years old, her father, a psychiatrist, could see that she wasn't learning anything. He brought her to two Americans he had seen on French television: Alfredo Corrado, who was deaf, and William Moody, who was not. They both signed fluently. They had managed to rekindle French interest in sign and the deaf theatre, although they had been unable to make any dent in the French teaching system. When she met Corrado, he seemed to her an impossibility:

—The man is deaf.
—He has no hearing aid.
—He's *alive.*

"It took me some time," she writes, "to understand this triple peculiarity." The only deaf human beings she had seen up until that time were her orally trained peers, since she was not allowed to see deaf adults, and she had concluded that she and all of her deaf schoolmates were going to die before growing up, a common belief among orally educated deaf children. Her astonishment was twofold:

> I was nothing less than stupefied when I saw that my father could understand what one man's hands were saying in the other's mouth. I didn't know that day that I was going to have a language thanks to them. But I came away with the formidable revelation that Emmanuelle was going to live to grow up! That, I could see with my own eyes.

When Corrado gave Emmanuelle her first class in sign, with other deaf students, it was an awakening: first came the signs House, Eat, Drink, Sleep, Table, Papa, Maman, Daughter. A miming of You are the Daughter of Papa, followed by the phrase in sign. A search for someone, a crouch, a hand at the forehead as if shielding the sun, followed by the sign Where?: palm up; hand cupped and moving rapidly sideways, back and forth; lips pursed. Maman: Helen's own home sign as a young untutored child, a single hand, a touch of the cheek. Then: Ma man, Where? The hand forms both signs at once, the phrase in a small, single swoop in space, subject, adverb, verb understood. And who was Emmanuelle?

> I became aware for the first time that you give *names* to people. This was fantastic. I had no idea anyone in my family had a name, apart from Papa and Maman. I would meet people, friends of my parents, members of the family, none of whom, for me, had a name; they remained undefined. I was surprised to discover that one [of my teachers] was called *Alfredo*, the other one *Bill*.—And I, especially, I, *Emmanuelle*. I understood at last that I had an identity. I: Emmanuelle.

She had probably fingerspelled her name before developing her own signed name (indicating, as is customary, a mark of her character, the shape of her hair, the brightness of her eyes). Emmanuelle could probably also speak her own name, once she discovered she had one, in her imperfect, deafened voice.

Emmanuelle had to continue her oral classes in order to get her French baccalaureate, but Moody and Corrado took her under their wing, and she learned to sign fluently. Once Emmanuelle learned it, she was able to express her ideas in written French, and in the French she had been forced to speak, far more easily. She taught her younger (hearing) sister how to sign, and her sister learned to switch "with astonishing facility" from oral French to French sign language, giving Emmanuelle immense pleasure and a sense of pride. She came to know herself and to develop her own voice:

> My voice, I do not know it. . . . [Nor do I know] my mother's voice. One can't miss what one doesn't know. I don't know the song of birds or the sound of waves . . . or the sound of a frying egg! What is the sound of a frying egg? I can try to imagine it, in my own way, the sizzling is something that undulates, it is hot. Hot, yellow and white, undulating. I don't miss the sound. My eyes do the work. My mind is surely more fertile, though I am a child, than that of others. Just a bit disorganized. . . . I am not handicapped. I am deaf. I have a language, I have friends who speak it, and I have parents who speak it.

Helen Keller, too, despite her almost unimaginable double difficulty, could, with her intellect and imagination, have had such a voice. With sign language teachers she would not have written of the colors and sounds of abstract pastoral scenes observed and heard through Anne's eyes and ears, of "a tide of green advancing upon a silver-grey stream," but of the same fried egg. Hot, spraying droplets on a hand held over it. Soft and greasy, two different tastes and textures. No yellow, no white, no undulation. But sizzling, as Helen could have tried to imagine it, in her own way.

CHAPTER 10

GLASS, STEEL, AND BABEL

IN MY THIRD AND LAST YEAR OF LAW SCHOOL, I continued to work through written lyricals, while not aware of why I had to struggle with them, and continued to do very well. I still knew nothing of deafness and very little of myself. I did relax a bit and wrote less in class, knowing that I could get most of what I needed from reading. The classroom discussions I recorded were decodable, and I had learned to spot the key issues with a careful review of the judges' opinions in our casebooks. I went out with women at random, save one at the law school whom I liked very much but who preferred my roommate. One night I met a Barnard junior at the West End Bar on Broadway; we spoke for a couple of hours and decided to spend the night at her place. When I woke up the following morning, she had already gone to an early class, leaving me covered with spots—red spots—all over.

I rushed over to St. Luke's Hospital for a test, and when I returned a day later, the resident, not much older than I was, opened the envelope with a flair and announced, "Ah, *Sisyphus!*"

"That's impossible!"

"It is? Well, since it's impossible, *your shadow I was adjust-ing.*" *your shadow you should just you should know—*

"What?"

"You should know I was just kidding!" the resident shouted. He raised his chin a bit (I was taller) and said loudly, theatrically, "Your spots are just spots, nonspecific spots! Just spots! And lo' and behold"—he lifted up my shirt—"they're gone! Maybe just a heat rash! 'Impossible impossible,' the boy says. 'Syphilis is im-possible!' for this boy, a wonder of nature." The nurses were laughing, and I saw Mary laughing among them.

When the law firms came up to Columbia to interview, they were pleasant enough about me, but they loved my grades, much like Andover did my times for the 100- and 220-yard dashes. In-telligence is a law firm's capital, and they saw academic perfor-mance as an outward sign of it. The interviews went well, for I could anticipate all the questions. One lawyer, Benjamin Boodle of Dewey Ballantine, became almost alarmingly enthusiastic ("*Kaw me men!*" *men Ben*). He had spotted me awkwardly putting my right hand over a hole in the knee of my crossed left leg: a hole he knew was no affectation, for these were my Sunday-go-to-meeting, dark-gray, flannel pants.

I'd heard that the leading firm was Debevoise & Plimpton, a place for men and women with other interests: a civilized, scrupu-lous, hard-working, intellectually rigorous institution, then and now at the pinnacle of the practice of law in the United States. I didn't have the slightest idea what lawyers actually did in large firms, nor how Debevoise differed from them in the way it did those things (though everyone said there was a difference), but I wanted to be part of it, and the success of my written lyricals, my private secret made public only in the form of As on a résumé, daz-zled them, though, it seemed to me, in a more agreeable fashion than they did "Call me Ben" Boodle, betrayed by his eager voice and acquisitive eyes.

That summer the bar exam and the bar review, the course for the exam, were almost fun, for the test was little more than a game of chance. The lectures were no problem, for the speakers said exactly what was in the printed booklets two feet thick and set in large type so as to be printed large in the minds of our impressionable group. Hypothetical questions, for example, are used in law school to test rules—illustrate exceptions, question their validity—not just to restate them. Freedom of speech is absolute, we say, and then we are given Holmes's example of the man who cries, "Fire!," in a crowded theatre when there is none, resulting in a stampede. Freedom of religion and equal protection of the laws are also absolutes under our Constitution. May the rules of conscription (the draft) therefore favor, ask the hypotheticals, a religious versus an agnostic conscientious objector in time of war?

But the bar exam course, given for about a thousand of us in an enormous hotel ballroom on the west side: What a different story! Speeding, for example, is normally negligent, as is running a red light. If a speeding car going one way hits the red-light runner going the other, the speeder may be said to be negligent, the light-jumper contributorily so, denying each the right to be compensated by the other. Clear enough. But the hypotheticals of John Bellini, *préparateur extraordinaire* for the bar exam, were there to engrave in the minds of his charges the rules printed in large type before us. His hypotheticals in a heavy New York accent, printed as well, were there to restate the rules, no more, no less.

> In the State o' New York, contributory negligence is a complete defense in a action for negligence.
> Example:
> A negligently runs into B. B is contributorily negligent. B sues A for the damage to B's auto.

Held:

B cannot recover from A. Why? Because—you got it—in the State o' New York, contributory negligence is a complete defense in a action for negligence.

At last I had a chance to laugh in a lecture hall—or at least to laugh at something I understood. I could even do imitations of the speakers, reveling in them, as in my *Gaudeamus* days. Knowing the words in large print, and looking hard at the speaker, I managed to pick up their movements and foibles, bring out the lower Hertzes of their voices, and invent the higher from lips and gesture. I would give my own lectures at lunch or dinner with friends—fellow applicants—in the voices of Bellini and his colleagues. I drew on the parallels in the Baltimore Catechism, in which, as an answer to a first question would have it, the four signs of the one true church are that it is one, holy, catholic, and apostolic. What is the one true church? The Catholic Church is, the next answer goes, because it alone has these four attributes, notably the third.

But the lecturers were well meaning and accomplished their task, and most of us, to our astonishment, in view of the great number of guesses we made—Do you have thirty days, forty-five days, or sixty days to appeal from a decision of the surrogate's court? *Go for the middle!*—passed the exam. The only test of my nerves during that time was on the day before the examination. An envelope arrived in the mail with Mary's handwriting on it, postmarked in Virginia. It contained a picture of my brother John and me at ages five and three in the days before the locusts, sitting on the staircase at my grandfather's house, which I had given to Mary. There was no return address, no note, just the picture of my brother and me smiling out at the world and, I used to like to think, at her. I was at a loss as to why she returned it without the slightest word. No affection, no memory, no salutation. Nothing.

~

MIDTOWN MANHATTAN IS NOT THE MASSACHUSETTS North Shore, New Haven, or even Morningside Heights. Debevoise & Plimpton's offices were in the ITT Building at Park and Fiftieth Street, which, like all other office buildings, would prove to be an acoustical nightmare. As I walked to work on my first day, October 2, I found the tall steel-and-glass buildings, mine and those around it, unimaginative and depressing. *Why can't cities spread horizontally?* But I rented an apartment a few blocks away, on Forty-Eighth and Third, to avoid taking the subway with its screeching wheels and brakes and echoing tunnels. I would work hard (*what do they do?*) and bring with me my acquired treasury of language, still unaware of the dead and wounded cells in my ears.

The firm had several floors. I took an elevator to the twenty-third and was led by a receptionist up the firm's spiral staircase to the office of Simon Harper on the twenty-fifth. He had interviewed me at the law school in the spring. "Welcome to the *fur*," he began, a warm, erudite, soft-spoken man, forty years old, white shirt, dark tie, horn-rimmed glasses, jacket hung on the back of the door. His hair and skin matched the pale brown color of his desk, and I guessed that he was as much a fixture in the room, day and night, as its furniture.

fur firm "Thank you."

"*Av a nye tummer?*"

"Sorry?"

"*Nye tummer?*"

tummer bummer no way—summer summer nice "Yes. Except for
the bar exam." We laughed. He took out a large spiral-bound
booklet, an introduction to the firm for new lawyers, and read
from it for the next hour and a half. On the twenty-fifth floor of
the ITT building, as on all the floors of all the glass-and-steel
office buildings in New York City, there is a permanent whoosh
of cold air in summer and warm air in winter. Though inaudible
to me without my hearing aids (and this was ten years before
their time), the airflow whites out virtually all high-frequency
sounds, acoustically camouflaging what little might be picked up
by the remaining high-frequency epithelial cells at the base and
into the first turn of my cochlea. I could identify each topic
Harper addressed—the keeping of time records, client confidentiality, avoidance of conflicts of interest, and so forth—but I
didn't understand the substance of what he was saying.

"By the way do you have any *such bans*?"

*such bans what's that such bans hutch bans god ok I own no securi-
ties.* "No."

"Excellent. We'll do it together." *do the bans? do the—*

"Now, down to business. Gerry, when you have a *litt unny, and
ink's about inventing, it's a sentient you avoid pi it any securities if used
by a verb science.*"

"Yes." *Inventing inv—securities—investing*

"You're clear on this?"

> a litt unny
> > a little money
> > > a sentient
> > > > if used by a
> > > > > verb science
> > > > > > firm science
> > > > > > > firm's clients

"Gerry?"

"Um—"

> *a sentient*
>> *it's essential*
>> *you avoid*
>>> *buying securities*
>>> *issued by the firm's clients*

"Yes, of course."

"You OK?"

"Yes. I'm a little nervous."

"Ha ha. Well, don't be. You'll loosen up *ooder tan you sink*.

At one o'clock I told Harper that I was late for a twelve thirty lunch date with Bob Goode, another starting lawyer. He looked mystified. "I thought you had no *such bans*."

dammit such lunch lunch plans totally fucked

"It's OK, Gerry, we'll break. But I thought you had said no."

"Sorry. I misunderstood."

I attributed the problem to nervousness, and when I did an initial legal memorandum on an insider's scheme to issue shares to himself to get 51 percent of a 50–50 company, there was praise from all quarters, particularly from the client, who called to thank me. Telephones seemed to work better, though at that time I had no idea it was the proximity and the whooshlessness. Thinking back today to my lack of awareness of how I was different from others, it seems to me that it is the variable nature of the problem that makes you feel you belong—or could belong. You can speak. You can read. You can write. You have been trained to think like a lawyer. And when you are listening to others, you can figure out what they're saying, but nowhere near as well as everyone else does.

I was allowed a brief interlude from work when I got a notice from the draft board demanding that I report for a physical, late in 1967. I was twenty-four and single, had finished law school, and was eminently eligible for the army. (This was well before the lottery.) Today's system of voluntary service is designed to keep the well educated (except for committed officers, usually educated by the military themselves) out of the service and their families and friends with no direct personal stake in armed conflicts, leaving politicians and the military a free hand and no accountability for their foreign adventures.

But in those days we had a citizen army. I was against the war in Vietnam, which most of my peers saw as a civil war for the unification of that country, but I wasn't courageous enough to flee to Canada. My only protest was to submit to the draft but to refrain from becoming an officer. I took the physical in Boston, thinking they would be more careful, and was ready to plead a heart murmur. But in Salem the draft board gave me my folder when I reported for the bus trip to the Boston army base, and the doctor in Salem I had asked the previous summer to write a letter confirmed the murmur but wrote that it was "of no clinical significance."

A fight broke out in the back of the bus as I finished the file and began reading the names of the (American) war dead in the *New York Times*, which I had picked up before boarding the bus. I was exhausted, for I had stayed with Mother the night before, and we drank scotch upon scotch and talked until three o'clock in the morning. She woke me up at five with four or five cups of coffee. "It will get rid of the hangover, Darling." When I arrived at the army base, I was terrified. Will they take me now? Would I be wounded? Killed? I thought of Bruce Warner, a friend and classmate at Yale, who was shot everywhere, it seemed, and took weeks to die. How many people would *I* be expected to kill? Do you shoot people in the head? In the chest? In the groin? Would I die, as the *Times* said some had, after falling into a deep pit of pointed pickets speckled with enemy shit? Do you use bayonets? When? There must be a lot of blood—and I looked at my hands. A voice shouted, *"Whoresounds!" whoresounds shore sounds shorts sound shorts down!*—We all dropped our shorts and were looked at for hernias and, I suppose, a variety of social diseases. It seemed to me not so much a medical examination as an inspection to determine our suitability for death. The hearing test was a brief, monosyllabic, readily lipreadable conversation, and of course, I thought my hearing, and everything else about me, was fine. I was a singer, a scholar now, a lawyer in New York's perhaps most notable firm. "Good morning." "Good Morning." "Can you hear me?" "Yes." "Good. Next!"

But when the time came to take my pulse, it proved to be stratospheric—perhaps this is what had given me the edge with the starting gun when I was a racer. It was 168 and irregular (*shit what's this guy taking*); the medics had me sit down in a corner. I was called back fifteen minutes later (*come back over here, recruit*), and it was 180—pulse three beats a second. I could feel it *thumpthumpthump thumpthumpthump thumpthumpthump* like a racing waltz, Swan Lake in triple time here on the banks of Boston Harbor.

I was recalling the beat of that waltz, the heavenly "do" down to "sol" of the basses in 3/4 time before the faint melody comes in, "mii re *fa* mi, mii re *fa* mi," when it was broken by the chief medic, who told me I was unfit for the army. His assistant gave me a yellow card (the cards of the conscripted were red, white, and blue) to turn in at the front desk as I left the inspection center. I had the impression they wanted me out of there as quickly as possible—before I dropped dead—but I insisted on the promised free lunch before leaving: a hamburger, Boston baked beans, and a glass of milk in the army canteen across the way. The

Tchaikovsky air lingered, and my pulse quieted as I ate the beans. It has rarely been so fast since. Today when I think of that day, I think about whether my skyrocketing pulse was caused by the list of the fallen in the *Times*, the doctor's treacherous report, the fight on the bus, or my fear of death and of killing. But I'm convinced it was Mother's handiwork—*six scotches, two hours' sleep, lots of coffee, and he'll be out.*

CHAPTER 11

ALL-NIGHTERS
AND ULCERS

WHEN I RETURNED TO THE OFFICE FROM SALEM, relieved and back to less mortal worries than being skewered in a pit of pointed pickets, I found that the physical environment at Debevoise, with its large conference rooms, noisy offices, and whooshes, was slowly becoming a nightmare. Ferdinand Berthier, the greatest deaf teacher of the deaf, once advised a graduating class of deaf students never to let the demands of difficult work make them neglect their maternal tongue. But in my case that tongue, or my extraordinarily complex version of it, was making the demands of difficult work intolerable. I should have sought help; even Berthier and his colleagues needed (and cultivated) help from the hearing during the age of enlightenment. What kind of help, I would have had no idea. What if my brain were simply not working? What if I were mad? Was I ready to face that?

At a meeting at the City Builders Association, of which one of our clients—a company president—was a member, proposed in his long afternoon speech that *"weasel out a tree to refuse to bay a dollar tour for the bent."* I felt the elbow of Bill Stein, a senior associate of the firm, who said, "OK, Gerry. You make the point." *No time to decipher. Why did Stein—why does everyone—understand so quickly? God weasel out we sel out out all we sell we shall we should all agree* I got no further.

"Can you do it, Bill?" Stein gave me a steady, disapproving stare. He stood and told the roomful of builders, competitors all (and we were there precisely to ward off any such moments), that "any *fissing of the pride of lament* would violate the antitrust law." *lament*
> *cement*
>> *pride price*
>>> *fixing the price*
>>> *of cement*

"I am sure," Bill said, "the speaker meant there should be a consensus on *safety* rules." *(Got it—nice slant.)* He said a few more words I missed. The speaker quickly agreed with him, and his proposal to *"weasel out a tree to refuse to bay a dollar tour for the bent"* (we should all agree to refuse to pay a dollar more for cement) was quickly abandoned. When Stein sat down, the conversation turned, as if the assembly were building a record, to the subject of safety rules for the contractors and their elevators, escalators, and stairwells. Much less fun—and less lucrative! A few contractors glared at Stein. Some stomped out. I had understood most of what he had said, standing beside me, but not the distant lyricals of the company president. In law school I would have written all of it down and deciphered what I had late into the night.

Stein was kind to me, but some of the rescues were embarrassing. At a meeting that included Bob Goode, an underwriter, and a manufacturing company issuing new shares, the company's treasurer asked whether it could just leave the problem of a large amount of missing funds out of a prospectus. "Can we *legal bottom out?*" I offered to "give it some thought," when Bob interrupted, saying, "Absolutely not!" and leaning forward, forcing me to sit back, hidden from the client by Bob's expressive shoulders, square head (he looked like Teddy Roosevelt), and wooden voice of reason.

I tried a number of different practice areas, as was the custom in those days, but the problem didn't seem to be the particular field of law in question, whether it was Mary Springs's tax assignment—*if the tire doesn't care a change with a dell or a subsection is sex-free* (if the buyer does a share exchange with the seller, the transaction is tax-free); a labor arbitration—*we are he in this proceeding to be German weather* . . . (we are here in this proceeding to determine whether . . .); mutual funds—*it's a doze and run* (it's a closed-end fund); and so forth. I felt like an outlier among the speakers of an elite language. Did all lawyers speak like this? It seemed different from the lectures at law school. Here, few if any were below the top ten or so individuals in their class—and seemed to be able to transform their lyricals as if they didn't exist at all.

During a labor arbitration I became so frustrated at the impenetrability of the testimony that I went down to Grand Central and boarded a train to Floral Hollow, Queens, where our client had an enormous smelting plant. I decided to interview the workers myself, one by one, about what happened to Charlie Walker, a black furnace worker who had been dismissed—wrongfully, he claimed.

"He said he was *it*."

"Was 'it'?" I asked.

"Was sick."

"Was he?"

"*Noah saw huh guessit.*"

"Who is Noah?"

"Whaddaya mean? Ain' no Noah here."

Noah no ah saw no one saw "Right. No one saw—"

"Saw him *guessit.*" *get sick*

"No one?"

"No."

I fled Floral Hollow after the interviews. Its name was the opposite of what it was: a burning reddish-brown horror of a place filled with sparks, soot, and molten metal. If Charlie Walker didn't get sick, he should have, along with everyone else who worked in that death trap. The place terrified me. On the refinery floor, bordered on each side by eight huge furnaces, the men worked smoothly together. All faces were masked, and the prisoners—for that's what they seemed—communicated by gesture. Maybe the perfect job for me. I went back to 320 Park Avenue and worked all night.

It turned out the fact that Noah (no one) saw Walker get sick to his stomach, and that he had told no one else at the plant at the time that he had been sick ("What color was it?" we asked him on cross-examination), was crucial. I wrote the brief, and we won the labor arbitration on that very issue. But I was not particularly proud of my slowness in digging it out at Floral Hollow that day, and I was troubled by the fact that people were working in an unspeakable hellhole. But at the firm I was gradually managing to find a narrow niche, developing a reputation as a good writer in a place that quietly prided itself on having the most talented draftsmen on the island of Manhattan, if not in the universe.

For a case in Washington, DC, two weeks later, I was looking through deeds in the public registry of Fairfax County, Virginia, where I discovered a land-use restriction that made our insurance company client's $50 million investment look riskier than it had previously appeared. I explained the covenant to Steve Clarke, who was with our client in New York. Clearly, we were going to use the restrictions to renegotiate the terms of the deal. "OK, Gerry. *Very good. Now get back here.*" I left the registry, grabbed the shuttle back to New York, and arrived in Clarke's office by four o'clock.

"What on earth are you doing here?! I've tried to reach you. I told you to stay put."

"*Very good. Now get back here.*" *Stay put. I'll get back t'ya—shit*

"Why did you leave?"

"I thought you *wanted* me to come back." He gave me a long hard look, angry, his usually jolly, chubby countenance clouded by a furrowed brow, but he looked puzzled, too.

"God, Steve, I'm sorry," I said, asking myself, silently, *Why don't I understand? Why am I so slow to get it? What the fuck is wrong with me?*

"Gerry, you *can* just leave" *can can't* "when—" He stopped in mid-sentence, seeing the fear in my eyes, not of him, but of the unknown, of something unknown, and I watched his anger dissipate, like an unwelcome physical presence in the room.

"It's all *rye*. Local counsel *say*." *say stayed* "You found the restrictions. They were helpful."

I looked for solutions to the mystery in the language of legal documents, the definitions sections and text of a complex lease, loan agreement, corporate charter, or common stock purchase warrant. If the language became second nature to me, then perhaps I'd be able to keep up with everyone else. I would search the form files for various examples of a document I was working on and then compare them: hereinafter called "Company," herein called the "Company," herein "Corporation," "shall not mortgage, lease or encumber," "shall not mortgage, lease or place any lien of any nature upon or otherwise encumber," "other than statutory liens," "a Delaware corporation," "a corporation organized and existing under the laws of Delaware. . . . "

These definitions are in the front; those are in the back; these covenants are here; those are there; "shall be multiplied by a fraction the numerator of which is 10 and the denominator of which is the number of shares . . . "; "shall be increased in the proportion that the new number of outstanding shares bears to . . . "; "whereupon the shares redeemed shall be retired and shall become authorized and unissued shares"; "shall no longer be issued shares"; "shall bear interest at a rate equal to a fraction, the numerator of which is . . . "; and so on and on into the night, the heavenly late night when the office was virtually empty, no need to talk, no other people, time just to bury myself in these documents, to learn, to find the magic, the other language, the secret to communication all these people held. What is it? What the hell is it?

How to bill the time? Hide it—work on the deal until eleven or twelve, and then look at the sample agreements from prior transactions—five, ten, twenty of them—until three or four in the morning and on weekend afternoons and evenings. Don't bill all the time. Solve the riddle! Do it! The next morning Bill Barnes's secretary called with the New York Trust Company on the phone. "Mr. Shea, it's Jeremy Costin for you."

"He doesn't want Bill?"

"Mr. Barnes is in San Francisco with Mr. Parkman on the Kaiser deal."

"OK."

"Hello?"

"Hi, Gerry. Could you come down here? We need to *lock to* a lawyer about *see us outing* mess." *lock talk to a lawyer—see who?*

"About—"

"The mess we have with *the outing*."
>*the outing*
>>*see us outing*
>>>*the us outing—shouting*
>>>>*clouting counting*
>>>>>*the accounting mess*

"Sure."

"This afternoon."

"I'll be there in half an hour."

I had been at two meetings with Costin before. I should never have agreed to go without Barnes, particularly since I seemed to have more trouble understanding what was going on in unfamiliar places. But I wanted to show Barnes I could do it on my own, as I had when I managed to discover the new facts at Floral Hollow. New York Trust's offices were downtown in the Chase Manhattan building, so I took the express train. In the subway car I put my briefcase between my knees and sat down as the train gathered speed and approached its first curve. I wanted to scream as the centrifugal force pushed its steel wheels against the rails, cutting into my locusts and sending a havoc of dissonance to the frayed hair cells that transmitted it to the acoustic nerve. I was not unhappy to have what I still believed was acute hearing, but I couldn't understand why the noise *hurt* so much, as did sirens, cutlery, horns, jet engines, whistles, crying babies. As the train approached the next curve, I held my hands over my ears—a blessing, for it's harder to deal with street noises while you're carrying a briefcase.

I left the subway at Fulton Street instead of Wall, hearing *all* instead of *Ful*ton, when I asked someone the name of the stop. I should've looked. I now saw that there were a few long blocks to walk. I started on my way, crossing with the light, but I was startled by the shriek of a horn to my left, on Fulton. I leapt back into the rush of gray to avoid the car, jostling a few people. "What's the matter with you?" a voice asked, for no car was coming. The traffic on Fulton was stopped and waiting for the light, and the horn, I realized, was going south on Broadway, thirty yards away.

I hate walking in the city, even at home in Paris, for all its splendor. The cars and the crowds are eerily silent, but the horns and the throttled engines of buses, delivery trucks, and motorcycles are deafening. New York is worse, as the reverberations play off the city's rising smooth surfaces and seem to come from every which way. I cringe sometimes, when the sounds slash into the dissonant notes that endlessly play in my head. Sirens can be unsettling, too; especially when I turn to the right looking for an ambulance or police car coming from the left or, as I had just done, jump back needlessly to avoid a car on another street, going another way, nowhere near me.

The Chase's (now J. P. Morgan's) ground floor lobby, designed by Skidmore, Owings & Merrill, is enormous and, in a public kind of way, elegant, with fifty-foot ceilings and marble everywhere. But halls like this, that were meant, I suppose, to inspire faith in the grandeur of the building's institutional inhabitants, make me dizzy. They are full of sounds—people's voices; footsteps; loud street noises seeping through revolving doors; industrial cleaning, waxing, and buffing machines; the whoosh of the air that heats or cools the giant room for all seasons. None of these noises comes to the partially deaf from its rightful place. Because the ear loses its ability to localize sound, the footsteps are on the ceiling, the floor polishers on the walls, people's voices and closing elevator doors emerge from the floor, and even your own voice seems to come from somewhere else. I steadied myself against a brass post supporting the red velvet loops that guide people into the hall. For an

instant up was down, out was in, and I started as the siren of a police car on Pine Street came racing out of an elevator.

"Costin," said a voice—my own. I'd moved from the post and
to the reception desk. "Mr. Shea for Mr. Costin of New York
Trust," said the voice again.

"Mr. Shea, yes, I see you're on the list. *Elevator bank C, vor C
tech and four.*" *vor C tech and four, no, floor vor*

"Mr. Shea?" *vor C and four four floor vor C and floor C and forty*

"C?"

"No, elevator bank *D*."

"B."

"Uh, D, like David."

"Thanks. Floor?

"*For tekand.*"

"Forty-second. Thanks."

I walked over to elevator bank D and caught one after two
false starts. I've missed more elevators than subways in New York.
When I manage to hear an elevator bell, it rings from everywhere
and nowhere, from the ceiling or another bank of elevators, a
group of people talking in a distant corner, from my briefcase,
from outside—so today I stand against the wall at the end of the
corridor between facing elevator banks and look for the light.

When the doors closed, I was alone in silence, heavenly silence
but for my locusts, which I now recognized not as the sounds of
seasons but as a permanent presence. The doors opened on the
forty-second floor, and Costin was there to greet me. We went
first to his office and then to the computer room, where he
wanted to show me how their records system worked and why
they had lost track of thousands of their affiliate's bondholders.

Costin was shrewd, and as I looked at him, I sensed he was
happy that Barnes wasn't there. I wanted to prove that there was
no need for him.

"So I've asked you to come down to *ease or foreswear was apt in.*"

ease or—

shit

was apt in

what

what's apt in

what's happened

"Gerry?"

see for yourself what's happened

"Fine."

"*The temperature was sued under the signature, but then some beaut her miss then up with the wreck tore for a northern copy, see? knee deep your help.*" The computer room was noisy—in addition, the subtle acoustical problem of rooms like this is that their hum whites out the remainder of middle-frequency sounds, just as the whoosh of the machine room's powerful air conditioners take out the highs. *Damn, Bill where are you what is Costin saying—maybe his office is better—damned noise—why is he so much quicker?*

"Jeremy, let's go back to your office." We walked between the two lines of computers and into the easy breathing whoosh of the hallway.

"Fine."

the tem—debentures were issued under the sig—?

under

the indenture

but then

some beaut

the com

puter

mixed them

up with—

what?

"So," said Costin, when we were back in his office, "we *deep your help.*" *What mixed up with, oh yes, a wreck the wreck records for a northern copy—for another company—we deep knee need we need your help* "Can you provide it?"

"We can try. What would you like us to do?"

"Well, we need *Europe in ya.*" *Europe in—your opinion—so tired* "Are you with me?"

"Our opinion. As to what?"

"Well, I thought you could look at the records *add ell a the odds—the in debt sure were to lease shoes.*" *wasn't the computer room— don't let your eyes panic—there's an idea, lease some shoes. Florsheims.*

"Could you do that for us?"

God, I thought to myself, *I must have the IQ of a plant.*

> *debt sure*
> > *indenture*
> > > *were to lease*
> > > > *shoes*
> > > > > *no no*
> > > > > > *to lee shoes*
> > > > > > > *duly issued*
> > > > > > > *bonds*
> > > > > > > > *tell us*
> > > > > > > > > *the bonds*
> > > > > > > > > > *under the indenture*
> > > > > > > > > > > *were duly issued*
> > > > > > > > > > > > *ah! good old indentures—*

"Gerry, can you or can't you?"

"We probably can." *wait! just because you understand him doesn't mean oh Christ doesn't mean you can do it—*

"Oh, good! You can do it! That solves the *bottom* then. Gerry, you rate!" *rate great am I? solved the problem.*

"Thanks, Jeremy. Glad to help."

Costin saw me to the elevator. I went down with the locusts into the upside-down lobby, for an instant catching my balance against a wall—so cold! I walked out to the street, waded through the surrounding sirens and horns, descended the stairs to the screeching subway, sat down, and clapped my ears.

Night was coming, blessed night, here at 320 Park, blessed to be left alone. *Let's see. The debentures are mixed up with others—thousands of them—and we have to give an opinion that they're all duly issued. I'll have to see the records. Where are they? I'll have to see the documents.* I made several trips to the New York Trust back office to look at the records, hoping that somehow I would find a way to issue the opinion I thought I had promised, though it was a trap, and an opinion the experienced Costin had no business asking me for.

"Gerry," said Simon Harper on the phone, "Bill's forever in *cacciatorian.*"

cacciatore
  in Kansas City
    everything's
     uptodate in
      calisthenics
       California
        here I come

"Gerry?"

"Uh, yes. Sorry, Simon. I was distracted. You said Bill's in California?"

"I saw your work report. What are you doing for Jeremy Costin? You've been over to New York Trust's *park awssis"* awssis *office back office* "several times now. *Who are you suing?!"* suing no doing *what are you doing*

"Uh—"

"Could you come up, please?" I grabbed my notes and took our stairs up to Harper's office on the twenty-fifth floor. Simon looked just as much a part of the furniture as ever, and, like his desk, he wasn't smiling. "Just tell me, Gerry, what this is. I *walked* to Bill," *walked to talked to* "and he doesn't know."

"Costin has asked for an opinion on the issuance of the debentures, and I thought we could—"

"Gerry, that's an accounting and records question—it's not *a boatee* related to any *bottom an up in ya could solve*."

> *a boatee*
>   *remotely related*
>   *to the problem an*
>   *up in ya*
>   *could solve*

"Well, I thought if I looked at the records, I could help them out—"

"Did you *ear* what I just said?"

"Of course. I guess you're right. But I had agreed—well virtually agreed."

"What did you *dell* him?"

"I'm not sure of my exact words, but I think I said we could probably do it. Then he thanked me."

"OK." Simon Harper picked up his phone and dialed a number, signaling me to pick up the phone near the couch in his office. "Hello, Jeremy, this is Simon. Gerry's on the other line. As I mentioned, this is an accounting matter. It's a record-keeping issue."

"But Gerry said you could do it—"

"*You, fair you*, Jeremy."

"He's not *that* young."

you youth fair youth

"And in any event he said we *probably* could do it. That's not a *sertea*. We've looked at it and concluded we can't. That's it. Can

you pass me to Monty?" Monty, I knew, was the chair of New
York Trust.

"He's out until around noon—you're not going to—"

"No. Another matter. But this one's closed. Right, Jeremy?"

"Closed."

Harper hung up and looked down at his desk in silence, as if
searching for words on his blotter.

"Simon, thank you. I, uh, I'm sorry."

"Gerry, when you're in a *baa* you've got to *taa to pee*, throw the
idea around, talk it through."

> *baa baa*
> *we are poor*
> *little lambs*
> *baa*
> *in a what*
> *a box*
> *taa to pee*
> *talk to people*

"You can't just *bury your head in butter cooking* for a miracle."

> *butter is records*
> *bury your head*
> *in records looking*
> *for a miracle*

God. What should I do?

"I don't know what to say."

"Well, let it be *lesser*." *a lesson*

Lawyers in the firm thought I was distracted or simply inflexible
in not moving along with the thread of discussion. The problem
seemed to many, including myself, to be intellectual, notwithstanding all those lyrically assisted As in law school—after all, I spoke
well, wrote well, and even did what was thought a brilliant imitation

of Whitney Debevoise (when he wasn't around). How could I not be hearing well? After three years the ulcers came, the repeated stabbings of a sharp knife just under the navel—*blood in the stool!*

Soon came the internists, white liquids to coat the stomach, probanthine to limit the body's production of liquids, valium to calm the nerves, and coffee to neutralize the valium. While all this time, deep inside my head, thousands of hair cells lay decades dead, and their invalid cohorts were sending to the acoustic nerve a barrage of lyricals growing in number day by day with the growing complexity of the work, driving me into the night looking for solutions in stacks of leases, charters, warrants, and prospectuses. Gerald MacDonald Shea, hereinafter referred to as the "Ulcered Lawyer," the "Hopeless Lawyer," the "Stupid Lawyer," or the "Lawyer Who Doesn't Belong Here."

CHAPTER 12

FRIENDS AND FOES

THOUGH I THEN HAD NO NAME FOR LYRICALS, I sensed their richness, energy, and flexibility. Auguste Bébian unveiled these qualities in sign language, but who would unveil to me the origin of my transitional language? Mary, and Beth before her, had tried to talk about my falling adrift, and Steve Clarke's eyes showed a glint of recognition of some kind of problem. But when you try to explain going adrift, you fall further adrift, and you suspend the discussion for fear that you are drifting into madness. You stay within the narrow confines of what you think, or hope, you can control.

I did occasionally join old friends outside the firm. At the wedding of one of my fellow Whiffenpoofs I was introduced to Emily Gardner, who had been in Mary's class in school. Emily was in many ways Mary's opposite: reserved, almost timid, ultimately in love but reluctant to say it, afraid from the beginning that I would leave her—and I did. She spoke little, and I heard less; there was no hope for us.

Emily and I lived in my apartment on Forty-Eighth Street for two and a half years. We were together, however, only to sleep. I would leave for the firm at nine AM and come home around one or two in the morning, sometimes later, and on occasion not until six o'clock the next night. I was wholly preoccupied, and Emily seemed willing, in effect, to give up much of her life for virtually none. To catch a glimpse of me in the morning she would bring her coffee into the bathroom, sit on the toilet cover, and watch me through the outlines of the hollow green-bordered apples in the transparent curtain, washing myself in the shower.

Sometimes she would come over to the Brasserie in the basement of the Seagram building across the street from the office to join me, in tears, for a quick dinner at the counter. I worked on Saturdays and Sundays, except for the occasional movie in the early evening. When in *Little Big Man* the cavalry obliterated an Indian village and put the children to the sword, Emily wept quietly—for our own.

It couldn't go on. I came home around three o'clock on a winter Sunday afternoon and said it couldn't. "It's not a life for you, Emily. Look at the circumstances. You never see me, I'm afraid to make love—"

"You *too* may love." *do make*

"Not the way you're entitled. I'm afraid, Emily. I don't want a child—I don't want even the remote possibility of a child. I don't want to bring *anyone else* into a life like mine or to condemn them to one. Do you hear me? Anyone!"

"I *doe dare*." *don't care*

"I'm sorry, Emily. I'm so sorry."

"I love you."

"I'm not fit for you. For anyone."

"We *ever deed* to get married." *never need to get—*

"I'm sorry. I have to be alone. Want to be alone. Alone."

When Emily went back home to Chicago, the apartment became her ghost, a sweater on the shelf, an unmatched shoe under the bed, a small bottle of perfume in the medicine cabinet, a bra on the hook in the back of the closet, and my own words, spoken to someone no longer there, *disparue*, as the French say of intimates who have died—"disappeared," in the sense that when I looked from under the shower's spray in the morning through the hollow green apple to see Emily sitting in her usual place sipping coffee, *poof*, she was gone. It had been eleven years since Andover, five years since Mary had left me, and four years since I had left law school. It was 1971, and I was twenty-eight years old.

By this time I was spending about fifteen hours a day in the office, seven days a week, and a number of partners at the firm were growing concerned that all that work, or what seemed to be work (I didn't bill all the time), might be the cause of my distraction. Various lawyers would try to pry me loose from the office on one pretext or another. One spring night Bill Barnes invited me with another lawyer from the firm and two from American Airlines, our client, to see *The Great White Hope* at the Alvin Theatre on Broadway. They stopped by my office, without warning, on the way out. "Grab your jacket, Gerry," Barnes said. "You're *dubbing willows*." you're dubbing coming with us.

James Earl Jones and his booming voice played the role of Jack Johnson, the legendary black prizefighter. I was astounded at the ability of the other lawyers to understand the ins and outs of the play, as they demonstrated during the discussion at intermission. I had digested just a few ideas, perhaps those pronounced in Jones's bass voice—I don't remember. I sympathized with Johnson, who seemed alone against the world. As I listened to the difficult script (no more difficult than *Rocky*), I longed to get back to the office to plan for the next day with a few more unbillable, futile exercises.

My sense of isolation even among the crowd at the Alvin Theatre reminds me today of Emmanuelle Laborit as Cordelia in
King Lear, performed at the International Visual Theater in Paris,
which I saw just a short time ago. Plays at the IVT are performed
by both deaf and hearing actors who are together on the stage.
When a deaf actor signs, a hearing actor speaks the signed part;
when an actor speaks, another signs the role of the speaker. Laborit's inspiration may have come from her own stupefaction the
day she saw that her father could understand what Corrado's
hands were saying in Moody's mouth. In the play, Lear himself at
a given time might sign the spoken lines of Goneril, a guard
might speak the words given in sign by Edgar, and Cordelia
would sign the lines spoken by Gloucester. Since my knowledge
of sign is limited and I could not hear the words, the play for me
had no language at all, other than the words or ideas I was able to
piece together from having read the play the night before.

I envied the deaf their voices of light, and for the speakers and
listeners I felt something like anger, which had been my senti-
ment that night in New York, as if they were deliberately masking
their lines and the later discussion to keep me from their secrets.
Today I am well aware of the aural origin of these mysteries. Still,
to many of us who are considerably deaf but can speak with ease
and are able to function in the hearing world, those who hear well
are our foes. They speak and listen with prodigious speed and
facility as we feel our way at a far slower pace, left to fend for
ourselves. If we can't, we glue our eyes to theirs, looking for a
miracle. When they lose us, we despise them.

Though I didn't know many signs, I was stunned by Laborit.
She held the public spellbound as she approached her father. Her
hands moved effortlessly, gracefully in her natural language, now
in full bloom, no longer signing, "Where is Papa? Papa is at
home," but giving Cordelia's ill-fated declaration of measured

love for her father: "You have begot me, bred me, loved me: I re-turn those duties back as are right fit, obey you, love you, and most honor you. Why have my sisters husbands if they say they love you all? Haply, when I shall wed that lord whose hand must take my plight shall carry half my love with him, half my care and duty." The flow of Emmanuelle's hands was like music, capturing every shadow of Cordelia's meaning.

The grace and visual clarity of those who speak the language of light are to me a wonder, and I feel a close affinity to it and to them. There are times, since learning my own secret, lodged deep in my inner ears, that I have wanted to be a part of them, far from the fast-talking world of the near meaningless noise and confu-sion of necessity. So perhaps the same is true for the many pro-foundly deaf children of hearing parents, like Helen Keller, who from childhood have been taught to reject those who are fluent in what is, in reality, their own natural tongue. They want to join the hearing, just as I, at such times, want to be deaf.

CHAPTER 13

POETRY AND BURNOUT

POETRY IN SIGN LANGUAGE IS AN ANCIENT TRADITION. In the early nineteenth century, the deaf of Paris gathered at dinners around town, in Saint Germain, Montmartre, the Marais, and elsewhere. They invited the hearing from all walks of life. Bilingual hearing interpreters (usually children of deaf parents) came, too, and served as interpreters for both the deaf and the hearing. The evenings included speeches, lively debates—and recitations of poetry.

The deaf poet Pierre Pélissier gave Lamartine's poems in sign, and his own as well, including one he had written for Lamartine:

> Let your poetry fall into my heart
> to dry the source of its tears,
> your voice to cradle its sorrows.

The deaf teacher Ferdinand Berthier borrowed Bébian's phrase to emphasize in sign language that it, of course, is the painting of ideas as well:

> Our language is rich in secret beauties
> that you who speak will never know;
> and have we not our own art of Phoenicia*
> to paint the words that speak
>   into our eyes?
> Your arts and sciences, save for sound,
> are they not open to our spirited minds?
> Show me the heavens
> I can't ascend with you.

There is poetry in lyricals as well, though they are not a formal language. They have an intrinsic unconscious beauty, one that writers of our spoken tongue consciously seek in their own prose or poetry. They are the reverse of writing, such as James Joyce's "the berginsoff, bergamoors, bergagambols, bergincellies, and country-bossed bergones," in which the word variations that I call lyricals are planned. The partially deaf have, as I read one day after setting down my lyricals here, our *mourningsides* for the artist's *of a thirsty mournin*, our *tie tear wassails* for Joyce's "wassaily Booslaeugh," our *clearasil sung* for his "clear all so"! There is a common grace at the artist's end and our beginning. We start with our lyricals, and Joyce leads us to his. Each of us has or is given his ultimate tongue; a poet's words become fixed as poetry, and our lyricals are transformed into a common prose. But I envy Joyce and other writers the luxury of their deliberate wordplay,

---

*The Phoenician alphabet (about 1000 BCE) is the source of virtually all modern alphabets.

for lyricals are not a conscious poetry, and when they arise in the commerce of necessity, they can be a hellish experience.

"I have you all, yes, I think," said the Debevoise operator, arranging a conference call. "*Less deck*."

"Mr. Smith of First National?"

"Yes." *less deck let's check*

"Mr. *Tricher of Tine Teapack?*"

"Yup." *tricher richer Prichard—Pine Street Bank*

"Mr. Estoril of *Very Tough.*"—*Paribas*

"*Oui*, yes."

"Mr. Legett of *Wrought Iron.*" *Rothschilds*

"Mr. *Bally* of *Planters Punch.*"

    Bally

     Bali hai

      Bali Hyatt

       Palfrey that's it

       Palfrey of Bankers Trust

She went on to confirm the presence of eight bankers and four lawyers on the phone who were about to discuss with fifteen others in Debevoise's main conference room the terms of an international financing: a loan of $2 billion for the purchase of a US appliance manufacturer. It was a beautiful Tuesday morning. "All there, Mr. Parkman."

"Thank you, Bess," said Silas Parkman, leading the Debevoise team, which included Simon Harper and myself, surrounding the speakerphone that sat in the middle of the long, oval, conference-room table. "The subject is security, gentlemen, what the banks will get in Europe to secure their loans. You have Simon Harper's short paper on this." Parkman's booming voice flooded the room with low-frequency sounds. He sat opposite me, his broad lips swimming in the sunlight that bathed our twenty-fifth-floor conference room. The shiny AT&T speakerphone's reflection of the sun would be of no help, however, nor would the sharp jab I felt below the navel, the first of many. I grabbed a coffee roll, took a bite, and slipped a probanthine into my mouth followed by a Gelusil tablet.

"So, as I understand it, it seems we can't give you *many eurydices inert,*" the lawyer for National Appliance began.

"That's not what the paper says," Si Parkman replied.

Eurydices inert
  Eurydice Orfeo
   sings che faro
    senza Euridice
     no
      Eurydices inert
       is security in Europe
       is we can't give you
        any security in Europe

"Gerry wrote this part. He can—"

I had it. "Well, you have a pledge of the subsidiaries' shares."

"There's a *tap, toe,*" said the Rothschilds lawyer, sitting just below the *whoosh.*

"What gap?" asked Simon.

"We want the *tet of an errant inured by the hubs,* not just the *cares of a dove.*" *tet tet*
     tet
      offensive
       the cares
       of a dove

"The cares of a dove." *the shares—oh lord lost it*

"The shares of the subs," Si repeated. Yet what did Rothschilds want?

"But we *dem in beckon,*" said Paribas. "Because if the subsidiaries have debt, the banks' interest in the shares *dem in beckon*" *comes in second "behind the other lenders." the pledge of their shares to secure National's own debt isn't enough because they come in second behind the subsidiaries' other lenders—that's it!*

"Gerry, do we have a solution?" asked Si, amiably, not really expecting one.

"Uh, the covenants. National and its subsidiaries could agree not to incur any debt except ours, so there'll be no debt ahead of the banks."

There was a pause as the twenty-five or so people in the room and on the call digested this. I was exhausted, and sat back. Silas Parkman, as quick as they come, looked across to me and down at my garbled, wildly written notes, apparently very casually, but it was a sharp and gentle eye, taking my measure.

"We can do that," said National. "We'll give you the covenants."

"Nope," said Pine Street Bank. "*Tone sink doe. Raid regidors are some instead a bust.*" *raid regidors corregidor get ahold of yourself goddamit*

"But they'll be paid currently," said National, very clearly, lips in the sunlight beside Parkman's. "There's no real risk." *raid regidors trade creditors will come in ahead of us*

"But if there's a problem," said Rothschilds, "they'll be out there, and *pari passu* with us. That's no good."

"Gerry?"

"That's true, but we can set limits in the covenants—and weigh the exposure. It shouldn't be much."

"I have an idea," said the Debevoise Plimpton lawyer on the phone in Paris, fifty years old and considered one of a handful of masters in international finance.

"Yes, Edgar," said Parkman, "we're listening." I was sure Edgar Platt was about to solve the bankers' problem, as he almost always did, with a new idea, something no one had thought of. "Take it slow," Silas added. "We're all still waking up here in New York, Edgar, and you're in the middle of your day."

Platt had his own way of making people hang on to his every word—the volume of his voice was inversely proportional to the importance of what he had to say.

"Well, *on tub tub borrow um a daren't a sieve connote add a sign to a blended intrusion a scruting* for National's debt."

"How does that help?" asked Harper.

"I've not made myself clear?"

"What you've said so far is clear enough," said Parkman. *Clear enough!?* "But be so kind as to bless our little group, your *low matadors* in these matters, with a little more."

"What's a *low matador*?" asked Paribas.

"Someone who works with someone else, usually in a subordinate *veracity*," said another. *capacity*

"Right," said Parkman. "Bless your coadjutors, Edgar."

"Yes. Well, of course," said Platt, "I'll try to make it simple. National will loan to the principal *tub, say on TV, which will tone down to a shudder a key will live notes on the TV and the TV henna sign* to National who assigns to the banks, and presto! The banks with the secured notes *on the band* come in ahead of the trade creditors and everyone else."

"Can you mortgage or pledge the notes in each jurisdiction?" Harper asked me.

"Yes. I think you can. I'll need to check."

"Good," said Silas.

"Brilliant," exclaimed Rothschilds.

"Great," offered Pine Street.

"Platt, I hate to admit it," said Paribas's lawyer from Cravath, Swaine & Moore, "but I wish you were one of us."

"Hell on earth," said Platt, before Cravath finished his sentence. Everyone in the room laughed, almost hysterically, not so much at Platt's retort as out of relief that he appeared to have saved the financing for a $10 billion deal.

"Gerry will write it up for us and circulate it—when, Gerry?" asked Harper. "I can't be here tonight."

"Tomorrow morning. I'll have to check on the pledges of the notes."

"We could do that here," said Platt, "but of course *a sake ear and every sung.*"

"Fine," said Silas.

> *a sake ear*
>> *it's late here*
>>> *and every sung*
>>>> *and Gerry's young*

"We'll have a paper in the morning—our morning—with Edgar's proposed solution and the news on the notes."

God, I thought. "It'll be here," I said, not knowing quite *what*.

I had all night to do the work. As I sat down at six PM, after the meeting, I knew I could pick off the Europeans one by one on the telephone, when they began work at three or so in the morning New York time, and have their answers by six. I could then complete the paper by nine, working with a secretary who would come in at seven. But I wasn't sure at all that I would be able to figure out the brilliant solution of Edgar Platt.

I sat down to work, starting with a diagram of National Appliance and its subsidiaries. The banks wanted to protect their loan to National Appliance and yet couldn't get mortgages or guarantees from the European companies because those would be considered unlawful "financial assistance" to a shareholder, favoring its parent, or so the rationale for the rule went, over its own creditors and employees. Reverting to my law school exercises, I copied the words of Platt as I had scrawled them and stared at the more orderly text for a few minutes. In a way I loved this "work"—it reminded me of my dark room at the law school, settling the riddle in time and place (on sheets of paper) while most of the riddlers were at home, asleep, silenced at last. I thought I would figure it out, though Platt's intellect was intimidating. This writing of riddles was, once again, what Bébian called the "fixing" of signs of sounds on paper or, in my case, the painting not of words but of lyricals to suspend them in time and to make them as readable as a sheet of music.

I began by comparing the riddles in my notes to words I had managed to decode mentally just after recording them during the conversation. *Tub*, for example was "sub" or "subsidiary"; *daren't* clearly the sub's "parent" or only shareholder. *TV*, however, obviously had no role in the negotiations, and our erudite Egor Platovsky (Platt was actually Russian) was not a transvestite and had probably never owned a television in his life. The "principal subsidiary" was not a TV, but a Dutch B.V., a Besloten Vennootschap or company with limited liability. The Dutch B.V. would borrow from National Appliance itself and lend to the subsidiaries funds they needed in any event. I reworked the text several times, until, at three in the morning, it finally made sense.

When it came time to call the Europeans, I had fully understood Platt's proposal: why the B.V., with its low tax on interest received from the other subsidiaries, was needed and how the security from the subsidiaries and the assignments of their notes by the B.V. to National Appliance and by the latter to the banks worked. If National Appliance defaulted on its own loan, the subsidiaries' notes would be triggered, and the banks would come in ahead of the subsidiaries' other creditors. I began calling at three thirty. By four thirty I had most of the answers and dictated the paper—essentially Platt's—to a secretary on the night staff. At six thirty I headed home for two hours' sleep, leaving an hour to clean up the text when I returned.

The next day, of course, the exercise began again, with new issues, new words, new voices, new obscurities, improvements on even Platt's ideas, and so forth. Toward the end of the afternoon, I went into the men's room to take some liquid, medicinal stomach-coating, which seemed to ease the pain more rapidly than tablets. Leaning over the sink and pouring the medicine into a tablespoon, I looked up at myself in the mirror, white and pale-green skin, red eyes circled in black—a faded flag of some occupied territory, twenty-eight years old and feeling eighty, and looking it, I thought.

"I wish I were dead."

I said it aloud, as I often did when alone, to dispel, I think, the mortal potential of the unspoken words. As I turned to leave, I noticed, under the stall nearest the door, the gray flannel pants and blue suspenders, tumbled around the silent but now agitated, brilliant black shoes of Silas Parkman.

CHAPTER 14

PARIS IN LYRICALS

SILAS DECIDED TO WATCH ME CAREFULLY. MANY IN THE firm thought I was better suited to work somewhere else, but his professional experience had made him unwilling to live with unsolved riddles. Ours was not a society of the deaf, of course, nor a conscious society of the hearing, but it was a society of lawyers, and Parkman was not about to let a hardworking, superbly well-educated lawyer, however troubled, sink without an explanation. He was determined to reconcile what he called competent drafts-manship with the apparent cluelessness.

When young lawyers join a law firm, they become "associates" of the firm, a title they keep until they either become partners or leave to do something else, either because they want to (every lawyer's hours are terrible in a large firm), they are told they have little chance of becoming a partner and that is what they had wanted, or they fail to get elected by the existing partners at the end of the usual seven- to nine-year term as an associate. It can be a competitive and ruthless system, though Debevoise Plimpton was and remains a collegial place, the competition being not so much one's peers as an abstract standard of excellence. Judgments at election time are made with great care.

I was ostensibly a part of that system, but I realized almost immediately, virtually during my initial meeting with Simon Harper, that I would never survive it. After my second year at the firm, my goal became not one of becoming a partner, or even an experienced senior associate, but simply being able to stay as long as I could, to become known, liked, helped along, a beneficiary, I don't know, of *misericordia* from some quarter in the firm, somewhere, of the kind for which I sought the intercession of powerful saints when I was a child. Partners at the firm weren't saints, but they were scrupulously fair and, by and large, very understanding. After my fourth year, with stabbing pains and medicines for them, and fifteen-hour work days, my goal became one of *physical* survival. Ultimately, I was not sure that even that was a desirable objective.

It was impossible for anyone to function in the unpredictable workaday world in the manner I tried, even if it worked in the mastering of law school classes and casebooks. Offering to a client an opinion we couldn't give, suggesting important information could be left out of a prospectus, fleeing a negotiation in Washington, and letting a group of competitors come to the brink of talking about fixing prices are not exactly the stuff of which good lawyers are made. And while the deciphering of Platt's opaque pronouncements may be a useful—if time-consuming—exercise, it would lead to double the effort the next night and triple the night after.

I don't know exactly how Paris came about, my Paris, which ultimately led me to the great teaching institutions of the deaf, to Bébian, to sign language, and to the full understanding of my own, quite different tongue. It was a kind of miracle. I do know that Silas Parkman was determined to get to the bottom of things. He invited George Marbury, his heir apparent as presiding partner, for lunch to discuss it. They went to The Century Association on Forty-Third Street, a circle of relatively lettered men and women. Parkman had been president, and although he was a lawyer, he was to some a man of letters because, early on in his career, he had single-handedly reduced the size of the average loan agreement and "trust indenture" from about 240 pages to just over 30, to the lasting relief of judges, the bar, banks, and corporate borrowers— just about everybody except the printers.

I do not know exactly what was said at that lunch. Silas turned the conversation to associates in general and then to me, and said that while he was sitting alone in the can, I came in to take some of my medicine over by the sink, I started mumbling something, and then I said I wished I were dead. I think it was at that point that Marbury raised the question of Paris, even though it was said to be the place where the firm sent its "best people." My colleague and friend Dominique Blanco, our French associate who was spending a year in New York before starting in Paris, had told Marbury I had the best accent in the office. Of course, I could barely *understand* Dominique in his own tongue, but that is often far less important to the French than one's ability to speak it more or less the way they do. But the key for both lawyers, I think, given the state of my stomach and my pessimism, if not depression, as overheard by Parkman, was that *something* needed to be done. The more the two discussed the subject, the more sense it made, and they both knew that if they agreed, it would fly.

"Uh is the rug of the comic A to Z in the light of federal law." what is the rug the role the comic atomic energy A to Z agency

Oscar Ruebhausen, another leader of our firm, had asked me to be secretary of the Atomic Energy Committee of the City Bar Association. Our group would have a drink, and then dinner, at the Association's nineteenth-century temple on Forty-Fourth Street and discuss the nuclear issues of the day. Debevoise, and Oscar in particular, had long been counsel to Nelson Rockefeller, and both Oscar and he had always taken an interest in the peaceful uses of nuclear energy, nonproliferation, research and development, and the need to assure the role of scientists and educators in decision making.

"Federal law does not preempt the role of *tate ate enties*." *role of tate state—state enti—does not preempt the role of state agencies*

"But New York just a *form to federal law to kill the plan*." *just a form must conform to federal law to build the plant*

"You don't even *knee to fly though*." *sees federal needs federal approval to build the plant fly though? apply?—*

The secretary takes the minutes. The chair, Maurice Lewy, began to badger me for them, and he was very close to Oscar. As I put them off for weeks, then months, my notes, taken in the high-ceilinged reverberatory committee room, became impossible to decipher. There is an inscribed plaque high on the north wall of that room that reads, "I would rather be with lawyers, drink with them, laugh with them, and fight with them, than with any other breed of mankind." *And understand them*, I thought, as I looked up at it during the discussions of *tate enties*, *plans to kill*, and *flying knees*.

"Hello, Gerry, it's Maurice. *Nee the mits—the last three mees*."

"Yes, I have the outlines—but I'm so tied up that I—"

"*Taa OK*. Send me the outlines, and I can *linn in a tale*." *details fill in the details*

"OK! I don't want you to think—"

"No, no. But we gotta get 'em done."

I rushed from Maurice's call to a meeting with Laurence Belknap to review my draft of a $50 million secured loan agreement from our client, New England Mutual, to a start-up paper manufacturing plant in Pennsylvania. The document was a distillation of what I found to be the best, among twenty different documents, of each of about forty sections in the loan agreement and many more in the mortgage, a selection of the best of 1,500 different approaches to the issues. Laurence was waiting in his office with Ed Masinter of Simpson Thacher & Bartlett, another New York firm. I sat on the couch in Laurence's office, looking at them in profile. Laurence was making or noting changes as we went along. I stood up, left the room, and went to the steno pool to check on a memo and returned to Belknap's office half an hour later.

"Where have you been?

"I thought you and Ed wanted to work it out together."

"Come, come, Gerry—I have the master, but *wet we after western* we shouldn't have to guess at what you *met in the raft!*" *western when we have a question meant in the raft the draft*

"No, I guess not."

My life, I thought the next morning, was days and nights of drudgery followed by abject apologies for fucking things up. I did manage to figure out at three o'clock one morning, examining the draft of a client's annual report, that because of the shifting values of its investments it had unwittingly become an investment company subject to special regulation. Charlie Rabin, who was responsible for the client, was not unhappy about my catching the issue—it was critical—but he asked someone else to help him with the exemption application. *Why don't they just kick me out, for Christ's sake?*

"Gerry, this is George Marbury." *This is it!*

"Could you join me for *such?*" *such such such bans lunch!*

"Oh, yes. Thank you."

"We'll go to the Century."

"Wonderful." *Lunch, a little wine, and I'm a goner. Maybe they'll find a job for me in the library at the bar association, or down in the basement of the registrar of deeds office, or working with Noah between the furnaces at Floral Horror.* I put down the phone, grabbed my tablespoon and medicine, and took my usual dose of probanthine and valium, with a boost of Mylanta.

We walked from Fiftieth and Park down to Forty-Third Street. "*Grade A,*" said Marbury.

"Yes. It is a lovely day." We walked up the front steps of the Stanford White building into its entrance hall, up two long cere-monial flights of stairs, then a smaller one to the dining room. I was terrified. How should I react? Make a plea to stay? Say I'm sorry again? Cry? The waiter came.

"Will you have some wine, Gerry?"

"Today, here, perhaps, yes."

"Good. We'll have a bottle of Bordeaux." *A last meal—enjoy it.* I ordered fish and rice and lots of cream sauce to soften the duo-denal sting of the wine.

"Gerry, I have good news for you." *Here it comes—God, I must look awful.* "It *is* good news, very good news." *You're going to work in the hall of records on Jarndyce and Jarndyce and Jarndyce and—*

"Good news?"

"We would *lie to you hoe to a pass off.*" *a pass off go to a pass off wait—to—*

"To pass off—"

"Gerry, would you like to go to Paris? Don't be nervous, my boy. It's good news!" *Paris Paris off—*

"The Paris office—of the firm?

"That's right, *our* Paris office!" *God, they must be crazy.*

"The Paris office."

"Yes, Gerry. The Paris *office* of Debevoise Plimpton, the *Paris* office, *the* Paris office!"

For once, I couldn't believe my ears. I had no inclination to discuss the whys and wherefores of the decision, and I sensed that George was a moving force behind it. They wanted me to go, and that was it. And that was enough for me. So I smiled, simply smiled—I bet the broadest smile I have ever smiled in a life that had been blessed with smiles in my pre-scarlet years.

"Well?"

"God, yes!" I said, almost shouting. "Yes, George. Yes. *Oui! Mais oui!* I would *love* to go to Paris!" I wanted to leap over the table and kiss George Marbury right then and there. He started to chuckle loudly, to the annoyance of a few of the newer Centurions around us who, not knowing who he was, looked from us to the wine bottle and back. George was probably thinking how fortunate he was to have the chance to offer such welcome news. He was beaming at the thought that Paris was his idea. He would tell Silas Parkman as soon as he got back that, given the way I jumped at the chance to go to the City of Light, it was unlikely I would jump out the window.

———

LANGUAGE IS THE CORE OF WHAT WE ARE, AND I WAS about to have another. The irony of appointing to a foreign office an associate who did not always appear to understand English seemed lost on George and Silas. My time for the next few months was full of blessed, shorter, winding-down days. It was a relief to deal with easy things, like terminating the boilerplate lease of my apartment and storing furniture, with a minimum of discussion and one-page legal instruments of the kind you find on the bar exam. Simon Harper gave a "translation" party for me, and a practical and popular French woman, Claire de Gramont, whom Laurence Belknap had invited with her husband for the purpose, sat me down on a couch beside her and wrote out lots of names and telephone numbers—"You want married women or single women? Do you like men?"

I flew to Paris via Boston, stopping for a few days in Salem to see my mother. My brothers were there, too, for the farewell. John, my older brother, was by then, in 1972, practicing gastroenterology at the Mayo Clinic in Rochester, Minnesota, and was married with two daughters. He was happy out there, except in the winter, when all you could see was snow (and patients). George had graduated from Northwestern Journalism School and was working for a small public relations firm in Stamford, Connecticut. Patrick was an actor and had played in David Merrick's *Child's Play* on Broadway, in the role of Shea, one of the schoolboys. He had gone to the American Academy of Dramatic Arts in New York.

It was extraordinary when I thought about it, how Mother pulled it all off, the four of us, with nothing but her wits and a few pennies to live on. Being together in Salem that weekend was a dream. Lyricals among intimates are almost words themselves, the right words, because you know each other so well: their eyes, their thoughts, what they are going to say. And if you miss something, you let it go, talk on, and then return to it, as if you were alternating between food and wine in the course of a long dinner you don't want to end.

Mother was pleased I was going; she had been educated by French nuns, and her own accent was sovereign—to the point of correcting the French themselves. At Logan Airport, I was turning around, waving, as she said, "*Good eye*, Gerry, *orfa bo peep.*"

au revoir

mon fils

I had been to France only once, with the Yale Glee Club the summer before my senior year. During the few days we had been there, I had thought of the French language itself as nothing less than a constant music. If you pay no attention to meaning, and simply listen to its sounds, you will hear a new variety of bird, or of flocks of birds, of another world. But I struggled to understand the taxi driver on the way in, and I was pleased when, as I got out, he asked me if I were Belgian—not necessarily a compliment, alas, in Paris. I stayed with Bill Barnes (the successor to Edgar Platt) for the first several weeks while I looked for an apartment. Bill was eager to give me a crash course in how to register companies under French law as we washed the dishes at night, but the high ceilings, the children, the clattering all had me smiling and agreeing to impossible ideas, like the *polishing in the shurful rediger* (publishing in the commercial register).

The Barnes's house was in the sixteenth *arrondissement*, the fancy west end of town, and the office was on the even more stylish place du Palais Bourbon, number 5, in the seventh. I inherited a yellow MGB convertible from my predecessor, and on the first day, going to work with Bill in the car, I had an accident that dented my yellow left front fender and the front of a large Renault. I had no idea who had priority, Bill spoke little French, and I couldn't understand a word of the man I crashed into, but we managed to fill out a *constat*, an amicable common declaration of the facts with a picture of the event the parties draw in the space provided. It was a festive moment, a beautiful day, with technical explanations of the *constat* by the Frenchman, and no one upset. I did think he spoke his language quite indistinctly, like the English. But in reality it was my first real introduction to the fact that the partially deaf can't read lips—at all—in a foreign language. True, you can parse together meanings from some sound, gesture, context, and, now and then, lip movement. But you don't have the fluid clues of your own tongue.

Our Paris office took up the second and third floors of a house that looks out on the *place* and, to the right, France's National Assembly. There is no whoosh in the office, just natural air. Dominique Blanco was an unqualified pleasure to be with. He would speak to me in English, and I to him in French. The firm's practice in Paris in those days was delightfully slow. A will for a wealthy expatriate here and there; an apartment in the seventh for Mrs. Hanna of Hanna Mining, or on the Île St. Louis for Miss Dodge of Phelps Dodge Corporation; entertaining visiting firemen or corporate clients from New York who came to Paris on the flimsiest of excuses. Iron executives from Montana, for example, came to review a reported gold discovery in the Haute Savoie; several lawyers from Cravath, Swaine & Moore flew in to help IBM's chief executive, Tom Watson, buy an apartment from our client; and the least abashed, a man who owned a large western sanitary-napkin company, came over to review, firsthand, the absorbent quality of French cotton.

All this allowed me to be home by six and to exhaust in two months of lunches the list of available French women provided by Claire de Gramont. There was no immediate rush, because I wanted to meet them all—*un train peut en cacher un autre* ("one passing train can hide another"). In fact, I was determined not to settle for anyone in particular in what I saw, and others in the firm saw for me, I think, as a return to the days of *Gaudeamus*. And, indeed, for the first time since the Yale days of Mary, Mory's, and music, I began to smile and sing.

Bill Barnes asked me to go to Brussels to help out with a sale of a large quantity of uranium by our client, Coastal Refining, to the Belgian state utility company. They were in urgent need of it for their nuclear power plants, and Coastal wanted to sell a chunk of its inventory in Wyoming before year end for tax purposes. New York law was to govern the sale, and Dave Smalley of our firm flew in from New York with the Uniform Commercial Code (UCC) under his arm. There were about twenty of us in the room. The discussions were primarily in English, and the lyricals on our side bore about the same degree of difficulty as those in the National Appliance deal. Dave went very fast, however, and when the Belgians spoke English, the message was obscure.

Smalley's use of the UCC was masterful and reminded me of my law school days, or rather nights, and eventually being able to call up the right sections with lightning speed just before an exam. Dave could still do it. He rapidly flipped through the pages just to assure himself, *after* he addressed a point, that he was correct. I had no idea what he was looking up, or why, or the bearing it had on the issues we were dealing with—price, transfer of title, date of sale, risk of loss, applicable safety standards, government approvals, and so on. But my fellow Belgians seemed to be following the issues with ease.

At the break, the Belgians began to speak French to me— "*Alors,* Gerry, *vous ahve ai tay à Paris?*" *have ai tay have a tea something in Paris*

"*Vous ahve ee tay là, non?*"

Dave said, yes, I did live in Paris, and that I loved it, right, Gerry?

"*Ah, oui, j'adore Paris.*"

"Have you *pins or brushes before*, Gerry?" *pins to been to brush bru Brussels*

"*Non, mais la prochaine fois, je vais rester plus longtemps pour visiter la ville.*" ("No, but next time I'll stay and visit.")

"*Excellent, très bien.*"

Foreign languages present a number of intractable problems to the partially deaf. As I first learned during the *constat* exercise, because the lip movement is so different, one hasn't the same facility to make informed guesses at their meaning. Moreover,

without an intimate knowledge of the foreign tongue, it is difficult to call on a stream of lyricals in that language as a transitional tool. So while, as at Andover and Yale, I could *speak* it
fairly well, when the conversation turned to French, I was of little help in responding to the mysterious offerings or responses of
the Belgians. Smalley, however, who seemed to have committed
the entire UCC to memory and knew some French, needed very
little assistance.

I found an apartment in the sixth *arrondissement*, a short drive to
our office in the seventh. The wife of the owner, a young woman
about my age, showed me the apartment. They were happy to have
an American expatriate in their pied-à-terre—guaranteed to leave
at the appointed time, with good credit and no complications. Her
husband was deputy prefect in a French *departement* northeast of
Paris, and on the telephone he asked me to pay the rent *on a tess. a
tess* "*Comment?*" "In cash!" he repeated in excellent English. "*En
espèce*," he had been saying in French. He assured me he wasn't
trying to avoid income taxes. I agreed to give the cash each month
to the concierge, and some years later, in spite of his little sins, he
was named a cabinet minister in the French government.

The Barneses went skiing for a week after my return from
Brussels, and they asked me to stay at their place because of a spate
of robberies of private houses in the sixteenth. They were particularly worried about their silver, which they padlocked in a cabinet
behind the linens in the locked closet of an unused bathroom in a
remote corner of the third floor of the house. I had the place to
myself, and it was wonderful, a large eighteenth-century house
hidden in a secluded garden off the boulevard de Beauséjour. I
loved being alone there at night, having some wine, making my
own dinner, and listening to music. On the third night I put on
one of the Barnes's records, a tenor whom I had never heard, Jussi

Björling. There was something about the voice—soft, secret, flawless—an ethereal sound. I turned the volume up, then up again, then higher and higher until I could feel the vibrations through the soles of my shoes and practically see the windows shake. Louder, louder, *what's he singing? What's*—

Aaaye yooeee feerr a ioooouu feeerooooor
doooo aaaah yaaaay yooray ooooo aaa raaaa sooo

I played it again and sang along with him. *What's he singing— what are Puccini's words? Is it "yooeee feerr" or "dooeee teerr"; "laaaaaa ssaaaa" or "paaaaaa ttiiii"; "aaaahhhhh raaaaa" or "daayyyyy zeeeeehh"? It doesn't matter.* I sang the mysterious words with him, went up a third when he went down, went down when he went up, singing in harmony with the great Björling. I could hear both voices together, his and mine—what an opportunity—but his voice, his voice, was so extraordinarily clear, a celestial voice I'd never heard before and—what's that sound up there? What's that up there—violins, flutes? Louder, louder, make the walls shake, make them shake!

When it was over, I put on Strauss at the same volume and waltzed, one two three, one two three, one two three, *thumpthumpthump thumpthumpthump thumpthumpthump* to music and heartbeats, around the living room, with the violins flutes piccolos harps, the basses in counterpoint, louder louder louder, into—*oh what is this wonderful world! Where have you been you instruments you music you heaven of vowels where have you been?* I let the music play on and on—the Emperor, the Tales, the Danube. The music was unearthly, the floor shaking, the reflections of the lampshades wavering like wary waxwings in the dark windows, buckled tight to protect the household silver from the Vienna Philharmonic. Then Björling again—what's it called on the jacket?

"Nessun dorma" ("Let No One Sleep")—the last two notes again of the Turandot aria, sung by the prince who solved riddles, "aaaahhhhhhhhhh raaaaaaaaa!," on and on and on and on and on and on and on. I sat down and—why on earth? I shed years and years of, an eternity of—why on earth these tears?

They were, I think today, a kind of homage to the sheer beauty of the music, the fullness of the voices and the orchestra that I was able to hear at volumes that would be intolerable for others. I was a singer, a musician of sorts, and yet I was listening to music for the first time—or at least since my father had given me a record of *Peter and the Wolf* when I was a child—listening to music as it should be, as it *is*. None of us, I think, can live without music. It is critically important to the hard of hearing because we can hear it, or at least important parts of it, and we don't have to search for its meaning. While music doesn't carry a message that approaches the precision of words, it has an immediate, readily understandable, profound message of its own. It may have saved Beethoven's life when the distant flutes were fading and he heard the sounds of speech but not words, because his own art survived. When the principal character in Vikram Seth's *An Equal Music*, Julia, a young pianist losing her hearing, failed to hear a robin, and her lover spoke to her of blackbirds and nightingales, she begged of him, "Don't pierce me so neatly to the heart."

I have known individuals born profoundly deaf who long to capture the sound of music, unknown to them, though they can, of course, be masters of the plastic and visual arts. "Your arts," wrote the great deaf teacher Ferdinand Berthier, "*save for sound, are they not open to our spirited minds?*" Some have considered implants just to be able to capture the sound of music, only to be told that the implants cannot help them do that. But the deaf already possess their own music, to be found in the beauty of their language. If you watch people signing, if you observe their eyes (if sighted), their hands, and their expressions, they look as if they're conducting mutually responsive, silent symphonies. And the deaf who are also blind, when signing with hands embraced, seem to be conducting a single symphony of their own. Music is thus in many respects, and in its various forms, as Julia says, the heart of the deaf. I now know the fullness of its beauty, and I cling to it as if to life itself.

The miracle of music at tempestuous volumes became my private secret—made me sing it and dance alone to it. The rest of the world seemed to me not to have discovered it, and the secret was mine. Perhaps it served to make up for the special codes for deciphering words that others possessed and I did not. I loved my flutes, piccolos, violins, and harps, and my discovery of the deeper structure of music, but where were the words? As to speech and librettos, the speakers at resounding volumes produced nothing more than louder lyricals. In any event, my night at Beauséjour marked the beginning of the new world I had been given. From Noah's furnaces, Debevoise all-nighters, and Mary's disappearance, I had now moved to Europe and had the time to enjoy it. I began to make love to French girls to whom a night in bed was like a warm after-dinner drink to be savored—subject, sometimes, to moments when I would stop just to dwell on how wonderful it all was.

When I was at home alone in Paris, after that night, I listened often to my newfound voices and musical instruments, discovering what lay behind the long intervals of silence in opera, as in the soft, heavenly introductions to the overtures of *La Traviata* and *Lohengrin*. One night when my speakers had been blaring, the seventy-five-year old man in the apartment just above woke me up with clumps and thumps on my ceiling. When I climbed the stairs and knocked on his door to see what was up, I found him wearing shorty pajamas and Dutch *klompers*, or wooden shoes (the clumps), and menacing me with an old shovel (the thumps) he kept buried somewhere in his fifth-floor apartment. I asked him what he was doing. He shouted "*Je me promène*" (I'm going for a walk), as his wife, in hair curlers and a nightgown, kept him from taking a swing. I concluded that he had very sensitive ears, like the French women staying in my apartment who, eager for sleep after a prolonged after-dinner drink, would jump out of bed in the middle of the night to throw my tickless alarm clock under my shirts and underwear. I finally bought some earphones and kept my heavenly secret to myself.

On occasion, for periods of a month or two, there was real business in the Paris office. In deals similar to those we arranged in New York, we represented the owners in the financing of five commercial aircraft for Air France and the French internal airline now merged with it, Air Inter. Our clients, comprising many of the large US insurance companies, were to "own" the planes and write them off for tax purposes against their US income, which reduced the cost of the aircraft—the "rent" (or, as a practical matter, the interest rate) paid to the Hartford and others by the French airlines. I rapidly found myself searching for English-language lyricals again, but the exercise was more complex.

"We need a *debtor a debit*." *debit debit credit debtor a credit of credit debtor of credit letter of credit*

"*Zat we dahnoe tee. We see a twara'ti.*"

The discussions were in English, and the fact that each side had a different native tongue could at times be helpful, as when the words spoken were repeated in French or in English, or both, for the other side. But often the difference was a hindrance, for though I was still ignorant of it, the proper pronunciation of words and, more specifically, the accents on the proper syllables—the meter of spoken prose—are, for the deaf who hear fragments of speech, indispensable keys to our understanding of language. All those iambs, trochees, dactyls, and anapests I had learned from Dudley Fitts, Longfellow, and Nabokov need to be in the right place: "*I'* was the *shad*'ow of the *wax*'wing *slain*' by the *false' az*'ure in the *win*'dow *pane*'." We need them all.

The above *dahnoe tee*, for example, yields a limitless number of lyricals, such as *ahnoe tee, hanoe dee, tuhnoe kee, ahdoe eee*. But even if the listener arbitrarily reached *kahnoe ghee*, it requires a leap to arrive at "cannot give," which is what the Frenchman said in his accented voice. The French way of pronouncing "not" as "know" and "cannot" as "kahnoe"—both resulting in a spondee (accent on both syllables)—rendered indecipherable both the first syllable of the normally iambic "cannot" (accent on the second syllable, *not*) and its following word, "give." He pronounced "give" as "ghee" here, which might have been recoverable as "give" if *dah-noe* had been understandable as "can*not*." In the second sentence (*We see a twara'ti*), the *see* I heard was another lyrical for "give," the same word (which I heard as *tee*) spoken in the first sentence. In fact, *see* would have done almost as well as the speaker's "give," though it did not convey precisely the fact that the French were ready to "give" not just to "see," or envision, a *twara'ti*.

But what in the world was a *twara'ti*? I finally asked George Adams, sitting beside me, who was present that day but running most of the deal from New York.

"'Guarantee,' Gerry, 'guarantee'! He says they can't give the letter of credit." *How did George get it!?*

"What is that in the *cuillère*?" asked a French banker from Paribas in the bathroom, as he saw me pouring myself a spoonful of Mylanta.

"It's for my stomach. I get these pains, ulcers, and I have to take it. It coats it."

"You are too *erfus.*" *erfus ervus I am too ervus nervous* "Relax a bit. Now we go to *déjeuner*. A good *such*," *lunch* "a little *vin!*"

Things were quiet after we closed the aircraft deal, and I took a ten-day vacation in Greece, on the island of Mykonos. The island was not such a tourist attraction then, in the summer of 1973, but a place where young people could go to find lovers. Everyone stayed in private houses or *pensions*, whitewashed and sparkling clean, invariably run by elderly Greek ladies dressed in black, universally called Grannies by the young American women, who comprised a high proportion of the *pension* population.

There were three principal beaches on Mykonos in those days: Paradise, Super Paradise, and Hell (the last phonetically derived from its name, *Elia*, in Greek), all of which looked south toward the sunlit Aegean Sea. To get to any of them from the port, you took an outboard fisherman's skiff, which held about fifteen people. On Paradise most of the people wore bathing suits. At Super Paradise, *the* place to go, taking off your bathing suit was de rigueur except when having lunch at the beachside taverna, where you had to put it back on. In the early 1970s Super Paradise was predominantly though not exclusively heterosexual, but soon thereafter became mostly gay. Hell was, even then, a lesbian beach, though gay men were tolerated. Heterosexual women were well received on Hell as potentially seducible subjects, though you were not welcome if you were a straight male. In any event, sailing down that happier, broad blue Styx to jump off the skiff to gawk at gay women would have been an oafish exercise, and if Hell had its Cerberus, he would have bitten your nose off.

I found a lovely lady on Paradise, a twenty-two-year old American named Stella from San Francisco, who said she called all her lovers Stanley in honor of Tennessee Williams. She had long curly brown hair and brown eyes, and smooth olive skin that reminded me of Mary's. Stella and I slept on the beach and swam in the turquoise water in the daytime and played in bed for the better part of three nights. But on the fourth day Stella disappeared because, like many other girls on Mykonos, she was looking not for some conventional blue-eyed American Stanley but for a dark-skinned, brown-eyed, curly-haired Greek "moment" to carry her off. Stella found hers and promptly vanished.

The next day I went off to Super Paradise alone. When the skiff arrived at the beach, I jumped into the shallow water, walked up into the soft sand, and found a comfortable spot, not far from some handsome naked ladies. I sat down on my towel and took off my shirt and bathing suit. I lay down, quite relaxed, hoping they were looking at me, ready to strike up a conversation. Stella had taught me how to look casual under these circumstances: on the first day, when I had tried to cover my hips with my T-shirt, she had promptly yanked it away.

There was no sex on any of the beaches, though gay men would often disappear among the vegetation and large rocks that lay just east of Super Paradise. It was a place to look and laugh and speak. One afternoon an Australian man and woman, who had gotten drunk on a gallon of retsina at the taverna, did make love splashing among the waves for a good fifteen minutes, came back, and collapsed in the sand. But even they were discreet and, unless you looked carefully, resembled a pair of frenetic water polo players.

As I settled onto my towel, I noticed a man sitting on a blanket to my left, who was reading from an Australian or South African magazine to the men and women around him.

The story was, I gathered, about Super Paradise itself:

palestine

　palestine

　　paradise

　　　the beach

　　　　pill with

　　　　filled with

　　　　　gorgeous women

I finally gave up on his words and let my eyes close, set my thoughts to drift. Five minutes later there was a sudden urgency in his voice, though he seemed still to be reading the article: "*at your lows at your lows oh the priest is ubbing quick quick.*" I finally opened my eyes, lifted my head, and was astonished to see that everyone else on the beach was dressed. *Get your clothes on—the police is coming!* There were two policemen no more than fifteen yards away, dressed in military-like gray uniforms, rushing at me, the only nude in sight.

I stood up, now the center of everyone's attention. It's remarkable how, once clothed, people can appear as if they'd never dream of getting undressed in public. *Who, me?* The police were still charging—and these were dangerous times, because the Greek junta was still in power and had no qualms about locking people up. I grabbed my bathing suit, but instead of turning to run, I ran backwards and tried, to a chorus of laughter from the innocents, to put the trunks on at the same time.

When I got them up as far as my knees, still running backwards, I fell into the sand, and the police were on me. They raised their arms and started whipping me with their switches. But it didn't hurt a bit, and I was more concerned about getting my suit up. They looked angry, and I expected to be arrested, though I had no idea whether being naked on a beach was lawful in Greece or not. After giving me about ten simultaneous lashes each with their mercifully pliant straw, they stepped back, turned around, plodded down the beach to their police skiff, and sailed away. When the next crop of bathers arrived in the public boat, they told us they saw the two policemen about a hundred yards out. They were practically in each other's arms, laughing hysterically.

"Take that suit off and relax!" said a lovely French, Belgian, or Canadian voice, as whoever it was slipped out of hers and lay down among her friends. I followed her advice and looked straight up at the brilliant blue sky. How wonderful it was to be alive and so far away—geographically, emotionally, culturally, professionally—from mergers, debentures, indentures, and the menacing furnaces of Floral Hollow.

CHAPTER 15

"SHEA'S NOT GETTING IT!"

MY THREE YEARS IN PARIS WERE JOYFUL, FLEETING ones despite the occasional daytime battles with *debtors a debit*, *twaratis*, and *kahnoe ghees*. When the time came to return, I dreaded the ineluctable, early-morning unraveling of mysteries in New York. In Paris I could afford to having *pins or brushes*, but back in New York the lyricals would all be professional, and they would be relentless. Though I would look like the hearing, act like them, talk like them, and think I heard like them, the effort to keep up would bring back the ulcers.

Shortly after my arrival Bob von Mehren invited me to lunch at the Harvard Club to brief me on the players in an ongoing negotiation for the transportation of liquefied natural gas—many billions of dollars' worth—from the Mediterranean to the United States. But in the large and noisy dining room I heard little of what he said, nodded at the appropriate times, and tried to ask a question or two whenever it seemed the moment to do so. I drafted the transportation agreement, but happily he and Laurence Belknap negotiated the deal. Sitting with them and about twenty others at the conference table of one of the shipping companies, I looked from face to face, sound to sound, lips to lips, as they all argued over scores of issues and arrived at terms. I made a half-hearted effort to work through the lyricals.

Oscar Ruebhausen at last called me to his office. There were occasional hints that I might be offered something at *omed oy, noble soy, bopil toy, Mobil Oil* Corporation, but I had been cool to the idea. One day I had been invited to lunch with six or seven lawyers from Debevoise's trust and estates department. We ate at a large round table at the University Club, but I didn't then grasp that they wanted to see whether, if I didn't want to go to Mobil, I might fit in with them, spending my life drafting wills and trust agreements. "*To you might to rye* imaginatively—*bend along the tile riding*, Gerry?" *to rye to write to spend a lot—*

"To spend a lot? . . ."

"I'm sorry?"

"Spend a lot of—what?"

"That's all right." *spend a lot of time writing! that's it. well, no—* "How'd you viss?" *you viss you fish how's your fish?*

At Oscar's office, his secretary greeted me and asked me to wait amid the whoosh of the building's cool spring air—"*Mitt reton it out town.*" *re-ton ree reeb ruebhausen Mr. is out is out of—*

"He's out of town?"

"No, Mr. Shea, he wants to see you! He's on the phone, but he'll be right with us."

This is it!

This was it, and Oscar was gentle. "Gerry, I know you've heard suggestions *abound more bills.*"

"More bills?"

"About Mobil, Gerry."

"Oh yes. I have. But I've not wanted to—did I become a lawyer just to lend a helping hand to the oil business?"

"Well, you're a corporate lawyer, and Mobil is a large, a *very wrong entomy*. You would like it very much. *Rust and a tate* is not what suits you, I think." *entomy tohny puhny p—company wrong? song strong company rust and a tate a tate tate gallery a tate a taste tastes tates a tates estates trusts and estates is not what suits you—*

"Yes. I guess I have the corporate background."

"And an international one, too, after Paris, and Mobil has *hopper rayshe* all over the world." *rayshe! raise? hopper raysha operations all over—*

"Yes."

"It's your decision."

"Should I take it?"

"I would, Gerry. You don't want to—"

"—to have others make it for me."

"I would never have put it that way."

"May I have a few days?"

"All the time you want, my boy. We *law* you here."

"You—"

"We love you here—all of us."

THE MOBIL BUILDING WAS ON FORTY-SECOND STREET between Lexington and Third, just a dozen blocks down from Debevoise Plimpton's offices on Park. I walked to avoid the subway's screech of steel wheels, and after the usual battles with receptionists and elevators I found my way to the twenty-fifth floor. I was met by the executive gatekeeper in the reception area—all of Mobil's principals worked on that floor. "*Is't her so what a will be two* now, Mr. Shea." *is't her mister of course Sorota will see you now*

"Thank you."

The gatekeeper showed me into a large office, about three times the size of Oscar's. Aldo Sorota was looking out the window at one of the giant gargoyles (1929 hood ornaments) that protrude from the corners of William Van Alen's Chrysler building just across the street. He turned around when he heard us and waved the gatekeeper out with thanks. Sorota was the son of a labor organizer and had gone on a scholarship to Notre Dame, where he majored in physics and was at the top of his class. From there he came directly to Mobil, and from the beginning he was groomed to be the company's chief. He had already run its affiliates in Italy and in India, and he was widely regarded, in effect, as Mobil's crown prince. He was about six feet tall, in his late thirties, good looking, solid as a rock, and partially bald with bright intelligent dark eyes, a moustache, and pitch black hair trimmed short. I was terrified.

"Hello, I—"

"Debevoise & Plimpton has sent you to us, Shea, because I need someone to write for me."

Despite the size of his office, Aldo's words were often readily intelligible partially because the thick rug and heavy curtains diminished the whoosh of the air conditioning, but mainly because of his distinct and relatively loud voice. Despite his moustache his lips were expressive, uttering words to convey ideas that had taken shape well before he spoke them. Auguste Bébian could have used Aldo if he had ever wanted to demonstrate that the idea comes first. Aldo's objective was to make sure he was understood immediately; he had no time to repeat himself. Alone with him, as I was at the interview, facing him, three feet away, no lighted windows at his back, I heard almost all of his words.

"They say you're good at writing."

"Well, I'm a lawyer, so—"

"I'm gonna give you a test," he said. *Jesus!* "We want a *getback* price for crude oil for the refinery we're building in *I'll raid ya*," *raid ya raybia rabia Arabia* "our new joint venture with the Saudis based on Singapore prices goin' east, and Rotterdam going west—we don't want to pay the *tony OSB* for the oil."

Though my eyes should have been looking into his, they were fixed on Sorota's lips.

"Whatta you lookin' at?"

"At you. I want to be sure I understand."

"Good."

"What is 'getback,' 'Singapore price,' 'Rotterdam price'? What is 'tony OSB'?"

"Good questions, Gerry, good questions. Lemme tell you."

He went on to describe how the market prices of refined oil products were determined at Singapore and Rotterdam. The netback price ("not 'getback,' though it is a sorta getback") was the *rice of brice of price of* crude oil "feedstock" to the refinery, determined by deducting real costs and a profit *endidid endidid elemid element profit element* from the market prices of the refinery's products. "OSP, not OSB. OSP is the official selling price, P for price, set by OPEC. *Howdy* not *phony* OSP is today the higher 'official price.'" *howdy howdydoo howdy do to saudi price* "We can't pay it. I gotta go. Meeting. Twenny minutes. When I come back, I wanna see a two-page contract. Got it? We're selling a *valid* barrel."

"A valid barrel?"

"You don't know anything, dammit. A balanced barrel!"

"What's a balanced barrel?"

"We get these supposedly smart, white-shoe, *ivy sea* lawyers from Debevoise Plimpton, and they're *itterant about the wirl that feeds them*."

"And so?"

Sorota explained that refineries produced both light (valuable) products and heavy (less valuable) ones, but the company needed to sell both. "Understand?" Sorota's voice and lips were a godsend, and I nodded.

"Good. Twenty minutes."

I sat down in front of the second word processor in his office, about fifteen yards from where he had been sitting, and wrote a two-page contract for the purchase of crude oil for the joint refinery, at a price calculated on the basis of the sale of a balanced barrel of refined products produced from a given volume of crude. I defined "netback price" by reference to product prices in the defined markets (Rotterdam and Singapore—Mobil could not legally agree with the Saudis, I thought, as to what those prices should be), and I listed the costs and profit element, throwing in as much as I could to lower the crude price. Mobil would want the joint project to pay the Saudi government as low a price as possible for its crude oil feedstock and to make as much as it could as a seller of the refinery's products offshore, not as a shareholder of the project whose profits would be captive in Arabia.

Sorota was back in eighteen minutes, puffing on an eight-inch cigar. "Goddam bankers don't understand the business either. No homework. You've got two more minutes."

"It's on your desk."

"Oh. OK." He picked up the two pages and read them in less than a minute.

"Shea, this is in English. A lawyer who writes in English. Amazing. Consider it done. You gotta have a *dezible*," *dezible decibel phizzible physical* "but it's routine."

"Thank you. And a physical's fine."

"I pay your salary."

"Yes." Mobil had already told Oscar the amount; Oscar had told me. Sorota meant that I would be responsible to him.

"And maybe, if you're any good, we give you some *clock sock-sens*. Much better than cash." *clock clock tick tock stock—stock options*

"Great. I've never owned any—"

"Figures. I can't understand you guys. Especially at Debevoise. You're somewhere between advisors—like my father used to have—but maybe smarter, I dunno—and saints, holy saints. No stock. Your *bunny's* prob'ly in a bank account somewhere."

"It is."

"*Earning roofer tent.*" *roofer tent 2 percent*

"No. It's in a money market fund. Three and a half percent."

"Three and a half percent! Like my Aunt Gertrude! As I said, Saint Gerald. No conflicts. Well if you're as good a lawyer as he was a saint, if there was such a saint, and he was a good saint, you'll get some stock. And you can pass it on to your kids."

"When I have them."

"Right. Find yourself a good woman."

"Not a priority."

"You don't like women?" Sorota took a puff on his cigar and smiled. "Of course, it doesn't matter."

"I love women, in general. But I can't find one like—"

"The *one-two sauce*." *sauce one you lost*

"Lost. Right."

"When?"

"Several years ago."

"She love you?"

"She had."

"You neglected her."

"School."

Sorota put down his cigar and looked steadily into my eyes. "'Several' years is a *song sie, derry*. You gotta move on."

> *song sigh derry*
> *song sigh, song*
> *time*
> *long time, Gerry*

I was flattered that a man who seemed to measure time by the millisecond was taking a personal interest in his new hire.

"And you gave her up to get As. All you Debevoise guys got straight As, or so they tell me."

"Finally, yes. I didn't realize what would be the price."

"Well, I'm sorry. *I* like you, for now, if it's *addy tuffelation*." *addy annie if it's any consolation* He picked up his cigar and took a final puff, signaling the end of the interview.

MOBIL'S MEDICAL EXAM FELT RATHER CASUAL, SOMETIMES careless ("at not much more than your age, your father dropped dead, but don't worry about it"). The examination Sorota had mentioned was a formality, and I was easily passing all the tests. In the last one, routine for Mobil, the nurse opened the door to a glass booth, inviting me to go in and sit down, my back to the door. There were headphones on the table.

"*Heifer dentist?*" she asked.

> *heifer*
> *a cow*
> *for a dentist?*
> *milk is good*
> *for the teeth*
> *but heifer*

ever

ever done this?

"I think so—it seems to me—a long time ago. In the first grade at my school. But there was no booth, just headphones. But not since—anyway, I'm sure I was fine."

"It's not done enough—a *candle* really."

candle really

candal scandals

in the wind

it's a scandal

"Well, I know my ears are very sensitive to sound. I *hate* riding in the subway, and horns and sirens are impossible."

"Good. We'll just check it out." The nurse put the headphones over my ears and told me to push a button whenever I heard a sound. The original device had been invented by Alexander Graham Bell in order to plot audiograms measuring residual hearing in the profoundly deaf. Mobil included the test in its physicals at the request of a former chairman, Al Nickerson, who, it was said, had to resign because of his partial deafness. The purpose was not to exclude from Mobil those who failed but to try to identify potential problems that might affect performance—a nice distinction. In any event, after I listened to five or six tones at different frequencies and pressed the button each time I heard a sound, the nurse said, "Thank you, Mr. Shea," into the headphones.

She came to the booth and opened the door. The sign on her breast said "Miss A. Oracle." She was soft spoken and had a gentle smile, though she seemed to be lowering her voice. "OK, Mr. First Grade, *we're on day?*" she asked.

"I'm sorry?"

"*We're are day?*"

are day are they were are they where are they "They?"

"Your *earring days.*"

"My earring days?"

"Your HEARING AIDS!"

"I left them at home," I said, laughing.

"Don't you have any?" She was smiling, trying to figure me out.

"Do I have any hearing aids!? Ha! Are you serious?"

"You pressed the *mudden vie tie*."

mudden

mudlark

button

vie tie

five times

you

pressed the button

five times

"Yes."

"But there were twenty tones."

"Twenty!"

"*Moly eyes* when you started missing them." *moly eyes! O, Mole, the beauty of it! moly mo—mostly—*

"Mostly—"

"Mostly highs. Higher frequency sounds. Mid-frequency, too. *Ow on avenue add is autumn*."

ow on

ow ow

how on

how long

have you

add

have you had this problem

"What problem?"

"You are—Mr. Shea, you do not hear well."

"I hear *you*."

"Well, you see me, and you're not profoundly deaf."

"Of course not. I'm not 'deaf' at all! I'm fine."

"But you are—you are partially deaf—*seriously*. What happened to you?"

"Come on."

Miss Oracle came close to me and was now speaking more loudly and slowly.

"I am—"

"*Considerably* deaf."

"That can't be."

"You should see someone."

"Well, some day. When I'm eighty-five maybe!"

"Mr. Shea."

"Yes, Miss Oracle."

"How old are you?"

"Um, you can see on the—I'm thirty-three."

"That's right. But your ears, your *ears*, are, are—perhaps eighty-five! This test is of course between us. But I urge you not to ignore it. If you do, it will be *do your fast reread*."

"My fast—my—"

"To your VAST REGRET. Please. For yourself, for me because I'm not writing it down. I'll just check that you took the test. Please see someone."

"You're really serious."

I could see that she wanted me to see that she was trying to get through, her lovely eyes staring out over her white dress, fixed on mine, like the double beams *hard a-lee* of some unearthly New England lighthouse. Miss Oracle pursed her lips for a moment.

"Do you hear any noises in your head, Mr. Shea?"

"Noises, no. Like what? Noises like what?"

"Like a whistling or a buzzing or ringing."

"No."

"Are you sure?"

"Yes."

"Please—there are things you can do—" Miss Oracle's toes were tap tap tapping on the ground, she was not smiling, and her eyes were full of questions.

I must have realized, at least subconsciously, that she was telling the truth, but I was of no mind to admit it. After all, were her *heifer dentists* and *moly eyes* but natural progressive steps to understanding, or did they have something to do with her message "you are considerably deaf"? But deafness is not hearing, and I hear! Just because I hesitated when she spoke? Yet the buzzer rang—twenty times!

It is no easy task, for anyone, to upset what he considers to be the longstanding, natural patterns of his life. For a young hearing mother, the acceptance of the fact that her infant is deaf takes some time, for it's fraught with feelings of guilt, failure, and the anticipation of a long isolated life for her newborn child. For those growing deaf because they are getting older, it is the acceptance of the advance of age that is troublesome, and the realization that they can no longer follow their peers, or fellow professionals, or those they love, without hearing aids, which, when they try them, don't seem to work anyway. For me, it would have been accepting the need to reappraise the past, an often hellish past too, but one in which I played a role that I thought was physically, if not intellectually, complete. So I tried to ignore Miss Oracle, in spite of the wisdom of her words. I was hiding, though—and you can't hide for long.

For the first few months at Mobil I managed fairly well, meeting people in the Middle East Department separately, slowly deciphering their messages, and—ploddingly—learning the oil business. But as I became drawn into meetings with two or three or more people, I became quickly lost as usual and reverted to trips to the bathroom for pills and some giganta Mylanta. People were starting to tell Sorota I wasn't getting it. At one staff meeting the group had spent twenty minutes on pipeline tariffs when I asked how much the Saudis would charge for our use of the line. Sorota wasn't present, but his second told him about it, though at the time he shaded my question and answered his own version of it.

Aldo's response was to have someone provide me with the draft minutes of the department meetings: "You know, to vet the thing, a legal review or some shit like that. The business is new to him—words like 'tariff.'" But he was beginning to wonder whether he had made a mistake. When I first looked at the minutes, with the admonitions of Miss Oracle at least in the back of my mind, I realized that they were more interesting than the nonsense I had been listening to. Reading the crisp words of a talented engineer turned oilman discussing technical, business, or political questions, I discovered that muddled ideas with an occasional "pipeline," "crude oil," or "refinery," were in fact thoughtful observations. I gave them back untouched.

I flew from New York to Boston to take a long weekend with my mother in Salem and told her about Miss Oracle.

"When this *it art*, Gerry."

"This it art?"

"When did this start?"

"I don't know. I think, I think I've always been the same. Frankly, I think my hearing's fine. It's just that sometimes I can't concentrate."

"You've always been a good student. But why don't you call John's sister-in-law, Geraldine, who works with that Greek ear surgeon. Go see her and—what's his name—Tassos, Tassos Alexander."

I gave myself a short tour of Salem the next day. I drove along Derby Street past Hawthorne's customs house and the house of the seven gables, as the dactyls Longfellow wrote for him danced in my head. I drove past Alexander Graham Bell's old place too, now a YMCA, and drove up the hill to the hospital.

Geraldine invited me into a booth, similar to the one at Mobil. I sat down, and she put the headphones on. She closed the door and went to her seat. "Can you hear me, Gerry?" she asked in the earphones.

"Yes."

"Fine. We'll star the *worse*."

"Sorry?"

"We'll start with words. You repeat them after me. Here we go—*Dart*."

" . . . Heart."

"*Flat.*"

" . . . That."

"*Again.*"

"Depend?"

"*Calm.*"

" . . . Tom."

"*Beach.*"

"Heat?"

"*About.*"

"A bow no—about."

"*Crawl.*"

"For . . . no, tore."

"*Church.*"

"Hurt."

"*Lawyer.*"

"Foyer?"

She kept on with the words and then said, "Keep facing away, and we'll *cow to the drones*, OK?" *cow we'll now do the tones*

"Yes." I took the button on the table. We went through the exercise, though this time I pressed the button more frequently, almost ten times. There were large intervals between the sounds. When we were finished and I stepped out of the booth, I wanted to ask Geraldine how I did, but she did not seem in the mood for questions.

"Dr. Alexander will see you now, Gerry."

I followed her to the doctor's office, and she left me there as she went into another room to give Alexander the results. She left that office by a different door. Alexander came after about ten minutes.

"Hello. How is your *other*?" *other, mother*

"Very well, thanks." He led me to a reclining chair and checked my nose and throat with lights and probes, and then looked into both ears.

"OK." His voice was flat and indifferent. I sat in a chair beside his desk. "I am afraid we have *mad ooze*." *mad ooze pad bad oo—bad news* "You are pretty deaf. Not in the lowest frequencies, but *ih sa bitter and I*."

ih sa bitter and I

"Gerry?"

"In the—"

"In the middle and high frequencies." He began speaking slowly and closer to me. "You don't hear them. In the verbal test Geraldine gave you, you scored *tebber tent*. You guessed eighteen out of twenty words incorrectly." *two of twenty is 10 percent* "You just happened to *get tea covers* right." *I guessed the others right* "Ow log have you add iss awesome?" *Christ ow log how long yes how long have you had this problem—*

"I'm not sure I believe this."

"Your audiogram shows that your hearing *tops rat city at vie unter terce*, at the level of the human voice, and keeps dropping. Higher sounds have to be increased by thousands of times for you to hear them." *tops rat city! tops dops drops rat city iddy drops rapidly terce terce*

"What is *terce*?"

"Hertz. Hertz. See?" *vie five hundred Hertz* "Here I am, my lips, three feet from your ears, speaking *race* at you—"

"Race at me—"

"Right, I didn't say that. And you can't hear some of the simplest things I say. If you close your eyes, or look away, as you did in the booth, it will be *mush were*. Is this recent?"

"I don't know."

"Have you noticed a change?"

"I don't think so—I think, to some extent, but it's hard to tell, maybe I've always guessed at words. But I think I was fine—I was tested—in the first grade."

"That's a long time ago. Still, this could be recent. You practice law?"

"Yes. I work for Mobil."

"So you *ten oceans ate*."

"Sorry?"

"So you negotiate—you do business negotiations."

"Yes."

"How long have you been doing this?"

"About eight years—five in New York and three in Paris."

"And without amplification you—and the French?"

"Yes."

"Yes what?"

"I do speak French."

"In Paris you spoke French—with the French—and you've been back—"

"Almost a year."

"Gerry, you know, you'll need to see someone in New York. I'm concerned that you may have *a bottom in your rain*." *bottom is problem in your rain, brain*

"You mean like a tumor?"

"Not necessarily. But it's possible. You see, a hearing loss—with both ears gone, or rather damaged—like this doesn't just suddenly appear."

"I feel fine."

"Good. But you should see a neurologist as soon as you get back—like—on Monday."

I thanked Alexander, but I felt, or tried to feel, as if he were giving the advice to someone else.

CHAPTER 16

A BRAIN ON OVERTIME

I MORE OR LESS HID MY FIRST TWO DAYS BACK AT
Mobil after the session with Dr. Alexander, saying little but
watching others carefully at meetings or at lunch, listening uncer-
tainly. I began to realize that I understood little if I avoided
people's eyes and lips. I made an appointment at P & S, Columbia's College of Physicians & Surgeons—north of mourningside,
I thought as I made my way uptown in a taxi and remembered
Mary as I passed the New York Hospital Nurses' Residence on
70th Street.

P & S is so far north, at 168th Street, that it seems not in the
city. I had an appointment with Raymond Chang, the chief ear
doctor—I wasn't quite ready for a neurologist—whose office was
in the administration building, a tiny place compared to Salem
Hospital. Chang was a jovial man. He was born, I later learned, of
Chinese parents and educated at Columbia. He spoke with a
slight accent when he laughed—and he laughed often. His audiologist did the audiogram first and then led me to his office. He

looked at all of the tests—Mobil's, Salem's, and his own audiologist's. "Aha!—Mr.—Shea—I—see!" He spoke slowly and loudly,
no doubt an acquired habit.

"What do you think?"

"Not good, not good! You're pretty deaf, to speak bluntly. Or
pretty hearing impaired, to be *berpity a wreck*." *berpity perfidy perfectly*

"Perfectly a wreck?"

"No! My accent sometimes. Politically correct. Though today
the deaf prefer the word 'deaf'—they are probably right."

"So—I'm pretty deaf?"

"Yes. Pretty deaf. Not *profoundly* deaf. You hear my voice.
Very good."

"Yes, I do, of course."

Chang leaned over his desk, now four feet from me, lips up,
aimed at my eyes. He closed the curtain behind him. "Daylight behind not a help. But you're *severely* deaf, Mr. Shea. In those high
tones anyway—you don't hear consonants. A I O U you hear pretty
good, except the high parts of them. E maybe no. But G H K N P
Q R S T V X etcetera—you don't hear at all. Receptors dead.
Many *airedales* dead."

"*Airedales?*"

"Hair cells! *Epic eely hotels*, Latin for 'hair.'"

"*Epic eely hotels?*"

"Epithelial cells. Tiny cells that interpret sounds, even amplify
them."

"The doctor in Boston—in Salem—thought I should be
checked for a tumor."

"Tumor. Tumor! Ha ha." I started to laugh along with him.
He was laughing, I hoped, because he thought Alexander's concerns way off the mark and, I think, because he wanted me to focus on the good news.

"So I don't have a brain tumor."

"No, no, Gerald—Gerry? Yes, Gerry, good! You have *two* ears. If you had a tumor, you'd have *two*. Twins! Identical twins, up there in your ears or in the nerve or in your brain, giving you same loss, both ears. Almost impossible—like two identical snowflakes, or fingerprints."

"So what is it then?"

Chang stopped smiling.

"Listen, Gerry. Listen carefully. You have *a fear censor in euro ear-ring loss.*"

"I have—"

"Severe sensorineural hearing loss. You hear because you hear some vowels, sometimes many vowels, and you read lips, plus you use your brain. You hear words, but you don't understand them unless—maybe with only one person, maybe two, very close, like me, you're in a quiet place."

"Alexander found this very sudden—"

"Not sudden, not sudden. You've been like this long time. I see it in your eyes, your way of looking at me. You *idolize* words. *idolize analyze* You have what the French call *le regard du sourd* while you figure it out. But you're pretty smart, so you figure it out most of the time. Very good! But you're tired."

"I am tired."

"You're pretty tired. Because you work long hours. Debevoise Plimpton you said?"

"Before, yes. Now I'm at Mobil."

"Debevoise great firm! All my colleagues at the law school say so. All very smart. All gentlemen. Impeccable! But hard work! How many hours?"

"A day? Oh about fourteen or fifteen, on average."

"Weekends?"

"Nine or ten."

"And you work harder than others because life's one big translation. You a walking UN. But it's nonsense English to sensible
English. It's natural," he added, as he kept smiling. "You look for
the meaning of words, of others, of life—we all do." His expression
darkened a bit as he said, "But meetings are very difficult."

"Well, yes. Before, I thought—"

"You thought people came together to mumble, say nothing.
Often true."

"But usually not."

"No, usually not. At Debevoise Plimpton probably never. At
Mobil, almost never. Except maybe when oilmen get together to
laugh about all the money they make!"

"I sang in the Whiffenpoofs."

"Good. Yale man. You have a good voice, musical brain. Excellent. Tables down at Mory's. You build on the low notes.
Good voice, but no violins, flutes, piccolos, no overtones. Basic
notes there for you, and you sing it all. Notes OK but hearing not
so good."

"This is so hard to accept."

"Yes. Complicated. You know Beethoven—not a Whiffenpoof
but pretty good, pretty good. He could hear music, I'm fairly
sure. His problem, once he realized it, was not hearing others
speak or not hearing music in the distance, a flute, a shepherd
singing. You think others are like you—because you have, or have
had, nothing to compare yourself to and had great confidence—
maybe too much—that you were *Norman*. Ha ha." *norman norman*

"*Norman* who?"

"Not *Norman*, Gerry, normal! You felt normal—at least physically normal."

"How did this happen?"

"Don't know. Maybe genetic. Maybe childhood disease. You
speak very well, so postlingual. No one knows for sure. Lawyers

know everything; doctors don't know anything. But you don't interest most doctors."

"Why not?"

"Because you can't be fixed! Too bad! Most *auto rare in knowledge is* like mechanical problems—fix bones in ear, operate, fix!"

"Most auto—"

"Most otolaryngologists. Like to fix. Wonderful! But your high frequencies are gone. Makes lower frequencies complicated too, while you figure out. Nerves dead, can't be replaced. Of course you must get hearing aids."

"I'm only thirty-four—just turned thirty-four!"

"Maybe you should have had them years ago!"

"Will they help?"

"That's for you and the audiologists. They are very knowledgeable. Sometimes I think hearing aids help, sometimes not. You'll have to decide." Chang leaned back in his chair, opened the curtains, turned slightly to my right, and spoke at a faster pace. *"Will I more a day from you, evening the quite rule, all you rain moos introvert tie tear wassail." evening evening even in*

"I guess it's—"

"Take your time, Gerry, dear boy."

   into overtime

     tie tier

      wassail

       to hear—

"I think you said, 'When I move away from you, even in a quiet room, all your brain moves into overtime to hear what I say.'"

Chang came around the desk to me, closing the curtains with his arm trailing behind him on the way without averting his eyes from mine.

"You have come a long way, my boy."

I put my head in my hands. The good doctor, the very good doctor, put his arms around me.

"A long way. I don't *allow who dit.*" *know how you did it* He said this, knowing full well how I, and how others, do it. My mind traveled back into the past, in search of lost time. Time lost as a child, a student, a lover. And lost in my later life too, as a lawyer negotiating transactions involving labor disputes, securities issues, antitrust problems, mergers, oil, shipping, aircraft, automobiles, billions of dollars as I struggled with voices in the air. I thought about the loss of so many ideas, in the near and distant past, affectionate or cross, complex or simple, subtle or brutish, unheard and never answered. Proust could at least *remember* times past; they were lost only in the sense that they had *been*, and he could find them, re-create them, adorn them with words worthy of his memory. The past I search for is one that in important respects never was.

Where have I been? I seem to have done so much, but have I been on the fringes of life, with all those words, all those words, using my every waking moment to try to understand these people so different from me, an alien world. And Mary—was she—was I—were we both—victims of those endless nights of studying, those thousands of mysteries born of silence, born of deafness? Years and years flashed through my mind, a lifetime of years, a quarter of a century, in an instant, the *plaa bencers, prides of lament*, and other lyricals of my personal and professional life, for I seldom forgot them. Though I had no name for them, I treasured them for their beauty and for their possible usefulness were they to appear in the air again. But they *weren't* treasures, I now thought, they were just the product of a—a deaf man walking. Miss Oracle's words were beating in my head: "Where are your HEARING AIDS?"

"What kind of a world is this?" I wondered aloud, as Dr. Chang, in a quiet, reassuring, proximate voice, said, "Easy, my boy." I steadied after a few moments. Dr. Chang let me collect myself and pulled up a chair beside me.

"I can write; I suppose that helps," I said, looking back and forth at nothing in particular and thinking about Sorota and *valid barrels*, *tony OSB*, and *raids*.

"I'm sure. And you're a good decipherer. Your mind moves a mile a second." He laughed at that point not just out of habit but to lighten the air, and to emphasize that I was not that different from others. "And you're a snappy dresser!"

"Snappy dresser?"

"Typical!"

"Of what?"

"Draws attention, down, away from your eyes, ears. Look at me, down here please." He gave me a handkerchief. I blew my nose.

"Am I that bad?"

"No, it's natural. It's good, if *it's worse*." *if it works* "But you're tired, so tired!"

"Can I continue like this?"

"Try the hearing aids; then see. But above all, and this is an *oh tight eeya*, you must know yourself."

"An oh—"

"An old idea."

"To know—whether I am hearing."

"Yes, that. But most of all, to know where to begin and where to stop."

"In particular or in general?"

"Both, my boy."

"I shall try to remember that. Does it get worse?"

"We're all mortal, all mortal. At Nanjing many died, died young. Life can be brutal. Don't be brutal with yourself. Sometimes, sometimes we have to go gently down the stream like the song. But—you said you were a runner—a sprinter, no?"

"Yes. Some time ago."

"Well, it's very hard to run a race—to run at all, for that matter—with an ankle always sprained."

"Very hard."

"So you must make judgments about the ankle, about yourself. Must be wise—hardest thing in the world. If not, events will control you."

"I love the law."

"I'm sure you do. And many other things, too. We should do what we like, do it well, as best we can, maybe with no sprained ankle." Chang paused and took my hand in his. "Keep eyes open, eyes always open, mind open. Ears are a bit closed. Don't kill yourself, my boy. Don't kill yourself. For me. For your mother. For some lucky girl!"

CHAPTER 17

HEARING AIDS AT LAST

S O I FINALLY GOT THEM, THIS NEW PART OF ME, MY
hearing aids, prosthetic devices, *appareils de sourd*, my indicia
of a deaf man, which have now been an integral part of my life for
thirty-five years. I know them well now, but when I first put them
on, they were an awakening not to an unknown language but to
the existence of a completed version of my own. The puzzles the
lyricals presented were to become less complex, to the point
where, assisted by an understanding of the nature of the problem,
I would be able to continue, or to begin, to practice law. It was
not the language of light but one of electrons.

How They Work

I was fitted with a pair of thick black-framed eyeglasses at a hearing aid center in midtown Manhattan. Hearing aids are relatively
simple instruments for the amplification of sound. They consist of
a microphone, an amplifier, and a speaker, powered by small bat-
teries. In the case of my glasses, the microphones were built into

the frames, just to the outside of each eye. These microphones, like the eardrum, have a diaphragm whose movements mirror the compressions and expansions of voices in the air (and ineluctably of other sounds). The diaphragm is extremely thin and is thus sensitive to the minute changes in air pressure produced by the transmission of speech. Originally, like the one in Bell's telephone, it was layered with carbon dust, which was alternatively squeezed and stretched along with the diaphragm as the sound waves passed through it, altering the electrical resistance of the carbon. A current was run through the carbon, its flow electronically reflecting the pattern of the sound waves mirrored in the carbon's resistance. Today the electronic conversion of the diaphragm's movements is made by electromagnets, crystals, and other devices.

Because the thinness of the diaphragm permits only a low amount of electrical current, the hearing aid has an amplifier that produces a more powerful version of the converted, mimicking electronic signals. The amplified signals are in turn transmitted to the speakers, which reconvert them to sound waves of corresponding amplitude (peaks and valleys) and hence of greater intensity than the sound waves that traversed the diaphragm. The amplified waves are then sent to the ear through tubes extending from the hearing aids (in the case of my first pair, the stems of the glasses) into the auditory canal. The eardrum (the "diaphragm" in our own ear) transmits the sound to the middle ear and on to the cochlea. In the cochlea the sound is converted, once again, into electrical current, which ultimately flows to the hearing nerve and on into the brain.

It is a complex voyage, from sound wave to electrical current to augmented current and back to amplified sound wave in the hearing aid, and from amplified sound wave back to electrical current in the ear and the brain. The journey, I would soon learn, produces a considerable distortion of natural sound—both the natural sound to which I had become accustomed and the sounds I had remembered from childhood. The problems undoubtedly stem in part from inefficiencies in this double conversion, but also from the fact that the amplified sound waves the hearing aid sends to the ear can neither stimulate dead hair cells nor elicit sharp signals from the damaged ones. Damaged hair cells responsive to neighboring frequencies do receive the louder signals, and they (and their counterparts organized by tone in the auditory nerve) struggle to capture their own frequencies and appear to make an empathetic effort to capture those to which their fallen comrades, and not they, have been finely attuned. In addition, in a healthy ear the background (irrelevant) noise is attenuated relative to the signal frequency. In a damaged ear, much more of this noise gets through and is dramatically amplified by the hearing aid. As a result, it is true that the brain's effort to find meaning is reduced somewhat, but it remains a struggle for the partially deaf who wear hearing aids to understand speech.

A Persistent Lack of Simultaneity

My glasses were thought suitable for me because they were designed to be particularly sensitive to high frequency sounds, and their microphones were in front, beside the eyes, closer to interlocutors than those that fit around the ear. That the device should be built into glasses was enlightening. People with poor eyesight usually have normally functioning retinas that convert light into electricity and transmit the current to the optical nerve. Normally it is the lens in the eye that is distorted. The addition of external lenses (the glasses) focuses the light on the healthy cells of the retina. If the glasses were to focus the light on a damaged retina, vision would still be blurred. And so it is with amplified sound channeled to damaged epithelial cells in the cochlea: the sounds are louder, but language is still difficult to understand. As a result, more often than not hearing aids fail to provide a critical element of speech to those of us who wear them. The partially deaf, even with hearing aids, lack the immediate merger of idea and sign (the word), the "simultaneity of circumstance," that Auguste Bébian identified as indispensable to fluent understanding. Nevertheless, the lyricals are fewer, the journey to the speaker's ideas a bit shorter, with them than without.

Surviving

It took me some time to become accustomed to my new devices. At first, in spite of all that Chang had said, I thought that I didn't need them, that I was someone else when I put them on, listening to unhelpful, inconvenient, uncomfortably high-pitched noises. I put them in my pocket after a day or so and reverted to my better-known world.

Three days after I first put on the glasses I was on a plane to Arabia to help out with a few odds and ends—the registration of our aircraft, a supply agreement for our lubricating-oil blending plant, Saudi taxes. On the last issue an Iraqi tax lawyer from Ernst & Young, Walid Chorbachi, called to arrange a meeting on the *tead mop as facts, the teed mop deem op deemed prop prof profits deemed profits tax*, the tax regime with which the Saudi government planned to assess the Mobil engineering company that was building a pipeline from the Persian Gulf to the Red Sea. I expected to learn little from Chorbachi and to write a memo with whatever thought or two I might gather from what he said.

At the last minute I decided to put the glasses on. Only Chorbachi and I were there. He was sitting across a narrow table, about three or four feet away, a wall behind him, his lips bathed in florescent light. As he began to speak, I flicked on the switches and heard crackles of speech, but as he continued his introduction to the problem, some words seemed to present themselves with simpler or fewer lyricals. *Mop as facts* would come out as *profits hacks* and then *profits tax*. *Byline* would convert to *pie-line* and quickly adopt its second *p*, becoming *pipeline*. *Tassable income* was clearly *taxable* income; *paren'tage of retinue* was *percentage of revenue*. Whereas, without my hearing aids, the phrase might have been *pass a pin some is a keener tendance of residue*—a long way from *taxable income is a deemed percentage of revenue*.

Whenever Chorbachi turned away, I would be unable to match the louder sound with his lips, and I finally asked him to keep looking at me. "Do they help?" he asked, glancing at the tubes in my ears; I said I thought they might if he could try not to look away. He slowed the pace of his speech and made a point of capturing my eyes with his all the time—in the way, he said, he spoke to his mother. When I went back to our Jeddah office, I wrote a two-page memorandum on the Saudi tax system. I had an English translation of their tax code in front of me but, most importantly, my notes on what Walid said—with fewer lyricals. At a meeting with one other person, at least, I realized that lips and hearing aids shorten the time needed to make the transition to the correct word or phrase before writing it down. When I sent it off to Mobil's tax department in New York, they praised it, and Aldo asked them why they hadn't written it themselves. The memorandum marked a beginning: my hour with Walid was the first meeting of my life.

The following day three of us drove over to the Ministry of Petroleum's office in Jeddah. Jack Butler, then the head of our Arabian subsidiary, sat in the front seat beside his driver, and our treasurer, Cliff Johnson, and I were in the back. Butler started to pepper me with questions; I had the glasses on. He didn't turn around but rattled them off facing the windshield. "What about our *bartered bankers?" bartered bankers darted anchors carted chartered tankers* I immediately understood that, with or without my hearing aids, I would need to see a speaker's lips in order to understand him. Johnson saw the problem, took out a pen and some paper, and mercifully, below the level of the rearview mirror, wrote down Jack's key words, with question marks or periods, to let me know what he was saying, sparing me, perhaps, from yet another lunch of the kind—*how's your fish?*—I had with the trusts and estates department of Debevoise & Plimpton.

My first meeting with Aldo after my return from Arabia, with my new glasses on, concerned crude oil and product exchange agreements with one of Mobil's most talented negotiators, Lawson Willard. There were only three of us, and the meeting became a rapid dialogue between Lawson and Aldo. Sorota suddenly turned to me and said, "What did I *cusstay*?"

"Uh—"

"*What* did I just say?"

"I don't know. You were talking to Lawson."

"But you're sitting right *here*!"

It was nine o'clock in the morning, and Sorota shouted to his secretary in the next room, "Shea needs *suboffy*. Get him some coffee!"

I had grown used to giving up on the conversations of others—with their lips in profile and the speech focused on each other. Discussions between third parties are less intelligible than conversations in which we, the partially deaf, are involved ourselves. In the latter case, lips are usually directed at us, full face, and our participation—our own words—reduces the number of ideas and words of others that need to be deciphered, providing a break and more time to try to catch up. So even with my new hearing aids and a better chance at getting the message, all I knew was that they were talking to each other about oil swaps—a swap of excess Royal Dutch Shell oil that Mobil needed in Singapore in exchange for surplus Mobil oil that Shell wanted in New York—to avoid each party's shipping costs.

The coffee came quickly. I moved my chair toward Aldo to get more of Lawson's lips, and I pitched in myself, if only to repeat what one or the other said, with different words, to slow the pace and decipher lyricals while I repeated the ideas I understood. The practice is a risky one—*I just said that!*—but with some practice the risk is manageable.

After the meeting Sorota, still angry, called to ask me to lunch the next day. We were given a table in the middle of the Mobil dining room. *What's Sorota gonna do to Shea?!* My hearing aids were on, and his voice had a high-pitched, tinny sound and competed with the amplified voices coming from the other tables. He nodded to a few people. His head came abruptly back to me. "What's wrong with you?"

"I have these new, uh, glasses."

"I can *knee tat*." *knee that see that*

"And I'm learning how to use them."

"You weren't listening! Not listening in this business is a very serious matter."

"I have to learn to listen."

"Look—"

"Aldo, listen. I'm pretty deaf. Not profoundly deaf—I still hear a lot—but I'm considerably deaf. I found out about it here first—a hearing test that was part of Mobil's physical. So I finally got these—hearing aids. They may help. They appear to help. I wore them at the meeting with Chorbachi on the tax thing, and they did help. How much they'll help in other settings I don't know. For example, with them on there's a lot of noise in this room, voices as loud as yours—that interfere with yours—even though they're farther away. I'll have to find out. I'll have to learn how to listen. But at least I know what's wrong—why I—"

I stopped speaking because I had to sneeze, and I had learned that sneezes with my glasses on, with the microphones in front and not far from the nose and mouth, and the tubes in my ears, sounded like an explosion inside my head. So instead of reaching for a napkin, I reached for my ears, flipped out the tubes, and sneezed into my boiled haddock.

"That was very interesting."

"Sorry. Look. I don't know where I belong, Aldo. I've lost a lot of my hearing. I'm a lawyer. Words are the heart of what I do. I hear the wrong words all the time, and then I have to translate the wrong words to the right ones, which requires some effort, so—"

"Good thing you can write."

"Well, good thing, bad thing. Maybe this crisis should have come sooner."

"They *do* help?"

"I think so, yes."

"Good. I understand. How *onionswill. onion unusual how unusual* I always thought you were unusual."

We left it at that. But after a long weekend in Salem, I returned to find that the knives were out—not Aldo's but a lot of the Middle East staff, who had grown tired of what they called my plodding along without getting it. He called a meeting in my office and phoned me just before coming to say, "You better get this done. *Use* those hearing aids!" He arrived with ten other people working on our refinery project with the government of Kuwait, a $5 billion dollar joint venture. I had drafted the agreement.

"OK. Questions," said Sorota. "Yeah. Rappaport."

"How can we *germinate—cat or if we* want?" *germinate is terminate cat ow get out how can we get out*

I said that Section 32 gave us a right to withdraw with board
approval. "But if the board doesn't approve?" asked treasurers.

"Under Section 37, withdrawal is a 'partner's event' and a 50
percent vote is sufficient. So it's not a deadlock—we can vote ourselves out."

"But we *grieve our intetment or enable.*" *intetment investment
leave our investment on the table*

"Well, we'd go to arbitration to recover it, and in any event,
we walk away without any further liability."

"What if *dayosee* terminates?" *day day K KOC (Kuwait Oil Company) what if KOC terminates?*

"They can't—they've waived that right, as the host country,
under Section 51, and we will have gotten our special incentive
crude oil up front."

"*Wah out fewer crude?*" *fewer future what about future crude*

"That's part of our decision—if we need the crude, we'll stay
in. They don't have the right to terminate our separate crude-oil
supply agreement if we withdraw from the refinery project under
Section 32, but as a sovereign they can do it."

The discussion continued along these lines, lyricals reduced,
and with the focus on points already in the contract—an easy task,
since few lyricals are needed for spoken words that are already
fixed on paper, stationary before everyone's eyes. At the end of
the meeting, Sorota was pleased. "I don't understand," he said,
implicitly rejecting the complaints about "Shea's not getting it."
He did understand, though; he was giving me a chance ("do they
work?") and alerting all of us of his support. The atmosphere
lightened a bit when I had to flip the tubes out again and sneezed
all over Section 32.

The Hearing Mind

Hearing aids can thus be helpful to the partially deaf by making words somewhat more accessible in limited environments. But the greatest asset for the deaf lies, I think, in the mind's extraordinary capacity for language and its unrelenting drive for meaning. This is a gift we all possess, hearing and deaf alike, but it serves the deaf in powerful ways. Oliver Sacks and Jean Massieu suggest as much in their respective phrases, "seeing voices" and "auricular sight." Sign, for the deaf who sign, and lyricals, for the partially deaf, define us as communicative human beings, as recipients of a common, indispensable gift.

Noam Chomsky suggests that language is but the surface of something more profound. A deeper, formative capacity resides in the fastness of our brains—a language acquisition device. It lies latent until awakened in us when we are just months old. It sets us apart as human beings in the age of science, though it was perhaps first identified in the early nineteenth century, when Auguste Bébian called it the "precious faculty" that unites us in what he called the commerce of souls. The language faculty doesn't enable us simply to mimic others. As Oliver Sacks has written, it no more originates from "experience" than the adaptation of the fin of a baby fish to the properties of water. Chomsky theorizes that it is an organic structure, located in the language-related centers of our brain. When an infant listens to speech, or a deaf baby observes sign language, he begins to speak or to sign himself, and before long he becomes a master at it, without any grammatical instruction and before even learning to read or write. The facility is strongest in the first few years of life and then diminishes until about age twelve, when our capacity to speak or to sign with native fluency disappears. But the element that impels us to understand *others*, I believe, remains with us undiminished for the rest of our lives.

Chomsky originally conceived of our language faculty as essentially a wizard of syntactical structure, an organ that triggers an innate grammatical exercise as a child begins to use a language. He emphasizes that language serves many purposes, such as to enable one to engage in creative mental activity, to gather one's thoughts, to gain understanding, and so on. He says little about hearing in his analysis of speech and language. He usually writes of a (hearing) child's first "exposure" to the language around him and his "use" of it, not his hearing and speaking it. He does not address the complex structures of the ear, though it is clear that language must conform to the ear's sensory characteristics, which enable most of us to identify with great precision the phones and words we hear in order to correlate them with the speaker's ideas, and to use them with the same meaning when we express our own.

Bébian, on the other hand, held that words and signs were fundamentally, and not incidentally, instruments for the conveyance of thought. Written language, he noted, was but painted speech and rooted in the need to convey our ideas. He stated his case clearly in 1817: the essential purpose of language is to give us a way of making our ideas known to others. For Bébian, our most "precious faculty" is our ability to communicate our thoughts and feelings, not simply to structure them and keep them to ourselves. It is the drive for communication that generates and enriches syntax, underlies creativity and intellectual pursuit, and reformulates lyricals and that, whether we are deaf or hearing, governs our linguistic selves.

In the case of the partially deaf who are able to speak and, with the benefit of sight and residual sound, to lipread, we necessarily engage our language faculty to the same extent as a person whose hearing is unimpaired. In any hearing environment, but most noticeably when we can't influence the flow and timing of the conversation, the brain immediately tries to formulate a syntactical structure for the combination of words that we hear. This is because the original structure is often lost, and we need a similar one, or to find the original, in order to capture the speaker's idea.

Our search for that idea is relentless. At the large meeting with Aldo Sorota and others in my office, I heard a Mobil executive say, "How can we *germinate—cat or* if we want?" We were not talking about cats, of course, but "cat" is also oil jargon for "catalytic cracker," an important part of a refinery. But the words "cat or" were syntactical nonsense. So the man may well have wanted a "cat" but never a "cat or," a cat plus a conjunction, without identifying something else. "Germinate" is grammatically correct, but one does not germinate a cat, whether animate or inanimate, and certainly not a "cat or." But "germinate" is a verb, so the trick was to find the right one—"terminate," which of course led me to its synonym, the verb phrase "get out," and the speaker's actual words: "How can we *terminate—get out* if we want?"

When another at that meeting said, "But we *grieve our intetment or enable*," my mind, this time, yielded a grammatical structure, but "intetment" is not a word. *Entêtement* is a French word, but this was an American speaking English. "Interment" was a possibility, but we were talking about oil, not burials. So the solution was to find the right verb, "leave" (not "grieve"), which led quickly to the object, the prepositional clause, and his actual words: "leave our investment on the table." The words "or enable" hadn't worked at all because the verb had no object, and, in any event, "leaving your investment on the table" is a common metaphor, particularly in the context of oil companies dealing with sovereigns.

For the profoundly deaf, the battle is won immediately when they turn to the language of light, as they inevitably do. Their language faculty is, of course, every bit as vibrant as that of those of us who hear. The hearing and speech centers of the brain are just as active when a deaf person receives or expresses sign language as when a hearing person listens and speaks. Victor Hugo made the point in 1845 when he wrote, "What matters deafness of the ear, when the mind hears," as did Lamartine when he wrote in his poem to Pélissier that the deaf had turned light into a sixth sense.

We, the partially deaf, are not as well off as those who sign, for we have to combine our dual paths of understanding, our eyes *and* our ears, to get the message in a medium in which we are not at home. The auditory and optic nerves transmit a portion of the information received from the ear and eye on to the brain. The brain then struggles to assemble and make sense of it, and more often than not manages to do so by constructing and moving through lyricals. As members of the hearing world—partly in, partly out—we have to make do with these imperfect paths to our mind's highly developed and sophisticated devices. But our effort to use them, every moment of our waking lives, helps us to remain members of Bébian's commerce of souls and to retain our sanity.

True, at times unresolved language does leave us dumbfounded, with messages that lyricals cannot make sense of. But even these sometimes have underlying meanings that we come to understand only years later and that seem to shape time itself. That Saturday night at Andover's George Washington Hall, after Lee Marvin seizes the badge of the sheriff and pins it on his own chest in *Bad Day at Black Rock*, I heard him say to Spencer Tracy,

"You gotta big mouth, boy—*makin' of today a song of a second peace.*" Whereas what Marvin actually said was "*makin' accusations of disturbin' the peace.*" Yet what I heard was a seductive idea, even on the lips of Lee Marvin's murderous character.

But what *is* that song, and what is a second peace?

CHAPTER 18

THE WIND IN
THE WILLOWS

THE MOST IMPORTANT ATTRIBUTE OF HEARING AIDS is not—for me and I suspect for countless others—their gift of words and simpler lyricals, but their evocation of what so enchanted Kenneth Grahame's Rat—the thin, clear, happy call of the wind in the willows. Though speech needs to be heard with precision and is made only a louder blur by hearing aids, they can unanchor from the depths of memory the sounds of earlier times—in my case, of early childhood.

When I turned them on during weekend visits to Main Harbor, the birds reappeared—not the one or two that for years appeared among the locusts, a crow in a tree or a seagull—but dozens, flocks of heavenly songs I had not heard since early Main Harbor, waxwings out of the shadows and skylarks over the shoreline. The amplified waves of cochlear fluids restored the ocean waves on rocks and sand, the rattling of pebbles down the beach with the retreating tide, rainfall on rooftops, and the wind, blowing through trees, or through willows when I was close to its clear happy call. My own footsteps were reborn, steps on a floor or court, or brushed across a rug, as were the nearby paces of a dog on a pavement. Silent rivers, the Housatonic in Connecticut in summer, the Arlberg in the Tyrol in the winter, now had voices—their own. And everywhere I went I reveled in the sound of a stream falling into still water.

Crickets had once filled each summer at Main Harbor until they died that seventh year. During the first August I wore hearing aids, just after returning from *mop as facts*, *pie-lines*, and *bartered bankers*, I rented a weekend house with friends in Dutchess County, about two hours up the Taconic Parkway from New York City. Millbrook is very much in the country, and the house lay in the hollow of a two-hundred-acre bowl of fields you could survey from a large backyard bounded by low hedges. My first Friday evening I made myself a gin and tonic and went out back to sit on a bench alone. I was wearing the hearing aids with the switches off. There wasn't a soul outside for miles. All I could hear was the buzz of the locusts in my head.

As I looked out over the waves of tall grass, I felt suddenly not alone. At first I thought it was the silent swaying of the grass in the wind, the breathless hush of evening that lingers on the brink of . . . I turned on the glasses. In a fraction of an instant, the fields came alive with crickets. Not one or two or ten or twenty crickets, but thousands upon thousands of them, with the glorious high-pitched trill of their wings, silencing my locusts. The chorus came from everywhere—north, south, east, west—stretching in from over the hills and fields and pouring into my electrified ears. I turned around in circles to hear it, a melody more hypnotizing even than Puccini's, coming from every direction. The hearing aids were reaching out to the orthoptera, real ones this time, crickets running the bows of their upper wings along the strings of the lower and amplifying the sound with the membranes along their surface as faithfully as the spruce and maple of a violin's hourglass.

I had not heard them since before the scarlet fever, and when I turned the hearing aids off, I became, suddenly, deafer again to them than the female cricket who, though deaf, has an olfactory sense that detects her lover when he lifts his wings. I turned the hearing aids on and off: from noise without and silence within to noise within and silence without, and back again. Thousands of real lives, out there in the field, restoring a distant past and raising a new present, born of the displacement of molecules in the air bearing those and other sounds that gentle Rat could hear and Beethoven could not. The birds, the rainfall, the footsteps, the breaths, the water, the crickets, the merry bubble and joy of my life as a young child.

The wind in the willows comes to us also in the form of music. Hearing aids didn't change my own voice, spoken or sung, other than to make it sound, to me, as if I were speaking or singing in a hollow tunnel or into a microphone because of the electric character of the signal. Nor did they alter the sound of lower-pitched musical instruments—the bass fiddles, cellos, oboes, drums, or low brasses of an orchestra—other than to make them louder. But they did bring with them the violins, flutes, piccolos, and upper strings of piano and harp, making whole what had been half-orchestras and introducing concertos, symphonies, and operas (except for the lyrics, unreachable lyricals) as completed musical compositions. The effect is spellbinding. The silent violins in overtures become audible; human voices appear in Wagner; sopranos, mezzos, and tenors come to life; bass fiddles and cellos playing harmonics or in counterpoint are relegated to their supporting roles as they lose the melody to the violins and flutes. Peter rivals the Wolf in Prokofiev, and here, too, I become a child again, as my long confusion is spiritually unraveled by returning, unrepentant, splendrous sounds.

Teaching Is Reaching?

After Chang's diagnosis, I made several subway excursions *steel wheels ripping into my locusts* downtown to the League for the Hard of Hearing to learn more about lipreading. The lessons were in the early evening, and I enrolled in a six-week course. Outside the building's front door I slipped my tubes into my ears and clicked the world back on. The woman at the desk told me the League was on the *tekah foe*. "The deck floor?" She smiled and held up two fingers, mouthing the word "second." I took the elevator and walked down a long narrow hallway, typical of many prewar office buildings. This one had been redone once or twice, and the corridor was well lit and carpeted. Several small doors opened into what seemed like classrooms. As I walked toward the right one, I swept one shoe back and forth over the rug to hear that soothingly soft *whoosh* whispering into my electric ears.

"Hello. *Missed her day?*" said a woman looking up from behind the reception desk.

> *missed her day*
> *mister day*
> Mr. Shea

"Yes. Hello." I leaned over the desk, close to her lips.

"I'm *Aria*. We've been expecting you."

"Hello, Harriet. Sorry I'm late."

"No problem. Have a seat." I pulled away a bit. "*This is summer's wilting youth in a Moma.*"

> *wilting youth*
> *in a museum*
> *what's her name*

> *Sommer*
>   *Mrs. Sommer*
>   *will see you*
>   *in a MOment.*

"Thank you."

I sat in one of three dozen plastic folding chairs in the large room. It was still early, and there were only three other people waiting. I took the *Times* out of my briefcase, along with the small blue spiral notebook Mrs. Sommer had asked me to buy for our sessions. I was catching up on a handful of disasters on the front page when a man tapped me on the shoulder. He was silent, pointing excitedly to Harriet. Mrs. Sommer was free and coming down the hall.

Jane Sommer was a short woman about sixty years old with dark hair still, almost blue but natural. She wore a bright red suit and black low-heeled shoes. I could see my audiograms tucked under her arm. At three feet away she smiled, looked into my eyes, and said, slowly, "Welcome, Mr. Shea. I am Jane Sommer. We'll be working together. Let's go to my office. It's small, but it'll do." When we got to her door, she gestured toward the seat beside her desk, to her left, facing her. Her desk was cluttered with notebooks, hearing charts, two hand mirrors, a magnifying glass, a box of Kleenex, and an empty pack of Ritalin tablets. On the floor around us were children's toys and blocks and an assortment of telephone amplifiers and magnifying glasses—tools for all seasons.

Jane wheeled her chair to the left, her lips now about three feet away, and stayed there, head turned up, speaking right to me, her eyes seeking mine. She tilted the metal lampshade on her desk toward her lips. "Let's see. I've looked at your charts here—thanks for sending them. Sixty-five decibels at 1,000 Hertz, 85 at 2,000, 95 at 4,000. Not so hot. You look pretty good for someone who's 150 years old. And you have a pleasant voice."

"I can sing."

"That's *ice*. You hear those *low dotes*. What happened to all those highs?"

"I'm not sure. Scarlet fever, they think. When I was six. But I found out that I was deaf late—in fact I just found out.

"Before, you must have thought everyone was *ike* you—heard like you?"

"Yes—that I was just slower—"

"I understand. Of course they don't hear like you do—most people don't anyway—and now you know."

"Now I know. And I just got these hearing aids. In fact, I have a name for them."

"A name! And what may I ask—"

"I call them *oiseaux lyres*."

"Wahzo lear—*oiseau*, I guess, that means *purr*, doesn't it?" *purr burr bird*

"Yes. They bring me birdsong and music, so I call them that, not so much when speaking to others as when I think about them. They're not much help with words. That's why I've come to you, as I said to the person over the phone—to learn how to lipread, or whether it's possible."

"It is possible, particularly if one has residual hearing like you do. Today we call it 'speechreading.' And I'm here, of course, to tell you about it." Jane took two sheets of paper from under a stack of charts and handed them to me. "This is all part of your 'vocabulary'—no doubt, already."

I took a few moments to read the two pages, uttering four or five sounds, conscious of the different shapes of my lips.

"Consonants." I handed the list back to her.

"Yes. We're starting with them—the visible ones—because they're the clues you look for first. They are the markers of our speech." Jane moved her chair opposite mine, our knees practically touching, and adjusted the light. "Do you know why I've come closer?"

"Sound is easier to hear."

"Right. Much easier. The intensity of sound is *unforesee tortion*"

tortion

bortion

portion

unforeseen inversely

proportional

"to the square of the distance you are from the sound. A voice two feet away is twenty-five times more intense than a voice ten feet away. OK?" She wrote it down. "Now, my lips are about three feet from yours. I shall speak slowly and with natural, unexaggerated lip movements. OK?"

"Yes."

"Look at me." She closed her lips and then puffed them open. "What do you see?"

"Two lips together, then a puff."

"Sound group?"

"*P*, *b* and, uh, I guess—*m*."

"Good. They're identical, usually *monotonous*. How do you tell the difference?"

"Sorry. Monotonous?"

"Never apologize. Visually homophonous—sounds that don't sound the same but look the same. So if you don't hear the sound, or don't hear it well, how do you know which is which?"

"Context."

"Right."

Jane pursed her lips as if, I thought, she were beginning to say the word "choo-choo." "When I pucker my lips like that, what sounds do you see?

"*Ch*, as in 'choo-choo.' And maybe *sh*?"

"Good. What else?"

"Don't know."

"Soft *g*, which we call or write as *j*, as in 'judge.' What about *y*?"

"It's like an *e*, *ee*, as in 'many.'"

"And at the beginning of a word?"

"It's a—pucker?"

"No. It is still seen on the lips as an *e* but leading into the following vowel, as in 'yes' or 'Yale.'" She wrote down *ee-ess* and *ee-ale*. "*Y* at the beginning."

"I went to Yale."

"Bully for you. Want some coffee?"

"No coffee, thanks. Can we take a break? I'm a little nervous."

"Down the hall on your right."

As I walked down the hall, a large arm wrapped itself around my shoulder. It was the man who had alerted me to Harriet. I laughed and looked at him more carefully, his closely cropped hair, white shirt, T-shirt underneath, black khakis, white socks, and basketball sneakers. He pulled me closer as we walked along. He was about thirty years old. He asked me how things were going by raising his left thumb, his head, and his eyebrows, as his voice uttered, loudly, a wordless question. I smiled. "It's great." He raised his thumb higher and hugged me again.

I asked him his name slowly: "What—is—your—name?" He double bounced the extended index and middle fingers of his right hand off those of his left and then pointed to himself. He uttered two syllables, one high, one low, as in "uh-oh." I thought, *Harold, Raymond, Peter—it could be almost anything*. He tried spelling it in three letters, but I didn't know fingerspelling; he then touched my shoulder as if to say, *Let's try this*, never taking his eyes away from mine. He opened his mouth wide, curled his lips into a snarl, and formed a claw with his right hand, which, beginning slowly, lunged into space, like a lion's. Biblical pantomime for my benefit, from a marvelous actor.

"Daniel."

He smacked the back of his right hand against his left palm, and pointed to me: "Good!"

When I got back to Jane's office, I asked her about the sound of water. "Why is it so . . . seductive?"

"It's all those liquid highs in your *oiseaux*. Beautiful."

"Right. Uh, I just saw Daniel again. You know, I worry too much—about myself; most people don't even realize it when I can't understand what they're saying. Mine is more like a spiritual problem than an illness. Sometimes I think it's not something worth—"

"Gerry. You live in two worlds, and you sometimes take the perspective of the hearing on your *dissipity. diss dissi diffi difficulty* 'They don't realize it,' you say. But you do. You're extraordinary. Don't forget that. You're a lawyer. Words are your trade. You're good at this stuff. Really good. And as to Daniel, he is doing fine. He's been profoundly deaf since birth. He is a fluent signer— fluent in his own language."

"His life is orders of magnitude more difficult. He can't hear anything."

"Probably not so. Virtually everyone hears something. A total absence of sound, total deafness, is called *govotis*, and it's very rare."

"Govotis."

"Cophosis. But Daniel hears almost nothing. He can't lipread at all, of course, or very little, because he hears virtually no sound. But he has the language he needs. He's in one world; you're in another. But as I say you're not entirely in that other world, the hearing world; you're partially in it. No way it's not a 'big deal.'

That is total bullshit." Totul Boolshit. She wrote it down as she spoke: at a normal pace, face up, phonetically.

"Now sit down. Here we go. We'll turn now to *bowels*; it's new."

"Once a day."

She moved closer. "Right. *Vvv*owels. Top teeth on bottom lip, no pucker." Jane was smiling. "There's been some progress in method over the past few years on vowels. To speechread vowels, Gerry, you look at two things. First, the shape of the lips, in this case smiling, neutral or puckered. Second, you look at the degree of opening of the lips: small, medium, or wide. So what vowels are smiling?"

"*Ee*, like 'meet.' And perhaps *eh* as in 'met.'"

"Yes. Also *ih* as in 'mitt' and *ah* as in 'mat.'"

"Let's meet Matt at the Met at midnight."

"Excellent. 'Meet' makes you smile broadly. 'Mat' opens up your lips. 'Let' and 'Met' less so."

"The opening at the Met."

"And after the opening at the Met, at midnight, lesser still. You know, you do this sort of thing, 'meeting Matt at the Met,' and so on, because you spend all your time—all your life, really—looking for the right words when you get the wrong ones."

Jane and I continued these sessions every other day for almost two weeks. But on the second Friday, on what turned out to be my last day, I was greeted by an attractive red-haired woman about forty years old. She was kind of the inverse of Jane, red at the top and dressed in blue.

"Where's Mrs. Sommer?"

"She had to go off to a meeting in Florida to fill in for my second, who's ill. We're opening an office in Miami. She asked me to hug you for her. This is your last day."

"But we have four weeks to go—"

"Nope."

"You're—

"The *pot*." *the pot the tot the toss the boss*—

"Pretty young! Let me turn on—"

"No. Don't switch on your glasses. We're going to *too iss*" *too do to do this* "without them. I want you to try to read my lips with almost no sound." She moved about ten feet away, down the hall. "Jane tells me you've been doing this for a *lone lime*." *lone lone lime time lone—long time*

"I guess so."

"I am going to whisper," she whispered.

"Right."

"What did I say?"

"You said, 'I am going to whisper.'"

"Did you have a good day at Mobil today?"

"A very good day."

"What *tapped*?" *tapped tappin tap tap tappin happin what happened*

"We got overlift rights at Aramco."

"Overlift?"

"It means we can lift—buy more barrels than our equity share of the company—Aramco—would normally allow us. I didn't, uh, do it, but I wrote it."

"Congratulations. Do you like your work there?"

"Yes. Now, I suppose I do."

"Would you *lie to kuh town* here to teach *is reaching* in the evening?"

"Teach is reaching?"

"Teach *lits reaching*."

"Teach lip reading! Well, I don't have the time, I'm afraid—but you've gotta be joking!"

"Can you *sir them ought*?" *sir sir ought ought on oiseaux lyres turn them on*

"Sure." I clicked on my glasses.

"Mr. Shea," she said, close to me, "you have a lifetime of experience in what we teach. You're really good. Like, I mean, I've never seen anybody like you. If you don't have the time, then that's a pity—for us. But remember this at work—remember it wherever: you're unusual."

"Funny. That's what Aldo, uh, Sorota at Mobil said—that I was *onionswill.*"

"Unusual. Yup. He's right. We can't help you here, except to tell you that you're unusual—perhaps unique—for us too. Remember this, when you feel like *drying in your coop.*" *coop coop.*

"Drying in your coop. Chicken coop. Harvard Coop."

"Nope."

"Crying in your soup."

"Right . . . you have no reason to. Don't. And come see us now and then." She gave me a hug—for herself and for Jane, she said—and she said good-bye.

CHAPTER 19

ALMOST WHOLE

THE MEMORY OF MARY, LINGERING FOR ALMOST A dozen years, was finally overtaken by the woman who had given me the names of eligible French ladies in Paris. Claire had offered me both single and married women, and men, and I came home with no one. Her list of single women turned out to resemble that of George W. Bush's charmless choice for vice president. Bush had originally asked Cheney to help sort out candidates, and in the end, Cheney helped choose . . . himself. As it happened, Claire, having introduced me to everyone she knew in Paris, was now separated from her husband and still in New York, working for the cultural section of the French embassy.

By the time I got back to New York at age thirty-three, in the fall of 1975, I had come to know in Paris most of her friends, her two sisters and brother, and her parents. I invited her to the opera. When it was over and we were standing on the sidewalk on Columbus Avenue, I looked about for a place to have dinner, a place where you might meet Matt at the Met at midnight, and remembered the Ginger Man across the way from Lincoln Center. But I heard a muffled bang and an *oh swaa oh swaa bow swaa bon swa bonsoir*, as the cab drove away with Claire in it. After that, I didn't see her for months. In May I spotted her at a buffet dinner at Laurence Belknap's and decided to avoid her. Having coffee on a couch after dinner, I felt someone sit down to my right, as I tried to listen to people on a chair to my left.

"Keh to feh cet aygay?" keh to feh feh fait cet aygay atay cet été qu'est-ce que tu fais cet été What are you doing this summer? It was Claire's voice, speaking to me. She meant what are you doing on the weekends, and explained that she was looking for a place for herself and her infant daughter, Pénélope. Since my early days at Debevoise I had seldom gone anywhere on the weekends other than to the office. But I didn't want to get another *oh swaa*, so I said I was trying to decide where to go. She asked me where I normally went; I said it depended and threw out all the chic towns I had ever heard of but never been to—"Oh, Southampton or Watermill, Tuxedo Park, Locust Valley or Watch Hill. It depends."

"Tu veux vay ta avec nous?" vay ta vay fay faire faire ça You want to find a place with us? I said sure, heart beating fast for this woman of few but unambiguous words, and agreed to call her. "Pick the town, and I'll come looking with you," she said. I knew no one in any of those towns but managed to reach a classmate I had not seen for twelve years who lived in Millbrook. I called him, we went up, and he helped us find the house where the crickets were to dance that night to the music of my *oiseaux lyres*. With Claire at my side, I was reborn too, and my dream of Mary somehow returning slowly faded away.

Claire's lyricals are a calm, sure-footed, musical French or French-accented English, and the transitions to her thoughts, apart from the untimely *boh swaas*, dreamlike. As for the lyricals of others, she would interrupt a conversation when she thought I didn't understand—not clumsily, but as if to clarify things for herself, though with a remark that was focused on points she knew I had missed. Her gifts were uncanny. Her father maintained that it was Claire alone in the family, whether in his generation or the generation before or after, who embodied what Proust wrote in describing her great-grandmother, la comtesse Greffulhe—that no element of her nature could be found in any other woman and that the mystery of her beauty lay in her indecipherable eyes.

Claire and I were already living together when the bows and strings of crickets returned to me. And she became first spiritually and later physically linked to my early memories in Main Harbor, where she ultimately insisted we buy a summer house. With her I was to live all seasons, my pre-scarlet summers at Main, the seasons of dragonflies and locusts, and those of the rebirth of music, wind, breaths, water, and footsteps. A few weeks after I started wearing my hearing aids regularly, she came to me at breakfast with her hands full of bottles and boxes, of Mylanta, Gelusil, valium, and probanthine, and put them all on the breakfast table.

"*Qu'est-ce que tu fais?* What are you doing? *Dur dot you oiseaux!*" I flicked on the switches. "*Je le chette?*" *chette jette les jète? Shall I throw them out?*

"But—"

"You don't *date* them anymore, dar-leeng." *don't take them*—

"I may need them again."

"Gérald! You *doe* what's wrong. You know! So they're *dishes!*" *dishes—finished they're finished*

She scooped them all up, opened the door under the sink, and threw them in the trash. For such a long time, at Debevoise and at Mobil, from New York to Paris and back, I'd taken medicine to coat the stomach, dry out the body, and calm the brain and nerves, and then coffee to wake them up and drugs again to calm them down—all to solve a problem in my inner ear. But Claire was right. The cause of the ulcers was not so much the constant wrestling with lyricals as not knowing why life among the hearing was so difficult. Once that question was answered, the puzzles remained, but lyricals became an identified challenge, something to overcome, a way to try to live like everyone else.

Three years passed, like the wind, and still I couldn't decide whether to marry her. It wasn't Mary's memory but my independence that was at stake, and the worry that the uncertainties presented by my need for hearing aids was not too great a risk for one person but a substantial one for three, and an even greater one if we decided to have children together. But she demanded that I decide. I said I couldn't make up my mind (all those elements of her nature notwithstanding), and she returned to Paris with Pénélope.

Over a period of several months I dithered. I got to know one other woman well: Andrea, a Hungarian harpsichordist. But as Andrea and I rowed across a lake on a summer afternoon in Austria, she proved to be afraid of the rain—the rain that, like everything else outdoors, on a lake, in a forest, in the street, on a mountaintop, Claire relished.

I drove up to Salem on a few weekends after Claire had left. My mother was unhappy with my decision about Claire. "You have to get married some time, Gerry, for heaven's sake; I'm getting too old to do all the worrying." On one of those weekends, I saw someone I hadn't seen for twenty years—since Andover—quite by chance. I was getting out of the car in Mother's driveway. As I closed the door to the car and looked up, there was—Elizabeth, Beth, still extraordinarily beautiful. *Gerry, your eyes and your mind are traveling separate ways.* She had seen me first and was only about two feet away. Beth looked at my large black-framed glasses and the tubes in my ears. She gave me that same gleaming smile, kissed me on the lips, and held me in her arms, for a good thirty seconds, rocking us left to right, right to left, just as, remarkably I thought, Chang had done.

"You're married, sweetheart. How did I manage to deserve that?"

"Two children, too. Your glasses—"

"They're hearing aids."

"I can see that! And I've heard. And so—?"

"And so now I can hear—at least hear a bit better. Life is, um, a bit less complicated."

"You poor boy!"

"What—?"

"You never understood anything! Me, my friends, the movies, your own family when we were with them together, even your mother. They never noticed—they were too into you. But I did. Not that I wasn't into you too, but for so short a time. And the answer was so simple!"

"Well, I've got the hearing aids now, and things are easier. And you, you're still beautiful."

"Chatterly forgets you tepperwear," chatterly no not a good idea Lady chatterly flattery will get you tepperwear everywhere—of course— "so you've come down to earth?"

"Uh, yes. Well, not quite. I still need to, to—figure things out." I was uneasy, standing there at the edge of the driveway, feeling at age thirty-eight the same way I had when I changed the subject the night we saw the incomprehensible *Lady and the Tramp.*

"But don't *daze*, Gerry."

"Don't daze, Gerry," I said, repeating what I had heard. "As you see, the 'daze' is still there. But you said, 'don't change.' Change from what?"

"You remember when I told you you were a curiosity—'member that?"

"I do."

"Your unusual—*spiritual* side. I hope you won't *ooze* it." *ooze ooze lose won't lose it*

"Won't lose what?"

"That side, that world."

"Did you—were you beginning to—?"

"Figure it out? No. I just knew you misunderstood things all the time, and I started to pay attention to it. It was fascinating. But whenever you spoke, joked, sang, you—you made even me forget your distractions. But not hearing—I understand it now— has made you what you are. Don Giovanni, maybe, but mostly Candide. I've heard all about you!"

"From Mom!"

"No, no. Lots of sources."

"I do regret—"

"You've gained more than you've missed. Don't look back. You'd have been someone else."

"I've my faults. I've just left—"

"That's romance, Gerry. You left me, too. You went away, and I never saw you again, you rat. I burned the scarf I was knitting you for the coming cold winter. That happens in love. But on the whole, and this is what I want to say—"

Several cars drove by as we stood on the sidewalk, a few Salemites looking at us curiously through their backseat car windows, imagining a scandal. "What I want to say is, that you think the world is a better place than it is, as you struggle to unravel its mysteries. You're a treasure hunter. Not material treasures, I don't think, but the treasures of everyday life."

Beth certainly hadn't changed. As she turned to walk the rest of her way home, her eyes stayed behind, focused on mine, just for an instant. Not to tell me, this time, that my mind was elsewhere, but to show me, I think, how beautiful the world can be when you use your mind to figure out what lies right before you.

TEN MONTHS AFTER I SAID I COULDN'T DECIDE, I WENT running back to Claire. On a trip to Arabia I stopped in Paris for a few days and wrote a letter saying that it was she, and not Mary's memory, that I could not do without, and would she come back to New York and marry me? I had a room at the Hotel Raphaël on the avenue Kléber in the sixteenth, where all the Mobil people stayed, and decided to leave my letter with the concierge on the ground floor of the rue d'Astorg where Claire lived, in the house that had belonged to the grandmother of the enigmatic eyes. I wanted Claire to read the letter before she saw me. I took a taxi over to her place in mid-afternoon and rang the downstairs bell.

The door opened, and standing there was not the concierge but Hugues de Montalembert, an intimate friend of Claire's, and mine, who is blind. Claire had given him the apartment for the summer. He faced out at me. "*Oui?*" Hugues wears a single band of silver over his eyes, so that when you look at him they appear to emit light, and he seems to see, as if its reflection were his glance.

"Uh—"

"Gérald." I flicked on my *oiseaux lyres*.

"*Bonjour*, Hugues, I—"

"*Écoute-moi, Gérald, tu mortes day o'lay?*" *tu mortes tu porte tes oreilles Are you wearing your hearing aids?*

"*Oui.*"

"*Alors, qu'est-ce que du* tou *là?*" *tu fous*—what the hell are you doing here?

"I have a letter for Claire. Is she here?"

"Ah! A letter for Claire. For Claire. How interesting, *mon cher* Gérald!"

"Are you OK?"

"Why, yes, I am quite OK. Quite all right. And how about you? That may be the *test 'em.*" *questem question* He began to laugh.

He had lost his eyesight in an assault by a street gang in New York several years before, and it was Claire, more than anyone, who had come to his rescue after the event, with the weight of the embassy behind her. His attackers had thrown acid in Hugues's eyes, and nothing could be done. He has narrated a film and written a book about it, *La Lumière Assassinée*, and wrote a second book in English, *Invisible*, just published, learned to play the piano, looks like Rudolf Nureyev in reflective sunglasses, and walks around New York and Paris with his white cane at a faster pace than any fast-moving, sighted investment banker on his way to work. He was once asked by a stranger, observing his long stride, silver eyes, and striking looks, whether he was engaged in "some kind of experiment." He laughed and said yes, it was—a *long* experiment. After all his suffering, and because of it, there is bitterness in Hugues's manner. There appeared to be a dose of malevolence in his *how about you?*, but I think Hugues's directness is, rather, his way of making others deal with him on equal terms.

"Is she here?"

"No, I *doe tea so*." ha ha ha

"Could you be sure that she gets the letter? It's important."

"I'm sure it is, ha ha! And you can be sure she will get it, Gérald. And how is *tour series*? Worse when you're living alone, I'd *rather, dough*?" *tour your series ear hearees hearing worse when you're living alone I gather, non?*

"Well—I've always said we'd make a good team."

"So you have! But today we are a *retail* team" *relay we are a relay team* "from the deaf to the blind to the woman you love!"

I thanked him and escaped into the waiting taxi. I stayed put at the Raphaël for two days and got no call. I sat beside a man at the bar the second evening, asking him whether he was French. "No, I am Italian." I said I thought I knew him and introduced myself.

"Perhaps, perhaps you do."

"And your name is . . . "

"My name is *A Cello Maestro Daddy*." *a cello—no like a B Bacello M Maccello God so charming—Marcello Mastroianni*. We talked about his movie *The Pizza Triangle*, and he introduced me to the director, who came down the stairs with a woman on each arm, headed out for the evening. Lucky them, I thought, all of them.

I finally called Claire, now worried about whether there was someone else in her life, and she reluctantly agreed to have dinner. We went to La Bourgogne in the seventh arrondissement, where I had last had dinner several years before with George Marbury when he stopped over, on his way to Italy with his wife and daughter, to see whether my stomach was still bleeding. La Bourgogne had now become a tourist spot, and Claire and I were surrounded by Japanese visitors. The waiter sat us at a central table. Claire put her napkin on her lap. When she looked up, I said, "*Alors?*" And so?

"*Alors, t'es un vrai con*, Gérald." You're a fool. "*T'es vieux, tu es trop vieux*. You're too old. I have a new *knife*." *a knife a life* "Tu *m'oblige de partir et puis et puis"*—you wanted me to leave, and now, and now—the tears came quickly.

My heart sank as I grew sure that this was the reenactment of my past. But she finally agreed to let me call her from Arabia every Monday night at the time I picked, seven fifteen, for the month I would be there, and when I got back to New York, I put together an album of our life together in New York and Mill-brook, with Pénélope and the crickets, the birds, the wind and the water, begging her to come back to America and adding captions and desperate assurances and promises, and sent the album over by FedEx. She asked a Swiss friend—really a Russian ballet dancer—staying with her to open it, who promptly wept her warm Russian tears and mascara all over the book, which I still have. I flew back on Labor Day weekend, 1981. Claire agreed to come back and *te barrier me marier avec toi to marry you.*

We bought an apartment on Ninety-Sixth Street, heavily mortgaged at the 1982 interest rate of 14 percent, and Claire had to sell her jewelry to help pay for food and other things our first year together. We had a son, Sebastian, in August. I was in Arabia; Claire had gone to Paris to have the baby. In the car on the way home from the office to the house where I was staying in Jeddah, the Yemeni driver, Ali, put on "For Unto Us a Child Is Born"—it was in the middle of the tape; it must have been set to play by chance. I thought of my words of ten years earlier, "I don't want to bring anyone else into a life like mine," and I couldn't contain the tears as I heard in the first verse, "and his name shall be callèd wonderful, *marvelous,*" the word I heard, still hear, for "counselor"—marvelous that she should give me our own American in Paris.

Ali was delighted and said, "Do not cry, *la domo,* Mr. Shea," for all of this was—"*Mumtaz!* Superb! A boy!" I think today of "For Unto Us" as signaling not just the birth of Christ but that of any child, all of whom may be called wonderful, marvelous, and perhaps one day, if we are lucky, counselors to all of us, as in my childhood my Infant of Prague was to me, and princes of peace as well. I began to feel almost whole, a variety of Bébian's whole person, with the memories of Mary virtually banished, a wife I loved, a stepdaughter and a son, and a second set of flawed ears with which, in the commerce of necessity, I would try to make it all work.

CHAPTER 20

LILACS AND MINARETS

Aldo had moved to Arabia to run Mobil's operations there on the ground, his last slot before he would return to the United States to become Mobil's chief executive. He seemed pleased that I finally got married. Most companies like to see their people married to avoid having them shot dead in unstable erotic adventures or having them waste, with a variety of loves, time and energy that should be devoted to the enterprise. "What are the chances," he asked me, casually, as if he were about to ask about the weather, during a break at our next meeting in Riyadh, "if I were to ask you to *give* here in Jeddah, *ring care and his askin'*, work more closely with me, like in New York?"

Ring Claire and—as ti tian seb astian bring Claire and Sebastian "Aldo, I've already said—the accents, the beards, the air conditioners, it's a—"

"What are the odds, *want a den?*"

"Two."

"Twenty percent. Not bad."

Eventually he had his way, of course, converting the odds of two out of ten into a reasonable possibility. In the summer of 1983 Claire, Pénélope, our baby, Sebastian, and I moved to Arabia. Aldo had a sense of my lyricals, ever since our lunch *what's wrong with you* on Forty-Second Street. "You gotta problem," he would say whenever I would lose my bearings at a meeting, as if encouraging me to find a way through it. If he was willing to take the chance on my coming, I thought, so should I be. In addition to the excitement in Arabia—still the center of the world as far as oil is concerned—there would be the beauty of its language I had grown accustomed to on earlier visits. As I walked down the street with my *oiseaux lyres* and heard it sung from the tops of minarets—the low, well-rounded chords of classical Arabic sung and spoken still, there in its cradle, I added the calls to prayer to my list of birds, crickets, water, wind, and music.

Our house, like all houses in Jeddah, was not far from a mosque, and we were awakened early each morning with "*la illah illa Allah*"—all those liquid *l*'s, the loveliest letter, I would sing to myself when I heard the song during the day, tongue between my teeth, imagining it, my childhood *l*—perhaps that was the memory—echoing in my palate, or in my memory as a schoolboy, "when lilacs last in the dooryard bloom'd," now *la illah illa allah* ("there is no God but Allah"), *wa Mohamed razuul Allah* ("and Mohamed is his prophet"). God or not, prophet or not, the song was hypnotizing, and the muezzin would vary its melody and prolong its call, singing out the *l*'s and *a*'s in a progression of notes that grew in number with the approach of sunset, as Whitman might have, had he chosen to sing about his lilacs from the height of a minaret.

Americans did not feel insecure in Arabia in those days, and our house was on a quiet street, with the head of the Saudi secret service on one side, the station chief of the CIA (the eponymous Ray Close) on the other, and the American embassy (until it moved to Riyadh) on the street just behind us. I snorkeled in the Red Sea, and Claire dove deep with a tank among the barracuda and the sharks.

Mobil kept a Gulfstream jet in Jeddah to take us to Riyadh whenever we needed to go, and to London and Paris for meetings there—often held with our Saudi counterparts, who, though they lived in Arabia as we did, sometimes preferred to negotiate in the more convivial and temperate climate of European capitals. Our relationship with the Ministry of Petroleum and the Saudi government in general was a good one. Although they were in the course of nationalizing Aramco, then owned by Exxon, Chevron, Texaco, and Mobil, they needed the majors to purchase their crude and market it overseas, as well as our technical expertise to help run their oilfields and build and operate their new in-country refinery and petrochemical or "downstream" ventures.

My principal function was to sit and listen and then to disappear after Aldo and the minister, or one of his deputy ministers, reached agreement on crude oil supply for the coming months, the offtake of refined products, joint venture terms, and the manufacture of lubricating oils inside the kingdom. The discussion would go on for some time, with the minister of Petroleum, Ahmed Zaki Yamani, or his deputy at the head of the table, flanked by Aldo and me, and a Saudi aide or two to my left. I wrote down everything I heard, looking at lips while writing, though proximity, the two familiar voices, and my *oiseaux lyres* were all helpful.

"When the *tie dynes down, we get the do dred byhip.*" *tie dynes pipelines get the do dred do dred?*

"We get the what?"

The minister put his hand on my shoulder. "Gerry, you get the two—hundred—by—ship—tanker—we'll ship it over. Two hundred *DDT*."

DDT TBD two hundred thousand barrels a day "Thank you."

He was delighted to walk me through things, to help Mobil's lawyer—Aldo's lawyer—with his English. After an hour or so, Aldo would say, "OK," and I would rush into the anteroom or down the halls of the ministry looking for a couple of secretaries. They were, of course, all men, normally either Palestinians, Pakistanis, or Indians, and I would choose the nearest people—any two individuals from the group to the extent that (not always the case) an Indian and a Pakistani could get along. I would dictate a page or two to the first secretary and then pass to the second, as I recited the formulas—so wonderful to speak in soliloquy as they wrote down my words in shorthand—without fear of having to hear and answer a question about what I was saying.

I would switch back to the first secretary one or two pages into the draft and continue dictating. When the dictation was done, I was given the typed drafts and marked up each section in writing as another was being typed or retyped. The exercise took about half an hour, and I would rush back into the minister's office with four or five copies in hand, putting them in front of each participant.

"*Ah eur*," said the minister.

Aa eur aa fast eur erd er fast work

"Thanks."

"This is his value added, Your Excellency. Shea's a bit deaf, but if he can hear it, he can write it, understandably, you know, like a rational human being, not like your average lawyer. He's more like a lawyer when he doesn't hear it."

The partially deaf may have an advantage at writing because lyricals give us an infinite vocabulary, far beyond that of our own

Randall went to the bar at the back of the cabin, broke the in-kingdom seal on it, and took out a bottle of Dewars. Aldo was raising another subject with the chairman, who was sitting beside him. I double checked the switches on my *oiseaux lyres*. *Christ, what does he want to know?* One of the most unsettling tasks in the professional lives of the partially deaf is searching for an expected answer to an unheard question, desperately hunting for cues in lyricals if you can, but if that fails, then in the eyes, expressions, pauses, reactions of others—anything at all that might provide a clue. *Are ee awe to owe ih ih eh ih rew ih all we gah . . . for a rev eye.* Randall handed me the scotch with an apologetic smile and disappeared into the cockpit.

Sorota turned from the chairman to me and said, "Drink it." I swallowed the scotch in less than half a minute. "Now," he said, leaning toward me, all eyes on us, "about the *rev eye ee*." *rev eye eee refinery*

"Yes."

"We got *ih seck tive roo*." *incen incentive crude extra crude oil for us*

"Yep."

"What else?"

"The offtake agreement. Destination options."

"So *what*," said the head of exploration and producing, two rows down, "*the par of the dee*." *deed eel part of the deal that's*

"I know, Bill. But as I wrote it, we pay the refinery based on the price of product at a combination of destinations if the average is lower, no matter where it goes."

"So we *bay* a lower brice. And we get *shoes* in the market." *shoes shews we get screwed in the market*

"No. We sell at market price but use the deemed price to pay the refinery."

forgot to put them on. He was sitting in the middle of the plane, and I had managed to sit diagonally across from him, on the other side of the aisle, facing backwards. We were flying from Riyadh to London with several members of Mobil's executive committee aboard. The plane took off at seven in the morning, and by seven thirty my eyes were half closed, calmed by the blessed silence, the engines now a quiet low-frequency hum, the words of others inaudible. Someone asked Aldo a question. I opened my eyes, and he turned his head toward me to repeat it.

"*Are ee awe to owe ih ih eh ih rew ih all we gah. Ady thee for a rev eye near.*" Not enough. I gave him a blank stare and attracted a festival of eager eyes. *So this is Sorota's lawyer.*

"Uh, what was that?"

Sorota cast a quick glance at my empty left ear and rephrased the question.

"*Ee ah extra koo, ah elle? extra roo crude extra crude we have what else?*" *Shit what else other crude other*

"Uh, what else, um . . . "

Sorota exploded. "Shea's no good unless he's had a *ring*! Get him a drink!" That I heard. The flight engineer, Joe Randall, came back from the cockpit. "Yes, Mr. Sorota."

"Get Shea a drink!"

"We're sill in *howdy air pay*," *howdy Saudi air pay Saudi air pay air space* "and I can't open the—"

"Well, we just left it."

"Yes, sir—we just left it."

"Get him a drink."

While everyone's eyes were on Aldo, I put on the hearing aids. Randall turned toward me: "Mr. Shea, what would you—"

"Scotch!" said Sorota.

"Yes, sir. Gerry, how would you—"

"On the rocks," said Sorota.

tongue, which enable us to slide from one word to another when we are in the more workable, limited, painted vocabulary of the English language. We take virtually every word or nonword we hear and substitute and interchange consonants and vowels forever, on the way to making manageable sense. Our lyricals leap to us as if from out of nowhere, involuntary, transitional, and spontaneous, as in *doe the parchment eyes* for *don't compartmentalize*. In fact, our lifetimes with lyricals make it relatively easy for us to write—a contract, a story, a letter, a song, these words themselves—when the input or idea is already expressed, not in lyricals but in our first language, right there, on the spot, in our minds, before our eyes, to be transformed into the same language, but in a clearer prose or in poetry. We may not be as eloquent as a poet, as Joyce, but the path is smooth, and the rearrangement of real words to reflect our ideas more fluently, or accurately, or poetically, is a defining element of our lives. It is our second nature.

There were of course difficult times. Even with the hearing aids, discussions on the airplane were always hard because the high-frequency white noise of the engines erased all but the lowest vowels (*a*, *o*, *u*) and a few consonants (*m*, *b*), so that *weh eye ih a me ee* would be the few cues yielded by "What time is the meeting?" This was true even on the Mobil plane, though it was smaller and quieter than commercial aircraft and flew in a thinner, loftier atmosphere. The setting was always a professional hazard, and I learned to put on my hearing aids just inside the plane, once out of the immediate reach of the murderous high-frequency blasts of its idling, screeching engines. I no longer wore the glasses but the more conventional crescent-shaped aids that curve around the back of the ear, now a bit better at picking up the screech of high-frequency sounds than earlier models. On one crucial day I was distracted trying to find a seat close to Aldo and

"But what about *deh baa*!?" asked Manufacturing, ever alert. *deh baa deh daa baa deh shit*

"What about—"

"What about netback, for Christ's sake!"

"Uh, right. That's the point. Under the formula we use the combined price, so we keep the difference. They know this, and they've agreed."

"Right," said Aldo. "Shea put it in. Thought they might buy all this, given our efforts at *elly then inderlize*. The minister accepted it; the *roll cow sill* approved. Gives us an edge. Big edge." *inder lize helly elping them inder indust—helping them industrialize roll cow sill sill cow crown sill royal council approved*

"Right," said S&D, "it's worth about a hundred million bucks a year."

"See what I mean?" said Aldo, holding up a glass of water, as Randall returned and took my empty glass to the back of the cabin. "Any more questions?" He looked around the plane, to blessed silence.

Our second son, Alexander, was born in May 1985, while we were living in Jeddah, though Claire went to Paris to have him, as she had done with Sebastian. I was in London working day and night on a new joint venture with the Saudis, and Aldo kept sending flowers to the Clinique Marignan, where she was having the baby, to the point, I am told, where her bed was in a lush maze of flowers, arousing speculation: oh where is this *bébé*'s papa? When I finally got through, three days after Claire's sister had called to tell me that Alex was born, the nurse was astonished—*eh le tata le tata! pata tata c'est le c'est le papa! It's the father!* Claire had kept insisting that "*mon mari*" would call (I had tried at night, but the switchboard was shut down), and they turned to humoring her, convinced that *le papa* had flown the coop.

It was with Alex that I discovered that our ability to speak languages can be hindered not just by the failure of the cochlea (in the profoundly deaf) but, albeit without harmful consequences, by exposure to a surfeit of tongues. For more than twenty months, Alex said not a word, not "Mamma," "Papa," "Daddy," "Mummy," *gâteau*, "cookie," anything. The woman who took care of him was Eritrean, and she shifted constantly among her three tongues when talking to the children—Eritrean, Arabic, and (a vestige of her country's departed visitors) Italian. Claire spoke to Alex in French, I in English. It was no easy task for Alex's young and fertile language acquisition device to exploit Bébian's "timeless and limitless principle" of a first language because he was confronted with five.

We kept waiting for him to say something, but we heard not a word until the morning at breakfast when, almost two years old, he finally picked up his wooden spoon and plastic fork, banged them on the table and said "*Allaaooo BaBaa!*" We lived near the mosque of liquid *l*'s, and this was his baby's lyrical for those sung out five times a day. *Allahu Akbar*—God is great! We stared at Alex in amazement, as he laughed, and we did too: a happy beginning, a baby's prayer—which would lead him to *Maman*, Daddy; counting in Arabic: *wahid, itneen, talaata*; *salaam aleekum*; *habibi*; *fratelli d'Italia, l'Italia sedesta*; trot, trot to Boston; London's burning; *Frère Jacques*; and an assortment of other phrases and songs until his two principal tongues finally occupied the field.

Despite Aldo's immeasurable help when needed, there were times when he was difficult, as when he threatened not to fire me but, half seriously, to shoot me, when I raised a problem with someone else and not with him. And the day he warned me to "control your wife," when Claire started telling Mobil people we would be returning to New York after two years, though my understanding with Aldo was four. Without him, however, I could very well have spent the rest of my life specializing in gas station curb rights on the third floor of Mobil's building on Forty-Second Street.

At the end of my third year in Arabia, Aldo was called back to New York. I missed him. Most of the critical issues for us in Arabia had been resolved, many even before I arrived, and I began to think about what I should do next. Go back to New York? I had been back on occasion, and on my last visit, just before Aldo's departure, I went to a lunch meeting of about twenty-five lawyers, eight of them new, in one of the private dining rooms on the fortieth floor. The general counsel, Ed Fowler, was there, and I gave a short talk on our operations in the Middle East. A few others spoke, and there were several questions from others, but even with hearing aids I understood very little. They were relatively far away, speaking from their seats in the large room, and the distant missing words were beyond recapture by lyricals. There were no accents or beards, virtually everyone was American, and they spoke the same first language I did; yet I didn't understand them. As I looked at their faces, I felt, perhaps for the first time, that my world was not theirs, that I was a member of Bell's different "species"—the deaf—and, if these hearing people who heard each other speak ever found out, they would drive me away.

How would I be able to function in New York at thirty-member board meetings? At lunch meetings? In side conversations? At Aramco meetings with the other majors—twenty or thirty people in the room? Being with Aldo, to the extent that I could be, wouldn't be enough. I went to see my New York audiologist, which I tried to do whenever I was in town. She imprudently suggested I choose another field—like *dacking wits tacking draft wits wills drafting wills* or something, just as Oscar and others at Debevoise had once considered that I might want to *bend along the tile riding* (spend a lot of time writing).

I said, almost shouted, "That's not what I do." She picked up my audiogram and her reference charts and showed me that though I was forty-three and had hearing aids, I still had the hearing, with or without them, of a ninety-year-old man—an exceptionally deaf one. I could imagine the quiet give-and-take with Aldo and a few other people in New York, but in major battles, the larger context of things, I would be next to useless to him. As the head of the Arabian affiliate he needed a draftsman, private counsel, and someone who could get along—even be well-liked—in another culture; as chairman of Mobil he would need a lawyer wholly ahead of the game—whatever the context.

I flew from New York to London to join Aldo at the closing of the outside financing for our joint refinery, a $450 million loan from a syndicate of international banks. This was a fairly large amount, but only 10 percent of the cost of the project. The negotiations with the banks had been done almost exclusively by exchanges of documentation and a few amplified telephone calls, and they were easy for me because of the Debevoise days, when I thought the key to understanding might lie in the definitions and covenants in every trust indenture I could get my hands on. The loan exercise in general (save for the crush of documents the last few days) boiled down to the question of sovereign risk: Will the Saudi government be around for a while? If so, lend the money.

We held a joint venture board meeting right after the closing, with about twenty people there, and the company's secretary taking the minutes. The matters were straightforward—acknowledgment of the loan, first disbursements, praises all around, crude supply, a new catalytic cracker. The written agenda was clear enough, but I was tired, couldn't focus on lips, and for most of the time was somewhere else. "*On graches*," Sorota said, amid all the noise after the banks wired the $450 million to our joint venture. I leaned forward. *graches graches on grach con grach congratulations*

CLAIRE'S FATHER HAD JUST DIED. I FLEW OVER TO PARIS for the funeral, worrying all the way. I was sure I would always have Aldo's confidence, but if I admitted, as I would have to, that most meetings in New York would be off limits, it might be down to the third floor for good. The taxi from the airport to Mortefontaine brought me back to my Paris days, when I'd drive out to the Gramonts, north on the autoroute, off at the first exit after the airport, the open country roads, then Mortefontaine, the château de Vallière, *du côté de Guermantes*, to la Ramée, the house built by Claire's father forty years before, into the salon with the wooden paneling of Claire's great-grandmother. Claire had come two weeks before, leaving the children in Main Harbor. The house was full of people.

The service at the family chapel was simple, though several hundred people were there, inside and out. The priest and a number of others spoke, but the words were swallowed as usual by the distances and echoes that are the hallmarks of tabernacles. As I finished my own words for her father, I thought again of my future as a centenarian: What am I going to do? Claire and her sisters easily managed the lunch, and I spoke to a number of friends, sticking to lipreadable English after the *bonjours* and *tu vas biens*. As I looked around, I thought that Paris, Mortefontaine, Claire at home, the children here, would be a wonderful life compared to New York, let alone Houston (if as was rumored Mobil was to move there), where the penalty for misunderstanding a Texas Ranger might be death itself.

CHAPTER 21

INTERNATIONAL
COUNSEL

A FTER THE SERVICE, I WALKED OUTSIDE TO LOOK AT
the lakes below, trying to listen for the swans and herons—
nothing, even with *oiseaux lyres*, but I could see them. I thought of
my years in Paris, those blissful years that ultimately brought me
Claire. Oscar Ruebhausen had asked me to come back a few years
before, but I suspected the firm was interested more in Mobil's
joint ventures than in me. But why not, after all, if it was possible,
finish here, back in Paris, back, though in a smaller environment,
with the great law firm, trying it alone, without Aldo but with my
oiseaux lyres now? And perhaps with others who would help in his
stead, doing European transactions in the English language, going
gently down the stream with a few other American lawyers who
liked to be in Paris, with talented and congenial French colleagues?

But the critical element here was Claire. Not simply for those
Proustian qualities she inherited from her grandmother, but for

her understanding—of my language, of the lyricals that she knew were coming often before I did, of the words that I would say before I spoke them. In the shifting, uncharted realm of language in the air, hers is the voice I could discern and understand, the ears that so often listened for and understood me, the embodiment of a permanence that has made my life, both personally and professionally, possible.

Claire already had an apartment in Paris. We would have the children, Mortefontaine, everything. We could see my mother at Main Harbor in the summertime and in Boston on stopovers whenever I had to go to New York. I spoke to a few lawyers in the firm about it, making it clear that I needed my hearing aids to function. Some were hopeful that we might boost the client roster in Paris with Claire's connections. That didn't trouble me, for getting clients was something I was sure I would be good at—keeping them, I hoped, might be left more to others.

I had no intention of reliving those long New York hours or their mysteries, though I didn't really know whether my *oiseaux lyres* would be able to help me escape them. They would certainly not have been enough in a Mobil board room or at an Aramco meeting with a host of oilmen and lawyers. But at least I had them, and there would be small meetings, amplified telephones, and, above all, Paris. I returned to Jeddah in late summer for two months, and from there I called Aldo to tell him I had decided to return to the firm. He said he was sorry *to choose to lose* me, and said good-bye.

PARIS HAD CHANGED DURING THE TWELVE YEARS I HAD been away: not the city itself, nor the charms of its countryside, nor the grace of its people, but the practice of law had changed

between 1975 and 1987. Debevoise & Plimpton had moved its offices to the avenue George V, from a quiet house on the place du
Palais Bourbon, a residential quarter except for the palace itself,
to a majestic avenue, with hotels, law firms, investment banks,
embassies, government offices, the international chamber of commerce, and a place in which we can all pray for each other, the
American Cathedral.

The firm's practice, like that of its New York competitors in
Paris, had shifted from finding apartments for dowagers and entertaining visiting firemen exclusively to the more serious business of large transactions, cross-border mergers, and acquisitions
involving scores of lawyers, executives, accountants, and bankers
and many billions of dollars. Even the lawyers in the French firms
were now drinking bottled water and eating sandwiches at their
desks. We represented a number of buyout firms, international
banks, and large corporations. Professionally, Paris was not to be
what I had expected.

I brought in a client myself, true to the firm's hopes, through
friends who were the controlling shareholders in a large French
manufacturing company in Allevard, a French industrial city
near Grenoble. They wanted to sell most of their shares in the
company and needed English-speaking advice in order to deal
with the English and American banks and buyout firms that were
the major powers in the market. Our first meeting was at the
Paris office of the principal lender, a British bank. We assembled
in the evening, and my heart dropped as we walked into the
large, ill-lit conference room in the basement of their building
on the place Vendôme. There were about forty people sitting
around a long elliptical table. I took a seat in the middle beside
our client, with Jim Kiernan, who ran our Paris office, beside me.
We were to negotiate and sign a letter of intent, a fifteen-page
document that would include all the major terms of the transac-

tion. The negotiations were in English, as is usual, but I had little light to read lips and too much air between myself and most of the others to allow my *oiseaux lyres* to wage any respectable battle against the inverse square rule.

"*Gooding*," said the lead English banker *gooding good ing good evening* and Jim responded, introducing the two of us.

"We *doe war a pretty sussdies, ah the junior day can call at a pall* without our consent." *doe don't war a pretty pretty don't want the printing subsidiaries*

"You get the *hole coy* or nothing at all," Jim answered, beside me. *coy coy company whole company junior day day debt can can't can't call a default*—

"If so, then only two-thirds of the *seeder tet seener senior debt* can call a default, not half," said the junior debt. "We *deed* the protection of *a high reshhole*." *deed need resh—need a high threshold*

"So *have can't gall*," said the company. "Good." *half the half can't call* "The junior debt need a higher threshold; that's OK *a fuss*." *a fuss us OK with us*

The negotiations went on in this fashion for about forty-five minutes, at which point Jim, who had been marking up a form of a letter of intent as the talks progressed, slid it over to me and said, "I gotta go."

"Jim, you can't go."

"I can't? Why not?"

"I can't really follow—adequately follow—" His eyes saw the desperation in mine. The pause brought all eyes on us, the same intense looks we got on Aldo's plane.

"OK," said Jim, "Right." And he stayed.

I revised Jim's draft pages as he passed them on, grafting them onto a clean copy of the Debevoise form, and passed it to the secretaries. To understand a document, particularly a scribbled mark-up, you need to know how the discussions went, but with the benefit of my hearing aids I found his compressed notes clear, like written lyricals but easily understood. "No B opt. on prntg evn if sub doesn't meet tsts, unl. dvn causes Allev. to fail all 3," for example, meant that the buyer had to buy the printing division even if it failed to meet the three accounting tests, as applied to the division separately, that were applied on audit to the business as a whole, unless the entire business failed all three tests but would have met them without the printing division. More often than not Jim's notes clarified the discussion by providing the keys to my lingering oral lyricals: *auction opt. option*; *pretty prntg printing*; *tosses all of it losses all of it causes Allevard*; *I'll see aisle C all see all three.*

In similar fashion, unexpected French subtitles to American movies can often provide the keys to American lyricals, for example *who gives Asa a ten* becomes *you kin say that agin* when you read the unprairie-like subtitle, "*C'est incontestable!*" on the screen of a Paris movie theatre. Merger negotiations are more complex than the gunfight at the OK Corral, however, and Jim's shorthand was available as backup for the first and last time.

The world of mergers and acquisitions and leveraged buyouts is a curious one. The negotiations are not much more than a clash of bankers' and investors' wills in common and repetitive games on a relatively circumscribed playing field. Had I witnessed these new games in my years before my *oiseaux lyres*, I would have thought the players all endowed with an uncanny ability to grasp and propose solutions to complex problems with lightning speed. But as I looked at them now back at Debevoise, with years of experience with hearing aids and ample awareness of my deafness and of the normal human weaknesses of the hearing, I saw them as the greedy enemy, the avaricious hearing exploiting, consciously or not, my slowness in our own tongue.

But are we all—the hearing, the deaf, and the partially deaf—an integral part of the commerce of necessity? With the Allevard transaction, I was beginning to hear, very clearly, the distant knell of my professional requiem. The ordeals were composed not so much of *dies irae, dies illa*, "days of wrath," from the liturgy I remember from my five-dollar, altar-boy Masses for the dead, as days of irremediable incompleteness. I now understand what Ferdinand Berthier, the great deaf teacher of the deaf, meant when he called Michel Maurice—the hearing, nonsigning lawyer at Ferdinand Berthier's first banquet for the deaf in Paris in 1834—an "incomplete man," for Maurice's predicament was the mirror of my own.

The next couple of transactions were done, mercifully, by telephone and involved the international segments of major transactions that were negotiated essentially by documentary exchanges between Paris and New York, Europe, Asia, and Australia. But it was exhausting: using lyricals and an array of inefficient telecommunications equipment, making lists of questions to ask allies after the meetings, in order to defend our clients at several hundred dollars an hour and sometimes billions at stake. About once a month I would escape to the quiet, empty pews of the American Cathedral next door to our office, to go over my notes in silence, with my *oiseaux lyres* drowning out the locusts, and, I suppose, though not consciously, to seek the intercession of my long lost saints.

I traveled from Main Harbor to Washington, DC (Mobil had relocated from New York to Fairfax, Virginia), on a lovely, warm summer day, in desperation, to ask Aldo Sorota whether he would consider taking me back to work closely with him, on his left, as his pen if not his ears, or at least one of his pens, though it would have meant uprooting Claire and the children once more

and abandoning Paris. Mobil, however, short of crude oil and
about to merge with Exxon, was shedding staff, not engaging
them. In any event Aldo felt—though he didn't say it, I could see
it in his eyes—that I had abandoned him. "Let me know," he
said, "if ya *caught a tee.*"

> *caught a tee*
> *let me know*
> *gotta tee*
> *let me know*
> *if ya gotta eat*

If I had no alternative, though perhaps not to the point of star-
vation, Aldo would have helped, as I think he would even today.
But I had an alternative, a highly desirable one, and of course
he knew it, and I did not want to tell him *you gotta problem*
what was wrong.

By this time, now 1991, I had doctors, audiologists, and other
hearing specialists in many places—New York, Boston, Jeddah,
Washington, Paris, and elsewhere. I was beginning to feel that
my place in the world of corporate law was precarious. I decided
to pay an unscheduled visit to my doctor in Paris, a highly talented otolaryngologist and surgeon named Gérald Ferrer. I had,
for years, been seeing Gérald and his predecessor Pierre Elbaz,
stopping during visits to Paris and Mortefontaine and on the way
to Arabia, and then periodically after I returned to the firm.

"*Alors, qu'est-ce qui ne va pas?*" he asked me in his booming voice
the sunny morning I came to see him, blinds drawn like Chang's,
lips in lamplight. He began every session that way, meaning not so
much "what's wrong" as "what needs fixing?," as if he were sure to
find a way.

"*Je—ça ne va pas du tout.*" Things are not going well at all.

"*Pourquoi pas?*"

"I'm missing too much. I'm not sure our clients formally know, but I do, and my colleagues do—and the individuals who work beside me do."

"Well, let's see." He gave me the usual test, and as I sat in the booth waiting, I saw flashes of Miss Oracle and Dr. Chang. The test tones Ferrer sounded seemed further apart than I remembered. He took some wax out of my ears—"Wax can affect your *earring days*, Gérald, what you call your *oiseaux lyres*."

"Is *that* it!?"

"No. Your *earring is a lid were lid were a little worse* but not much—not very much."

"Not very much. Perhaps not. But I—it's difficult. Microphones, my *oiseaux lyres*, distance, numbers of people, it's hard to keep up—and I'm supposed to be leading—"

"So?"

"So clients rely on me to—what do I do when I don't understand? I know it's a little late to ask that question, but what do I do if my lyricals—what you call transitional language—don't work, or if there's not enough time—?"

"You *pre-dead*. And then you *get a dater*."

> pre-dead
>> preTEND
>>> dater later
>>>> then get it later—resurrection!

"Pretend with a lot of money at stake and our fees mounting up?"

"So what. They're lucky to have you. *To try it to*."

"To try it to—that's not what you said, Doctor."

"I had said your firm is lucky to have you. And then—" *too try it client*

"The client, too."

"Exactly. See? Excellent. Keep up the good work, Gérald. Say hello to *tare*, your handsome children."

"Claire and the children."

"Right. Good. *Tout va bien*. Everything's OK. Promise me you'll keep up the good work."

"I can't promise that."

"*Si*. Promise me."

And I did.

CHAPTER 22

PRAGUE, BUDAPEST, AND THE LIMITS OF TECHNOLOGY

THE SOVIET UNION HAD JUST FALLEN APART, AND BY 1991 a number of people at Debevoise & Plimpton were eager to expand our practice into Eastern Europe. Its landscape was already studded with American lawyers and bankers, bedecked in suspenders and double-vented suits, symbols of Western financial enterprise, scanning the countryside for deals in the former satellite states. Those nations welcomed Western advisors, particularly Americans, since their governments were eager to develop relationships with the United States that might help prevent their being ruled, yet again, by the Russians. It was a real advantage for us. The Czech Republic's sending troops into Iraq (just as Poland, Romania, Bulgaria, Georgia, and other Eastern Europeans did), whether the United Nations authorized the invasion or not, was more than anything else testimony to their fear of their old Soviet nemesis.

Some of my longtime friends at the firm in New York encouraged me toward this work in Eastern Europe. I'd returned to Debevoise Plimpton as international counsel, a title I invented and everyone at the firm seemed to like (there are several international counsel at Debevoise today). I then became international counsel/partner, a hybrid title I described to my secretary one day as meaning "deaf partner," though I now had the opportunity to give the position some substance by taking charge of our Eastern European practice. *They must be nuts.*

Other, perhaps wiser, but unkinder heads, told me flatly I was not their choice. I knew Jim Kiernan was worried because of the Allevard deal *I can't really follow—adequately follow* and because he could see how I functioned every day. Fiona Fields, a partner in the New York office, was particularly blunt. When I paid her a visit in Manhattan, I talked about the morning and the weather as I put on my *oiseaux lyres* and connected them to the telex microphones I put on her desk to hear her. When I was ready, Fiona seemed to awaken suddenly from what appeared to be a quiet morning and leapt into an alertness that reminded me of Saki's terrier (in *The Quince Tree*) and of our dog in the country, Figeac, when they swap their bored indifference for the excited anticipation of an imminent rat hunt. Fiona said that, now in my late forties, I had reached an age at which many people *to knit her adiring. knit her sit her consider atiring retiring* At thirty-nine or so, Fiona had become a kind of queen of leveraged buyouts (LBOs).

LBOs are transactions in which many financial companies (today, "private equity" firms) like Kohlberg Kravis Roberts and Blackstone set up a shell company to borrow billions of dollars and use the money to buy a large industrial company (called the "target"). They merge the target into the shell, thus sticking the target with their own loan, and then mortgage the industrial company's assets to cover it. Federal and state governments in effect subsidize these deals by allowing enormous tax deductions for the interest on the acquisition loans, giving the merged company tax-free income that, if all goes well, it can use in addition to sales of assets to pay off all the debt. The private equity firms pay themselves handsome dividends from excess loan proceeds and "streamline" these industrial companies by firing and outsourcing for cheaper labor and materials, not infrequently in foreign countries with unrestrictive labor laws. Then they sell what's left, and do it again.

Fiona's suggestion that I retire, coming from someone at home in that brutal world, was unpersuasive, but Ferrer's encouragement notwithstanding, I was virtually sure I couldn't do Eastern Europe. Getting off a plane left my ears numb, with locusts ringing loudly for hours, and deals there were bound to move very quickly. The accents, the voices of translators, the reverberating halls of high-ceilinged Stalinist ministries, the loud ventilation systems: it would all be hell, and I would have to rely heavily on lyricals and lipreading. But New York carried the day, and I couldn't turn it down without giving the reason. Only those who worked closely with me, most of whom were supportive, understood the depth of the problem.

Claire and I flew to Prague and Budapest together a couple of times in the fall of 1991 to measure the climate, and I to meet with lawyers and potential clients. Andy Sommer, an American, ran the Budapest office, and we had gotten along very well since one of our deals done over the telephone when he had been in our London office. The meetings with Andy were quiet affairs in the corners of well-carpeted restaurants in Budapest and Prague and discussions across his desk, where his lips, though bearded, guided his deep, clear voice.

It was not to last, however. Wearing a couple of serviceable English suits and presentable French shoes, I came to feel like the Eastern European cities themselves, with their freshly painted seventeenth-, eighteenth- and nineteenth-century concert halls, palaces, and other structures—agreeable enough to behold on the outside, but dilapidated within. Moreover, I didn't have their future—as buildings whose crumbling walls, polluting fuels, and antiquated heating and plumbing systems would ultimately be fixed. I knew that the damage to my most critical infrastructure, the cochlea, would never be.

My main efforts for the next three years, from 1992 through 1995, were in Prague. After the success of the Velvet Revolution and the fall of the Iron Curtain and with Vaclav Havel as prime minister and later president, Prague's possibilities, despite its ramshackle condition, seemed limitless. It was a particularly exciting time for Americans—not unlike our symbiotic relationship with Arabia. Though the Czechs had no oil, they had many resources—automobile and aircraft manufacturers, other industrial companies, airports, large commercial banks, and much else—and we had the legal and financial skills and ultimately, of course, if it came to that, the guns to protect them from the Russians.

The Czech government and its Ministry of Industry selected Debevoise & Plimpton to represent it in a large transaction involving the privatization of Česká Tool Company, a large manufacturer of industrial machinery with holdings in the rail and air freight sectors of the Czech economy. I had prepared our written bid, and others handled the firm's competitive interviews while I sat in the background. Once we had the deal, however, I had to run it. I decided to find a better assistive listening device, and I called Stanley Resor of our firm, who had been secretary of the army, to ask for his help.

"So I thought perhaps Army Intelligence or the CIA might have some sort of listening device and you could—"

"I *wowed* it." *wowed it wowed what? the CIA? doubt it* "If they had anything that good they wouldn't give it to you."

"So it's not even worth—"

"Don't think so."

I had better luck with my cousin Maureen Shea, an old Washington hand who had been married to the (now late) secretary of defense, Les Aspin, and worked for the Democratic National Committee. "I'll call *Tim*."

"Tim?"

"*Jim*, Gerry, Jim Woolsey—he's the head of the CIA."

Woolsey referred us to the National Institutes of Health. NIH gave me the name of an electronics company in New Jersey that made an "omnidirectional" microphone, which I bought and ever since have called my Woolseyphone. It has a handsome hexagonal wooden cover and looks like a large, upscale pencil box. It was less conspicuous than the string of telex microphones I had been using, and the quality of the sound was better, though the principle was the same. The microphone converted the mechanical sound of voices in the air at a conference table to electrons and sent them as FM radio waves to a receiver clipped to my belt, attached to a magnetic loop around my neck. A special switch on my *oiseaux lyres* picked up the signals from the loop, treating them as they do all sounds by augmenting the highs a bit more than the lows and sending the sound waves through the ear canal to the eardrum and then on to the oval window of the cochlea.

One of the problems of the hearing-aid trade is its vocabulary. "Omnidirectional" implies a capacity to capture sound from all directions, but here again the devil is in the inverse square rule. My Woolseyphone was good at receiving and transmitting the voice of a speaker two or three feet away from it, but all other speakers still require extensive lipreading and lyricals, and their words are obscured by any conversation around them.

In the tool company deal, a Belgian manufacturer and a group of British, Dutch, and Austrian investors, financed by English,

French, and American banks, were to buy a significant share of the Czech company, which we all called Toolco. The banks included some of my old friends, including Citibank, BNP, Rothschilds, and Bankers Trust. The Czech government would keep a small piece of the company. Private Czech investors would hold a minority interest through their voucher program, originally designed to place the ownership of industry in the hands of Czech citizens.

Boarding my first Tupolev 154, the Russian-made aircraft in which the Polish president and a number of officials were killed in 2010, was an unsettling experience. We all took our assigned seats but were then shifted around the plane to make sure it was *allen talen talent balanced* on takeoff. Once aloft we could regain our original seats but were again hurriedly reassigned for the landing. We landed and the race was on.

The Bankers Trust representative launched the meeting in English: "The *secree be of lad, plaid and—" secree siarity lad?* Before the end of the banker's sentence, a translator with a high-pitched voice gave the banker's words in Czech. Translators present a particular difficulty for the partially deaf. People who hear normally are usually able to *anticipate* the end of a sentence—to know its conclusion before the words are actually spoken because of the fullness of meaning provided by the earlier words. But the partially deaf generally cannot, because of the poverty of the earlier input. Thus, when translators break in at this point of "cognitive anticipation," as they usually do, they cut off subsequent words—or lyricals—that can be critical to our understanding. This often happens in normal conversation as well, when another speaker responds before the first is finished. But with translators there is a special urge to break in early, in order to diminish the retarding effect of translation on the pace of the discussion.

"I'm sorry, the what?" I asked.

"The security, *lad, plaid and ee diptych.*"
> *lad, plaid*
> *land, plaid*
> *land, plant*

"Uh—to have the land, plant, and—the what?

"Equipment—plant and equipment!" said BNP, loud and impatient.

After several weeks of negotiations, I found myself reverting to my law school practice of taking copious notes, translating them deep into the night. Following my calls to Claire and the children in the evenings over the crackles of the Czech telephone system enhanced by my Nuvox—my portable telephone amplifier—I took long walks in Prague to clear my head for the day to come.

On one occasion, at the Ministry of Industry, Bankers Trust insisted that "*the vows her own the key for decent.*" *Accents! DE cent deCENT cent percent the KEY TIIIR-ty 30 percent 34—*

"Got that, Gerry?" asked Citibank.

"Uh, the vouchers take—34 percent. That means they have a blocking vote."

"Bravo."

"Is it wise?"

"They're not a *pox.* Just a *pitch of Dorsets.*" *pitch what a bitch a— they're not a box a bock a block*

"They're not a block?"

"Exactly," said BNP. "Just a bunch of poor citizens." *got it dorsets poor citizens*

"Well," I said, "if 34 percent is held by a group acting in concert, say in an Investment Privatization Fund, they'll have a blocking vote—and leverage over all of us. It's *gotta* be less." The voucher percentage was reduced, and I took a deep breath. *I can do it.*

Another day, back at Toolco's offices, our client, Bronislav Sikora, leading the Czech side, asked for my advice on the *kwara'ti*. The Austrian investor, Austinvest, was supposed to place and keep $10 million in a Czech bank account as evidence of their financial substance.

"*Rye gear*," said Austinvest. *right here* He read it aloud in English quickly, and without the natural rhythm of unread speech, I lost him after a few words.

"*Cowed wood*," said Sikora, in English, to the evident relief of Citibank, Rothschilds, and Bankers Trust.

"Sorry?"

"Sounds GOOD, what do you say?"

"May I see it?" Austinvest, with some reluctance, handed me the letter. It was from an executive vice president of Wienbank A.G. and stated that the bank had deposited $10 million in its account with Komerční Banka in Prague at the request of Austinvest. "Well," I said, "the $10 million is there, certainly."

"*Gray*," said the Austrians, "so we *can tissue toward* the consortium." *can tissue tinnue continue toward*

"Gerry?" asked Sikora in translation. "Is that right?"

great, so we can continue to run the consortium "The problem, though," I added, "is that the money is not Austinvest's—it still belongs to Wienbank." There was a long silence. *I can do it!—well, at least I can fucking read.* The Belgians took over the lead from the Austrians, but they were to prove to be redoubtable adversaries.

One free Friday morning I went to a conference on privatization at the Forum Hotel on the edge of town. Under the Czech program, "vouchers" (of the kind discussed at our meeting) were distributed to the public to enable them to bid on the companies being privatized. But foreign investors were buying them up through Czech proxies (non-Czechs were not allowed to hold them) in order to gain effective control of the state companies.

Yet another opportunity for a killing by our distinguished Western bankers. Talks on the program were being given by a panel of those bankers, and I sat in the second row. My *oiseaux lyres* gave me very little, however.

I headed for the airport after the meeting. In the terminal I spotted two of the British lecturer-bankers, headed to London. I joined them with a cup of coffee, put on my *oiseaux lyres*, introduced myself, and started to listen, ready to ask what they thought about Czech proxies for foreign investors. Airports, like cathedrals, are difficult because they are echo chambers. "As the *ballast is only 600 rounds . . .* " *rounds rounds crowns ballast ballast*

"Where?" I asked.

"At the palace," said Barclays Bank, looking annoyed.

Kind Warts & Son (Kleinwort Benson) said, "*Well, of the intercom's rental is nicer, say a thousand for any earl on the voucher with a hobby*, but the quality is better." *voucher with a higher quality? a thousand crowns*

"I'm sorry," I said. "Vouchers are priced by the government— at the palace [the seat of the Czech government on the other side of the Vltava River]. I thought they were priced at a hundred crowns each. But you say they have a higher value elsewhere?"

"What!?" said Barclays. "We're not talking about vouchers, man! We're talking about women! The price of women!" *intercom's rental Intercontinental* "At the hotels! There's a big difference, and the *park it is sufficient.*" *park it market market's inefficient* "They're cheaper at the Palace than at the Intercontinental, but the Palace is a much better hotel! Did you *go!?*" *go no know did you know*

"Uh, no. I've seen them, of course." In fact, the bars at the Intercontinental and the Palace were full of beautiful young women from Eastern Europe, principally Russia and Bulgaria, looking for men who would pay them in hard currency—or abundantly in Czech koruna. I avoided them, not so much out of sexual scruple as because they were known to be lured from home with the promise of work and coerced into prostitution by mobsters. The message of the West should hardly be that its lawyers have come to Eastern Europe with cash in order to bed with the victims of organized crime. "Come on, man, get with it," said one. "Sixty pence on the pound at the Palace!" said the other, as I headed for the plane.

I spent every Saturday in Paris going over the terms of the Toolco acquisition or its financing and preparing memoranda I developed to try to shape the vocabulary for the coming week's negotiations. I had the memos typed and duplicated in the office on Sundays, with no time for prayers for myself at the cathedral, and got home for dinner by eight o'clock. On Mondays I would get up at five and arrive at the airport by six thirty. The Czech fleet was slowly converted over time to 737s, and the Tupolev balancing acts, ultimately viewed by the Czechs (but unfortunately not the Poles) as an exotic exercise of the past, were over.

At a late stage in the transaction, on one of these Monday morning flights, I was seated beside an attractive young Frenchwoman. When the plane reached cruising altitude and the seatbelt light went off, she stood up and, looking back at me with a slight smirk, went to another seat, which, as it turned out, had been occupied by Bill Cramley, an Englishman and one of the junior people in the British company in the Toolco consortium. I hadn't seen Bill at the airport, and at first I was baffled as to why he'd moved to the place beside me or how he'd arranged the switch. And why switch? I said hello and decided to take a nap, which seemed to make him unhappy. When I awoke an hour later, Cramley was babbling something, and I put on my *oiseaux lyres*.

Cramley said, "Oh, *tone ih edding err espedd it*. Gerry?"

"Sorry?"

"I said, the loan *ih eddy eur espedd it*." He was covering his mouth intermittently as he spoke and often turning away. I sensed he was up to something and should have gone back to sleep. I took out a newer set of hearing aids that I had not really tested yet and listened intently. "*Tay dine, tay all the dime*—" he turned away as he finished his sentence.

"It doesn't take long, Bill," I said as I switched them on and heard an even louder whoosh of the 737's Rolls Royce engines under the wings beside us. "You were talking about the loan."

"Yeah." He repeated the incomprehensible phrase and turned away again as he began, partially covering his lips when he turned back, and spoke more softly. I turned down the volume, and the engines became softer, but his voice was gone. I finally told him we would discuss the issues at the meeting and gave him a list. I took my hearing aids out and pretended to go back to sleep.

I had been too slow to see the trouble coming. Cramley was English, so I could not plead a Czech accent or the difficulties in translation, and in spite of the notoriously hostile environment of airplanes for the partially deaf, they are a usual place of engagement in business. The fact that he had looked away from time to time, or covered his mouth or coughed occasionally, was also quite natural and should not be a problem for a highly paid lawyer with a prominent law firm. And this would be the urgent message, I finally feared: his Western superiors would urge the Czechs not to pay attention to their deaf counsel (especially since that deaf counsel was well aware of the pitfalls of the transaction before them).

When we landed in Prague, I went to our office, meeting up with our local Czech lawyers there at nine to plan for the day. The meeting with Toolco was scheduled for later that morning; the consortium and the banks were to join us at noon. Walking into Toolco's offices at eleven, I put in my older pair of *oiseaux lyres* and said hello to Bronislav Sikora and his colleagues. Two people from the ministry were present. Cramley and the heads of the Belgian and English investors in the consortium were sitting there, Cramley with an unsettling smirk on his face. They had clearly been meeting *your deaf counsel didn't understand a word I said* with the Czech group. I handed out my list and analysis of the issues and took everyone through it.

"And as to the generator division contributed by the Power Authority to Toolco a few years ago," I said, "I understand it's now going to continue in Toolco, so there's an adjustment—an increase—in the price, which will go to the Authority upon sale. It's part of Toolco in this deal."

Sikora responded in Czech, and the translator began, as usual, before he finished, "*Gerer business has been off for the dore ermet,* Gerry." *business has been off for the government*

"Right, Bronislav, the government no longer wants it, so Toolco keeps it and—"

"*Ne ne ne,* no no no, Gerry! *Gerer business has been off*" *spin-off to the government*

"A spin-off?"

"That's what I said."

"OK, Bronislav, a spin-off."

I went on to discuss a spin-off of the division back to the Power Authority before the sale, but Sikora was anything but happy. The larger meeting began at twelve, and there were thirty of us in the room. I took out my list of issues, handed it out, and took a deep breath as everyone looked it over. But I had the sense that people were only vaguely interested. I said, "Let's start with the matter of the government's limited guarantee."

"No," said the Belgian investor, as the Czech translator was finishing what I had said, "*ah ree our pro tole.*" The air conditioners were blowing, smothering his voice. *ah ree ree read read*

"Um, you'd like to—"

"READ OUR PROPOSAL!"

"Right. But let's stick to my list," I said, "because—"

Sikora interrupted me. "No, Gerry. *Get ear wa ee had today.*"
today to day to say let's hear what he has to say

The Belgian went on to read it as everyone listened carefully,
but with his accent, the air conditioners, the translators, and the
lack of dialogue, I was able to grasp only a few rudiments of the
proposal. He appeared to be announcing a deal. He glanced at
Cramley and his British and Dutch colleagues a few times, then at
me, both times with unsettling expressions of triumph and, for
the now vulnerable lawyer who had too often gotten in their way,
a degree of contempt. Some discussion followed, notably among
Sikora, BNP, and the British investor, but I had no lyrical base.

In fact, everything had been decided that morning, or the
night before, or the day before, I didn't know. The Ministry of
Industry had been looking for a way out of the privatization of
Toolco and had decided to use a German company as an advisor
and to finance its modernization and keep the company for itself.
The foreign investors and the banks had been asking for too
much, and the Czechs had agreed to pay them off—handsomely.
At the end of the morning session, when most had left the large
conference room, I pulled out the loop's wire from my receiver
and turned to Sikora, who had come to sit beside me. I told him I
was thoroughly puzzled—

"It's OK, Gerry. OK. Understand," he said, "you do the best
you can, *utter her romances.*"

> *utter under*
> *romances*
> *romances*
> *moving shadows*
> *music in the night*
> *no—circumstances*
> *under the circumstances*

"Under—what circumstances?"

He looked, though with a degree of empathy in his eyes, at the loop's loose wire sticking out of my shirt, the receiver on my belt, the omnidirectional microphone on the desk, and my hearing aids. He paused as my eyes brought his into focus. "You have been a great help to us. Thank you."

Thank you and goodbye? Not quite, for I went on to help them wrap up the deal on more favorable terms. Nevertheless: *pretend to hear,* Gérald Ferrer had said; and while I wasn't *pre-dead* (the lyrical I had heard Ferrer utter), still—this masquerade of understanding wasn't working. But *no* one's perfect. Remember *vouchers, no blocking vote; the money belongs to Weinbank, not Austinvest; a hundred million bucks a year. Shea did it!* Solve the riddle. *Fuck* Cramley. *Don't cry in your soup. You gotta problem.* Find a solution. Do it!

I called Claire and the children when I got back to the Intercontinental that night, after smiling at the now more evident beauties for whom the bankers were trying to fix a fair price. After the call I had dinner in the room, enjoying the relief of not having to listen to anyone. At ten o'clock I took a walk as usual over to the Karluv Most, the Charles Bridge, which crosses the Vltava River in the middle of the city. The bridge was named in honor of Karel IV, Bohemia's greatest king. Thirty-one stone statues stand guard over those who cross it to go in and out of the old city.

Many of the great minds of the church are there, including Bernard, Thomas Aquinas, and Augustine. I wondered which of its saints carved in stone or cast in iron and spanning both sides of the five-hundred-meter bridge might hold in their breasts the conference table's secrets of the days and weeks past and those yet to come. *Where in this city may I find my Infant of Prague?* Not Augustine, who thought the deaf could never learn to read. Perhaps Hildegarde of Bingen, the twelfth-century German abbess who kept in her prayerbook the image of Christ, the Word made flesh, curing a deaf man. *Come to the meeting tomorrow, Hildegarde, armed with His wisdom, and enlighten me*, I prayed aloud, drawing some curious glances from a cheerful group of students from Charles University strolling across the bridge, singing and drinking *pivos* and looking forward to their future.

My life, I knew, looking over the railing, was simpler than that of the profoundly deaf. I could speak and listen to speech in air, the language of the hearing; I could live in their world, and understand and advise them, however imperfectly, for a sizeable fee. And yet the signing deaf, though they have to continue to fight hard to keep it, have their language of light. I have no such language. I am often, as I would be that night at *Lear*, hearing the voices neither of light nor of air. Neither I, nor my locusts, nor my lyricals, nor my *oiseaux lyres* are fully at home in the world of those who hear speech in air. Before too long, would I be expelled, become an outcast, from their world? Not if I could help it! "Sever the links," Bébian had warned, "that bind man to man and his life becomes an unbearable burden." I was determined to keep my own links intact, but I was feeling *their* burden as I looked from Hildegarde to the Vltava and back, searching in its reflection beneath her eyes for the tears that, as Bébian comfortingly tells us, are able to heal our hearts.

I finally turned away from the river and walked slowly back across the bridge, well above the water. I flew to Paris the next morning, Saturday. Claire met me, and we drove out to Mortefontaine. Everyone was there: the boys, Pénélope, Claire's sisters and their children, the forest, the lakes, the swans, the heron, all that I had come back to France for. Now was the time to consider further and perhaps renew my promise to Ferrer, but how peaceful it would be, I thought, to put an end to my constant battles—my war—of words.

I had to return to Prague at six on Monday morning, and we drove into Paris Sunday afternoon. I slept fitfully through a recurring dream. I was meeting with a man who, in his wide-brimmed hat and long overcoat, looked something like Orson Welles in *The Third Man*. He was leaning against the reception desk at the bottom of the staircase in a crumbling hotel. The man asked me to *voh* him. *to voh to tow to row to*—

"To FOLLOW me, you idiot! What's the matter with you?"

"This lobby is upside down." I was catching my balance against a wall—so cold!

"Counselor, what the fuck is wrong with you? Follow me."

"Can you tell me what I am doing wrong? Do you have the—?

"I do not have the answer, but I will take you to someone who does."

"What is the answer?"

"Do you want it now?"

"Yes."

"The answer is—you are NOAH!!"

I woke up to Claire's voice. "Gérald, *tu rêves, t'as eu un cauchemar*" ("you're dreaming, you've had a nightmare"). It was three o'clock in the morning. My pillow and neck were cold and soaking wet. She put her hand on my chest. "Your heart is beating a hundred times a minute—two hundred! What's wrong?"

"The Toolco deal is—"

"Forget it! You know, for months you've been having nightmares, just like in the middle of that—that Allevard deal and, before, over Mobil and those words, Sorota's words—*what's wrong with you?*—and your heart beats like this *quand tu dors*, when you're asleep. You're going to kill yourself if you keep this up. I won't have it! I'm not going to lose you over some bank or some—some tool company, for heaven's sake!"

"It's all right."

"All right!? It's not all right! You can't hear. You never could, really, if you face it, *si tu fais face.* That's the problem! You can't hear me, unless I'm inches away and in broad daylight. And at the office I'm sure you can't hear the words at fifty miles an hour with your eyes and brain and *oiseaux lyres* and Woolseyphone and your racing heart, which wakes you up at night freezing with sweat! You're paid by your clients to analyze words, but since you can't hear them, you have to figure them out with your brain and your heart—and one of them is going to—*exploser.*"

I succeeded in calming Claire down, as my focus on her quieted my own heart and turned it toward the future. It wasn't like the old days, I insisted—I knew, as she had said when she threw the pills away, what was wrong, and I could deal with it, as I had for years. At five o'clock I got dressed and kissed her, still sleeping. I headed for the airport looking forward, after meetings with clients in Prague, to a forthcoming trip to the United States.

I got to our office in Prague by nine as usual. A joint venture of two large British and Swedish tobacco companies had asked us to help them with their proposed investment in the government-owned Czech tobacco group. The transaction reminded me that our larger meetings, in Warsaw, Budapest, Prague, or elsewhere, were all affairs in dark and smoky rooms. The evolving habits of the West had not yet reached Eastern Europe, and after a few hours a number of us would take an air break, slipping outside to clear our lungs. It didn't help much in the winter, when the air was heavy with the odor of coke, still used to heat houses in those cities. But when I came home to Paris, my clothes would reek for weeks of the odor not of coke but of smoke. In Prague it is the lungs of its citizenry that are lined with both.

Our meeting with the tobacconists was a short one, with only four of us, and with the Woolseyphone and my hearing aids I managed to hear much of what was said. No one was smoking, and the conversation was all about how to maximize profits from the country's addicted population. It turned out that the foreign investors were doing almost all the work with their internal lawyers, so our contribution to the spread of disease in the region proved to be minimal. To our discredit, we did help on a collateral issue, sent the tobacco folks an opinion and a handsome bill, and left it at that.

From the meeting I went back to the airport and then on to London to spend the night at Heathrow on the way to Washington for a meeting with the World Bank on the financing of a Hungarian hydroelectric project. The trip to Heathrow was about two and a half hours, and at about nine PM I checked into my hotel room on the eighth floor of the Heathrow Marriott or Radisson or some such place. I called Claire to reassure her that all was well, ordered up dinner, and watched the mumblings of a variety of television newsreaders as I sat on the bed eating well-done roast beef (declining the "vegitarian" menu) and drinking half a bottle of wine from the "Claret region" of France.

I turned off the TV, propped my head against two pillows, and sipped the final drops. I had kept my *oiseaux lyres* on, but with the television off things seemed eerily quiet—nothing but locusts. I opened the door and heard the faint sound of a vacuum cleaner toward the end of the hall, where there were two carts of sheets and towels braced against the open door of the linen closet. I became alarmed by the profound silence, beginning to think *fire* as I went to the window, drew open the curtains, and, to my great surprise, saw a couple of hundred people outside, many of them wearing their bathrobes. They were looking up at me, waving and moving their mouths, but the windows were sealed.

I ran to the door, looked out again, and listened more carefully—the vacuum cleaner was a fire alarm, and I was alone in the building. I rushed back into the bedroom and put on a bathrobe and a pair of loafers. I found the exit quickly, as the sign we all see ran through my mind ("in case of fire do not use elevator"), and vaulted down the stairwell three or four steps at a time, grabbing the railings. There was no smoke, no fire, no screaming, just emptiness. I burst through the ground-floor doors into the courtyard to a round of applause—"Well done, lad, *ferry vah.*" *ferry vah very fast*

It was not a fire but a bomb threat from a group claiming to be an offshoot of the *prior aide. the buyer aide the dire aid the IRA.* We all adjourned to a nearby pub, set among the glass-and-steel airport hotels but designed to look like a Red Lion Inn in the middle of the New Forest, and drank free pints of bitters. The British accents were difficult in all the clatter, but everyone was friendly and relieved, more so as the beer flowed on without an explosion. In fact I had little to offer to the pub discussion, for it was centered on the horrors of the Irish, and it was not the time *what is your dame your tame your name* to talk of Cromwell.

We were back in our Heathrow hotel rooms in less than two hours, and I took the plane the next day to Washington. When I arrived, I got a taxi to my cousin Maureen's house on A Street near the Capitol. We walked around a bit before dinner, which she planned for six o'clock so I could get some sleep before the meeting the next day. It was a beautiful spring day, one on which Anne Sullivan might have encouraged Helen to write that "soft veils of mist, spun of wind and dew, were drawn around the shoulders" of the nation's marble-white monuments. I had never had such a close look at the Capitol.

"It's overwhelming."

"Yes, and it *houses your gullet*, Gerry." *gullet gull'et cull'et*

"It houses my gullet?" The locusts that followed the flight were overpowering the hearing aids.

"Your CONGress."

"I wonder what the acoustics are like in the—"

"Forget it. You're too naïve ever to be a politician. By the way, how is *Tim's eye* working?"

> *tim's eye*
> > *jim's mike*
> > > *the woolseyphone*
> > > > *working?*

"Oh, shit!"

"What's wrong?"

"I think I left it in the hotel at Heathrow. There was a bomb scare, and I had put it on a corner table to get out some papers. I left it there."

"Will it *take a since?*" *take a make a mince dince make a difference*

"It can—if it winds up in front of the right person. Usually it's a matter of luck." The meeting was at ten thirty the next day. Starting at eight in the morning, Maureen made the rounds, beginning with Woolsey's office, to try to find out where to get a replacement. She finally called a place in Chevy Chase called SHHH, an odd acronym that shaped the organization's name, Self Help for the Hard of Hearing. They had a couple of them and agreed to provide me with a loaner. It was waiting for me when I got to the Debevoise office on Thirteenth Street.

I took a taxi over to the IFC, the International Finance Corporation, which is the investment arm of the World Bank. The conference room was on the third floor of its building at 2121 Pennsylvania Avenue, and when I arrived, our clients, personnel from the Hungarian Ministry of Energy, were there with the

IFC's translators. As we were introduced, I was relieved to hear their American-accented English, the result of their years of living in the United States. Also present was the usual handful of commercial banks.

I was to lead the Hungarian side. The two IFC people came in last, a Japanese man, Yoshiro Sakakida, and *Dayo*, a woman from Singapore *dayo day o star a come an' me wan' go ho-ome no not day pay? No—may*

"Hello, May Oh," I said.

"*Gomorrah*," said both. *and Sodom to you!*

My heart sank as it became clear I would understand neither one. Sakakida asked me whether I had a *DIEdee diedee you have to put a nightie on Aphrodite to keep all the married men home accent accent dieDEE deep treep nice trip* "Yes, thank you very much."

I was tired, but we had only the one day to resolve the IFC's concerns. I put the Woolseyphone in front of Sakakida, pulled the loop from inside my shirt, and plugged it into the receiver on my belt, which everyone in the room seemed to find entirely normal. I got out my notes.

"Two real *tissues issues barter barter bother* us," said Sakakida. "First, the *kwara'ti*." *Whew! a guarantee thank you*

"Yes."

"*Muss pee huck Indian guttent kwara'ti not just a power oughtee.*" *muss pee must be*

"Must be—" *must be Hungarian government guarantee not just the power authority's* Our client, Attila Ermai, pointed out that the government does not give guarantees, but the Power Authority's guarantee is enough. "Yes," I added. "Hungarian law does not allow a government guarantee, but the government stands behind—"

"Change the *rah*!" said Ms. Oh. *the raw*

"We can't change the law," I answered. "It's in the Constitution."

Bankers Trust said that if the IFC gets the guarantee, so should the *latertial packs.*

> *packs is banks*
> *latertial*
> *laertes*
> *brother*
> *of Ophelia*

"Gerry?" asked *Bell and Back*, Mellon Bank. *latertial commercial banks'll want a guarantee too, so if IFC gets a guarantee, so should the commercial banks*

"Uh, the issue is not who gets it, because no one can. But it shouldn't be an issue because you don't need it. If the Power Authority's guarantee is triggered, the government will be legally obligated to fund it."

"OK," said May Oh.

An American voice far away from the Woolseyphone, I think it was J. P. Morgan, said *"And the fecund igloo?"*

> *fecund igloo*
> *fecund second*
> *the second issue*

"*Been led news, teed at reese errefen a bunch,*" Sakakida said, through three voices around him. I was almost lost. Going through my mind were textbook clues: R *and* l—*in Asian languages* r *and* l *are allophones of the same phoneme pronounced somewhere between* r *and* l *and difficult to distinguish. Hence "rice" can be "lice," and so "reese" is "leese" is "least." What did that lady, Maki, say? That people who make fun of the difficulty the Japanese have with* l*'s and* r*'s are ignorant, racist, mouth-breathing cretins who deserve to be choked with a big wad of mochi. reese is leese least need at least led is red is red new is revnew is we need revenues need at least errefen eleven yes we need minimum revenues of at least $11 million a month*

The others were watching me.

"But," I finally said, "if you have the equivalent of a government guarantee, then you shouldn't insist on a minimum revenue standard—it should not be an event of default in the loan agreements."

I sat opposite Sakakida with SHHH's Woolseyphone between us. At times he spoke very slowly and cast an empathetic eye toward it and the wire protruding from my shirt. Ms. Oh was gentle as well, and while I welcomed the understanding and help, it occurred to me that my equipment and its shortcomings—and mine—were becoming a matter of common knowledge.

By the end of the day I was exhausted. The IFC finally gave up on the guarantee and asked only for a nominal minimum revenue stream. Sakakida put his hand on my shoulder as we left and said something in my ear. "Uh, sorry, Yoshiro, I didn't hear you," I said. "I need to see your lips."

"Yes, yes. Of course. Sorry. Sorry, Gerry. You very *glayshus*."

"I am gracious?"

"That, too. Yes. Very gracious. You naturally gracious. But I say you very courageous!" And I blessed him, his accent, his compassion, his colleague, the IFC, the World Bank, Japan, Hungary, the power project, and the day.

I got back to Maureen's on A Street at about eight o'clock to find that she had invited a number of colleagues from the Democratic National Committee over to dinner. "Gerry, what happened to you?"

"Do I look that bad?"

"You're ashen. You're shirt's hanging out, and that loose wire down there looks like you're *unsung*." *unsung unpung unplugged* She took my briefcase and jacket, gave me a drink, and took me out to the small garden in back of the house to introduce me to people. As I stepped onto the porch, I leaned back against the door. *locusts there are locusts out here everywhere locusts the locusts God what's wrong*

"What's the matter?"

"The locusts!"

"*E tartars.*"

"E tartar?"

"CIC-A-DAS, Gerry. "It's that time of year. Once every fourteen years or so, they come out in DC. They're not locusts, but they might as well be." She moved closer. "They are a shrill, buzzing creature, and your *oiseaux lyres* are picking them up."

"My *oiseaux lyres* are supposed to drown them out."

"They're the loudest insects in the world. The males make sounds with their bellies to call the females. The sound can be over 100 decibels. But there are *no* locusts inside—inside the house."

My head was spinning. *God steady steady against a brass post holding the velvet loops that guide you into the Chase Bank my locusts aren't crickets the female cricket is deaf and though the chirp of the male is territorial and heard by other males he attracts his loves with the scent he emits from under his wings but the locusts are different the descendants of singing men who needed no other sustenance and sang themselves to death*

"GERRY! Take them out!" she said. I did, and there was silence except for my own. "Let's—Gerry—LET'S GO—INSIDE! You'll turn on your *oiseaux lyres*, and all you'll hear is us. OK?"

"INSIDE. Yes."

She led me inside. "Are you all right?"

"Yes. I'm fine. I'm so sorry." She came into focus. "It was just—the reversal of things."

"Well, they're gone now. I'm going to bring everyone in, and we're going to have a party—right side up."

CHAPTER 23

LIFE AS A LYRICAL?

FROM WASHINGTON I CAUGHT A PLANE TO NEW Orleans. There I had an appointment with a specialist, Paul Berle, who people at Gallaudet thought might be able to help me. In New Orleans the French signs and shops along the way made me feel at home. *"Bienvenue à la Nouvelle Orléans,"* read a sign as the taxi followed the south shore of Lake Ponchartrain. But who exactly *was* this man, I thought to myself, and why did Gallaudet send me all the way down here to see him?

I checked into my hotel, across the park from the LSU Medical Center, went to my room, and ordered up dinner. I wanted to see Bourbon Street and the French quarter, and to make a trip upriver to see the lyrical lakes of the Atchafalaya and the boughs of Wachita willows. But I had planned to look at the terms of a client's investments for a meeting two days later in Prague. I needed to review the deals, set the agenda, and develop a lyrical key. "Warrants" might appear as *was*; "Brno Plastics" as *turn oh has ticks*; "Bratislava debt" as *has a lotta rent*. You never know exactly what the lyrical will be, of course, and an important reason for looking at a deal over and over again—notably its unfamiliar proper names—before a meeting is to try to enable the brain to make as rapid a transition as possible.

I gave up at one o'clock and went to bed after calling the desk to make sure the hotel wasn't on fire and to wake me up at eight. The LSU Medical Center is a five-minute walk from the hotel. Paul Berle proved to be an amiable man. Then in his early sixties, he spoke slowly and softly. He was not a physician but a scientist and the head of LSU's Kresge Hearing Research Laboratory. With my *oiseaux lyres* I had relatively little trouble reading his lips. Berle (pronounced "burly") specialized in hearing aids and other communications equipment for the partially deaf. He introduced me to his assistant, who gave me an audiogram.

"Well, let's see," said Berle. "You're at 85–90 decibels in the middling to high frequencies. Difficult. Do you have an omnidirectional microphone?"

"Yes. Made in New Jersey."

"Good. You know where they *kay for*?" *kay foh from came from*

"Yes. NIH, and before that, I think they were a CIA discard. I call it my Woolseyphone."

"I imagine you know a lot about your hearing, Gerry. Do you have a family?"

"Yes. A family. A French wife, a stepdaughter, and two sons."

"Excellent. And you live in Paris."

"Yes."

"And how is life?"

"How is life!?" I considered the question trite at first, but after giving it some thought, I let him have it.

"Life is, uh, my professional life—is a long, lamentable, unbearable torture. I hate my life."

"I am so sorry. Look—"

"Is there anything you can do for me? *(Do you have the answer?)* Gallaudet sent me to you." I would have said that Bébian and Clerc had sent me as well if I had then known who they were.

"Yes. I think there is something, though it may not exactly be what you expect. Do you have a large *traditional angle?*" *traditional angle anguo languo lang—transitional language*

"Yes. Always, always. I have it. A transitional language? I think this is what I call 'lyricals.'"

"That's a *uticil were* for them. Lyricals." *uticil beautiful word* "Lyricals. Do you remember any, for example?"

"I do. I always remember them—I mean almost every lyrical I've ever—I could write a dictionary of lyricals. They have no intrinsic meaning, of course. They're keys to other words. The ones that just made an appearance are *kay fuh* for 'came from,' and *traditional angle* for 'transitional language.' At the DC airport there was *doe de to doo or. Song of a second peace* is a lyrical from an old movie."

"And the words the latter two were seeking were—?"

" At the airport *doe de to doo or* was 'going to New Orleans'— 'I'll be gone five hundred miles when the day is done.'" I sang the line from the song. "*Song of a second peace* is from *Bad Day at Black Rock*, which I saw as a schoolboy. Lee Marvin spoke the actual words, which were a commonplace threat to another character."

Berle began to speak more slowly, and louder. "Why did you just sing, Gerry?"

"I've always loved that song, and they were among the few words in it I understand, and five hundred miles is a long day."

"A very long day. As I recall, Guthrie's words in 'Ridin' on the City of New Orleans' are unusual, hard to anticipate. Hard to—"

"Lyricalize."

"Do you play the piano?"

"Well, yes. Why?"

"Would you *say* something?" *say say play something* There was an upright piano in the corner of Berle's office, to the right as you walk in, and I hadn't noticed it. I went over to the bench to play; he got up from his desk, drew up to my stool, and sat down beside me with a pen and notepad.

I played a piece from Schumann's "Scenes from Childhood." When I was finished, he said nothing, so I followed with—why not—the first of Mendelssohn's "Songs without Words." They are both easy pieces. I couldn't hear the highest notes, but I imagine them when I play, as my fingers strum the right side of the keyboard, as if a table. I had no idea why he had asked me to play.

He was jotting something down. "You play well."

"Thanks. I'm not very good, but I love to play. I memorize pieces because I can't sight read."

"Perhaps some *say*" *some say some day* "you'll take the time to learn."

Fat chance, I thought. "I'll never have the time."

"Oh? Could you hear what you played?"

"Most of it—except for some highs, but they were there."

"Excellent. Now—"

"Why did you ask me to play?"

"Well, you seemed musical to me. After all you sang for me, and New Orleans is a musical city, and the piano was right there."

"Yes—but why?"

"I—have a theory about the deaf and music. To take a preeminent example, you can hear Beethoven's deafness in his music."

"The low notes—"

"Well, they're certainly there, but it's perhaps not so much the lows—it may be the highs that you have to listen for—that he heard with such difficulty, that he missed so profoundly. Music for the deaf, for the partially deaf, in my clinical experience, appears to supplant the music others hear in words themselves, the fullness of each word and of all of them together. Music is not a language, but it has overwhelming *immune if a tic fours." a tic tic icatica icative imunica*—*communicative force.* "Mendelssohn himself said it about what you just played. When a friend offered to write words for it, he emphasized that the music expressed ideas not 'too indefinite' to put into words but, on the contrary, 'too definite.' That's why you find it—why Edison, to take another example, though he was not a musician, found it—"

"Irresistible." *The birds the rainfall the footsteps the breaths the water the crickets O burly gentle mole the call in it is stronger even than the music is sweet, the merry bubble and joy of my earlier life*

"In the case of the profoundly deaf, the music lies in the play of their visual language itself. Their eyes betray that music; that is, they let us see it as they 'speak.' And when you were playing, your eyes gave you away as well. They were somewhere else. *Lots of dessert.*"

"Lots of what?"

"They were not of this earth." Berle straightened his back a bit, his demeanor shifting from a relaxed and collaborative one to a more earnest, even insistent posture, squaring his shoulders and voice to show he was coming to what he most wanted to say. "Now, Gerry, I have someone I want you to meet, and I will take you to him. *(Does he have the answer?)* He's over in the surgical bloc."

"Do you want me to have an operation?" I asked with a nervous laugh.

"No," he chuckled. "You know as well as I do that the cochlea isn't operable. But I want you to see him." He stood up. "I believe you and I are through. It is a great pleasure to meet you. You have the best hearing equipment available, at least to date. You have a family you cherish, and you are in love with music."

"I am a lawyer!" I hesitated. "Uh, a good lawyer—"

"I'm sure of that! And I bet you have other qualities I'm not aware of yet—and perhaps you aren't either. Perhaps, Gerry, it is time you were—time that you made yourself aware of them."

"Who is this person?"

"He's a doctor. Come with me." *I do not have the answer, but I will take you to someone who does.*

We left Berle's laboratory and building and crossed the lawn to the operating section of the hospital, took an elevator to the third floor, for which Berle took my arm to keep me from heading for the wrong one, and then walked through receptionists and nurses to a conference room. There was a long narrow table in it, looking disturbingly like the one at the World Bank. All of this seemed so wholly improbable that I wouldn't have been shocked to find Dr. Jekyll sitting there. The man turned out to be a young doctor, about thirty years old. He got up to greet us. "Gerry," said Berle, "this is Peter Melanson, one of our ablest young physicians at LSU."

"Well, one of the doctors, anyway," said Melanson. He had sandy hair and small, wire-framed glasses and was wearing a tie and a white coat. His smile was broad and attentive, and his bright blue eyes looked directly into mine. "Hello, Gerry."

Berle shook my hand, and told me to stay in touch—to call if I needed him for anything at all—and left us.

"Let's have a seat," Melanson said. I sat to his left at the end of the table, he at its head. We both shifted to a forty-five-degree angle to face each other.

"It's good to sit down," I said to Melanson. "As you can imagine, I am terrified. You are a surgeon?"

I didn't know it yet, but my own words were lyricals racing through the mind of the young doctor. My word "terrified" registered in his mind, transitionally, as *everside*, *everfied*, then *terrified*.

"No," he replied, "but I used to be. I was a *pray* surgeon."

> *pray*
>
> *pray to*
>
> *St. Hilde—*
>
> *problem in*
>
> *your brain*
>
> *a brain surgeon*

"What do you do now?" I asked.

"I am a psychiatrist. I *lay tear*" *lay tear lay take take care* "of people's *byes, or dry dew*, but I don't operate." *byes byes mize minds dry dew try to*

"Do you *deter society?*" *deter ciety kiety psych—do you prefer psychiatry*

"I loved being a brain surgeon or becoming one. But it proved to be impossible."

"Why?"

"Because of the *offering* room. You see, Gerry, I am *clued in my Erie.*"

clued in lewd in lose in losing losing losing—my hearing! the timing of his responses God He reached into the left pocket of his white coat, took out his hearing aids, and put them on.

"Is this OK?" I asked.

"Maybe just a bit closer—to be sure we understand each other!" We pulled our chairs closer to the corner of the table, our lips now about three feet apart. "That's fine. The intensity of sound, as you surely know, is inversely proportional to the square of the distance."

"Yes. Not here, though. There's no distance."

"I couldn't understand what others were saying in the operating room—both because of the masks, which of course make lipreading impossible, and on account of the hurriedness of speech in what is often, as you can imagine, a frantic environment. If you'll forgive me—I believe I am like you." He pulled back a few feet and looked away. "*As a tick hyater I read wuh person on a dime, at loos warders.*" He came closer again.

"*Tick hyater,*" I said.

"Psychiatrist," said the brain surgeon, turning to me.

"*I read.*"

"I treat."

"*Wuh person.*"

"One person."

"*On a dime.*"

"At a time."

"*At loos warders.*"

"At close quarters, like this, it works quite well. The change has, in a real sense, saved my life."

I looked away and spoke softly. "You gave up the field you loved most," I said. "When did you decide to change?" I translated his lyricals as he pronounced them aloud.

"*Cay uh,*" said the doctor.

"Gave up," I replied.

"*Veal stew dove boat.*"

"Field you loved most."

"*Derive do chain.*"

"Decide to change."

He raised his voice slightly and spoke more slowly. "I guess I realized my hearing was declining when I was about twenty-five, still in medical school. No one knows what has happened; it's probably congenital, but there are no deaf or hard of hearing relatives that I know of. It took some time, but eventually I realized that in the operating room I was wholly inventing what others were saying. There was no transitional language at all, as I came to understand later, with the lips of the others masked."

"Everything was a blank—you had no lyricals."

"No 'lyricals'? You mean the—yes, that's right. Nice word. The lyricals were gone. Just about. But this is not at all the case if you sit close enough to and facing the individual patient, just as we are here. I could have done research or become a pathologist or even a coroner! But I wanted to work with people, and what I know about the brain, of course, can be helpful. And you? I understand that words are your profession."

"Yes. Written words too."

"But I guess not *potem*." *potem totem modem*

"Potem?"

"Spoken."

"Not spoken words."

"Right. Lyricals are your profession. That's very difficult."

"I—"

"In the operating room they can be lethal. Elsewhere too, I imagine."

"What are you suggesting, Peter?"

"Only that you face things, squarely. Lyricals shape your language, but you can't let your whole life become a lyrical. You may be hiding. I miss my scalpel and what it could do—could have done. Giving it up broke my *arc*." *arc art heart* "But I'm all right now."

"But I'm perfectly capable—"

"Of course. But at what cost?"

"I have rarely—

"Not the cost to the client, Gerry. To you. *(don't kill yourself my boy)* Don't be afraid to break your own heart. It will mend, I am sure very quickly. *Used lots of Allen.*"

"Lots of Allen."

"You've lots of talent. That's obvious—except perhaps to you." *Don't be brutal with yourself.* Melanson smiled, though his eyes were sparkling still for his own heart in spite of its mending. He looked at his watch. "I'm sorry," he said, "I have *Truro*." *true row to go to go* He could see that I would have stayed with him for the rest of the day, if not forever. He gave me a hug, a big Cajun hug, "bigger than a bear's," the surgeon said, and wished me luck.

I walked out of the hospital and into the park that led back to my hotel. It was a heavenly June day in New Orleans. As I think back over that morning, it occurs to me that, with poorer luck in my search for an answer, I might, like so many others, have run into the modern successors of Bell and his ilk, whose numbers are legion. But in Berle I found the compassion of Bébian, and in Melanson the wisdom of Bérthier, to both of whom, to my exceptional good fortune, I had been sent by the institution founded by Clerc and Gallaudet.

CHAPTER 24

FREEDOM

I TOOK AN AFTERNOON PLANE FROM NEW ORLEANS through St. Louis to New York, and from there a Lufthansa plane to Frankfurt for a connection to Prague the next morning. When I arrived at the meeting in an old building in downtown Prague, not far from the Karluv Most, there were eight or nine people of various nationalities waiting in the conference room. Through our New York office we had been asked to help a public investment fund restructure some of its investments in the Czech Republic that had gone sour. The fund, jointly owned by the United States and three European countries, was called the European American Investment Group and known as EAIG. The language at the fund was English, which everyone spoke, so there would be no translators to cut off speakers at the point of cognitive anticipation. The chief financial officer, a German woman, was about to give the presentation, and I sat down two seats away from her. I placed the Woolseyphone on the table, wondering whether the lyricals—through my hearing aids for those close to me and switching to the Woolseyphone for those farther away in the room—would be workable or out of reach.

The fund's officers stared at my Woolseyphone in disbelief, as if it were an unwelcome participant at the meeting, while I explained why it was there. *Are we to be saved from our misfortunes by a deaf man?* The financial officer *is she called Hildegarde* was soft-spoken and her English heavily accented—*zie tei guPANny is ESSen schlie bahk rut*—phrases that lyricals would normally master with the help of the Woolseyphone and my *oiseaux lyres zie tei gut (look at the list of deals!) rut bankrupt the tire company is esSENtially bankrupt*—but they were rapidly spoken and cumulatively unmanageable. The lyricals would be out of reach.

About ten minutes into her talk I grew indifferent to the fact that the entire presentation was being given for me, and lapsed into the mode of my years before *oiseaux lyres*, hoping that I would somehow get it later. She completed her review in about an hour and a half, and I asked a few peremptory questions that elicited a simple yes or no. I agreed to study the transactions and come back for a closer review in a few weeks. I was going to be spending several weeks in Paris to work on the European segment of the refinancing of an American automobile company, mostly on the telephone, and was eager to get back.

I planned to spend two hours a day on the EAIG transactions, using spare moments I could wrest from what would no doubt be fifteen-hour days on the refinancing. When the Carcorp deal, as we called it, was completed, I was to take a sabbatical from the firm, traveling to California and Wyoming with Claire and the children and then on to Main Harbor for two months.

Jim Kiernan and I had dinner with Carcorp's executive vice president in a two-star restaurant in the seventh arrondissement, where there was too much noise for my *oiseaux lyres*. The conversation quickly became a dialogue between Jim and our client. "*So we deed to subvert most on a set.*" *on a set on a set debt—*

"*But we dan the loot de-deck of tea.*" *de-deck of tea is de the eck equ the equity*

"Right." At the end of the dinner, Carcorp turned to me and asked, "Are you OK? You haven't said anything." He meant that the meter had been running (it hadn't) for nothing.

"I'm fine," I said. "I want to learn about the deal before I jump into it." EAIG had put off our meeting because of management changes in the fund and asked me to come over a month later than planned. I worked on Carcorp for the next six weeks, mostly with Americans over the telephone, lawyers, bankers, and the client, and with the help of three young lawyers in the firm managed to get through the closing. I flew to Prague the morning after Carcorp was completed.

I got to EAIG's offices at ten. It was early June in Prague, and the room was already very hot. When we started, the windows were wide open, with street noises *dobre dobre dobre* ringing horns and roaring truck engines coming into my hearing aids at over 150 decibels. When I got up to close them and saw the looks on people's faces, I suggested we move to another room I had spotted that had a small circular table, around which everyone would be seated equidistant from the Woolseyphone. There were some grumbles, but they agreed. Two of the four windows were half open. We had fifteen transactions to go through.

I handed out the agenda, with a list and analysis of issues and possible solutions. Most of the problems were financial, not legal, like the need to get lines of credit or change suppliers, and those proposals were taken up by EAIG managers as I looked at their lips and took notes. With the microphone in the middle an outsider would have thought us a cell of spies listening in to *the lives of others* under the direction of Hildegarde, the chief financial officer. By about two o'clock the lyricals and, for everyone, the heat, were becoming a burden. *"Wha za siurdy for the bridge dance?"* dance bridge dance siurty security what's the security dancing financing bridge financing

"There's no interim or bridge financing on this deal," I said. "It's straight long term, to renovate the plant."

"Gerry, we've *skipped town." skipped town slipped down* "We're talking about *the ridge ban in turn oh." turn oh Brno the ridge ban ridge ridge bridge dance the Brno bridge span* "the real bridge, for heaven's sake." At five o'clock a secretary came in to say I had a *bow tall bow poe tall call phone call* that I could take in the now-empty main conference room. There was a sigh of relief, and as I left, people bolted toward the windows.

"Hello?"

"Hello, Gerry?" I recognized my brother John's voice and clapped the Nuvox to the receiver.

"What's wrong?"

"Things are OK, but Patrick and I have taken *Bob* to the hospital."

"Who's Bob?"

"Mom! Mother."

"What's wrong?"

"Well, you remember her cough. She has, uh, she has lung cancer. It's very serious."

"Lung cancer all of a sudden?"

"She's been hiding it—I see her every week, but she's been able to suppress the cough for an hour or so, perhaps with a shot of vodka or two, I don't know. In any event it's finally overwhelmed her." He explained that she had called him earlier that day.

I told John I would call her the next day. I walked back toward the place people were calling the "oval office" because of its American tyrant and round table. All the windows were open, and everyone was breathing easily. People froze as I came in, and there was a momentary pause in the humming clatter of their words. They cast furtive glances at the windows, the Woolsey-phone, my stack of papers, and me.

"I think we've finished," I said to visible sighs of relief. We agreed that I would write a note summarizing the key points and that we could take them up at EAIG's annual meeting in Washington in July.

At three o'clock the next day I called Mother from the Paris office.

"Goddam telephones—*suddens suddens*—too small too many." *suttons buttons*

"The buttons—the keys—on the phone are too small?"

"Yes. Can you hear me?"

"Yes, I can. Mother. How are you?"

"I am *tuck tether.*" *touch much tether much better* "You'll come to me after your vacation."

"No—"

"Yes!" I heard a few tones in the Nuvox—she was pressing the numbers instead of the volume controls. "Dammit! This is exactly why I don't have a *zap*!"

"I'm on my way—"

"No, you're not. You are taking Claire and the boys out west—where is Pénélope?"

"She's going to Spain with her father."

"Fine. And you are going out west. Then you *ka kuh do be.*" *can come to me*

We took the trip to Wyoming, and I made daily calls to the hospital. Jackson was as beautiful as ever, and we rode horses, took long hikes, and shot the rapids with guides in a large raft-like boat on the Snake River. At last I had some time with a family I had been neglecting for years for the sake of—what? I relished being with the boys. Though their voices were still high, they thoroughly had the hang of talking to me, getting my attention first, coming close, looking up, sticking to English, and rephrasing things if they didn't work the second time. How wonderful it was to see them, day and night, night and day, and not just for breakfast, between trips, sound asleep in their beds. Claire kept commenting on my dry pillow and slow-beating, contented heart.

We arrived in Main Harbor early in July. Our house, which Claire and I bought in 1990, is at the end of the peninsula overlooking the harbor and the bay. As soon as we arrived, we all put on our suits, rushed down the wooden steps that lead to the beach just below the house, and splashed into the sea. When we are bathing in the water there—it seems the one place in the world this is true—I hear Claire and the children fairly well without my *oiseaux lyres*. The sound of their voices in the harbor and bay is extraordinary. While the words can be unclear, their timbre and rhythm make me feel as if I am hearing as I did as a child at Main. I am not sure why this is so. Coupled always with my memory of those heavenly early days, perhaps it is the water's spectral reflection of Claire's or Sebastian's or Alex's or Pénélope's voice, or the thermal inversion in the air just above the water that keeps the sound waves close to the surface, or all these things, I don't know.

The next morning we all went over to Salem hospital—or rather to the rehabilitation clinic adjoining it, to which Mother had now been moved. She had combed her hair and put on some lipstick. I could see that she was giving a performance, for the contours of her face were hollowing. "*I wan to deeper sensible* for the boys." *sensible sentible du per sentible sentable be presentable*

"Mother, you look terrific." We approached the bed to kiss her. Behind us a voice shouted, "I'd bust my ass for you, Grace." We turned around, and on the bed behind us—which I had not noticed as I came in—was a woman in her eighties, smiling broadly, showing her remaining three or four teeth. She bore an unsettling resemblance to the witch in Snow White, not the image to have in a city that had hanged a score of its women for it. Mother introduced her, "This is my friend, Agnes," and Agnes said, "You bet your sweet life I'm your friend, Grace. I'd do anything for you." Mother was about ten years younger than her roommate, who had been at the clinic for years and decided that Grace was a welcome addition, "the best we've ever had." I shook Agnes's hand and thanked her, and she fell into a deep sleep.

"How do you feel, Mom?"

"Much better. The boys are handsome."

"Look like you."

"How was Jackson Hole?" she asked the boys, and they told her about our shooting the rapids. "Your grandfather and I went on our honeymoon to Lake Louise, in Canada. It is beautiful, too, and when you go there one day, you will think of us." Her eyes closed; I kissed her forehead at the centered dip of her hairline, which I hadn't lingered on from so close a distance since I was a child. We went back to the house for dinner. I asked John how much time. He said it was difficult to tell, but the illness was taking over her lungs and was metastatic, a word we all recognize, but I looked it up anyway: metastatic, from the Greek, standing in another place or way, spreading in the bloodstream or in the flow of lymphatic fluid from one place in the body to another. Nothing could be done.

I had the whole summer to be with her. Each day Claire made dinner for her—*soupe, poulet à l'estragon, escalope de veau à la crème, bar* (sea bass), or *homard à la crème*. We sailed out in our whaler as usual to buy lobsters from boats pulling traps in the bay. I took the dinners over to Salem on a hot plate. Between small bites, her lips said *ah uh oo oh uh* not for any failing of my ears, for I was well within the sphere of maternal intimacy, but because of her inability to say the words, quickly transformed by lyricals into *I love you so much*.

          ⌒

In early August I took an early morning plane to Washington and a taxi to the Hay-Adams Hotel, where the EAIG board meeting was being held. It is an old hotel with ancient lower ceilings and abundant curtains and rugs—far less daunting, though more expensive (notwithstanding EAIG's troubled transactions), than the glass, steel, and marble tombs of our modern chains. The hotel sits across the street from the White House. Henry Adams once owned the property along with John Hay, Lincoln's secretary of state, and you feel as if you're walking into the American past as you enter its lobby.

  Hildegarde introduced me to about twenty-five people in the Windsor Room. My sole objective was to deliver my presentation to them as quickly as possible so that I could deliver to Mother by the end of the day her *escalope de veau*. I didn't understand their names, but at the conference table we all had nameplates in front of us: Mr. Thompson; Mr. Blazek; Mr. Schwarzenberg the Prince, a real prince now following the restitution of his castle to his family; Mr. Bata the shoemaker, his Czech company restored to his empire; and so on. The American chairman went through the minutes of the prior year's meeting and praised the current venue. My mind was wandering.

  "*Erry? Derry? Gerry!?* Are you with us?"

  "Oh—yes. Sorry, I was distracted." I covered the transactions in about forty-five minutes, three or four minutes each, a good clip. Don't let them talk. The few questions—"Will *submissing the tet liquidy ell?*" *ell help submissing converting the debt to equity will it help?*—were soft ones from a deferential board more removed from the issues than management itself. I took a deep breath when it was over and rushed for the airport.

When John and I went over to see Mother early that evening, she was crying out in pain.

"What did she say?" asked the nurse who was with us.

"You've got to stop the pain!" I shouted. She looked at John, a doctor, who looked away. "Listen," I added, in a quieter, more reasonable, more urgent voice, "make her comfortable. Can you do that?"

"Yes, we can." As we left, I clasped the ball of her left foot, which was warm, and her toes responded, as did the toes of the other. We went home, and I called the hospital at ten that night.

"I'm calling about Mrs. Shea."

"*Oh! Oh yeh. I yet the tocker.*" *yet the get the doctor* She looked for him forever, and when she found him, he left it to her. "Mr. Shea, I'm so sorry. I can't *vie it.*" *vie it fie it find it I can't find him* "*Tea kye jus a few mints ago.*" *tea kye she die she died she—died*

TWO NIGHTS AFTER THE FUNERAL, AT MAIN HARBOR, I fell into a deep sleep and dreamt of Claire. I seemed to be able to hear her well in the dream, although, as Tomas Tranströmer has put it, dreams (like some lives) are often composed of nonsense words to which one can later give meaning. Perhaps I understood the dream only as I awakened, after complementing it with my own conscious thoughts. Claire and I stood, in the dream, on the steps to the beach looking out at the bay and the harbor, a forest of masts in August. Without looking at me, Claire said, "She's still here."

"Mother?"

She turned to me. "Your mother loved you very much."

"I know that."

"Your brother Patrick gave me one of her last poems. She called it 'Midnight Angelus.'"

"It sounds like a prayer to St. Hildegarde."

"Perhaps it is. Gérald. Listen: I have something to say to you."

Claire's eyes were unblinking and now fixed squarely on mine, demanding their undivided attention. I had never seen that look before; it was as if it were not she standing there but someone who had taken her over.

"Something to say to me . . . "

"*Il faut que tu arrête*. You've got to stop."

"Stop—what?"

"Stop your trade of spoken words. Stop practicing law. If you don't—if you don't—it will kill you."

"But . . . "

"*I'll* be your life. The children and I."

"You're asking me—"

"*Je ne te demande rien*, Gérald. I'm not asking you anything. *Tu n'as pas de choix*. You have no choice!"

I woke up, startled, perspiring into a soaking wet pillow, heart beating fast, *thumpthumpthump thumpthumpthump*. Claire was still asleep beside me, but her words were echoing in my mind, as if we were together in a sleeping car and I were listening to them to the beat of the train tracks—*pas de choix, pas de choix, pas de choix*. I got out of bed slowly, lightening the mattress little by little to avoid waking her up as I shifted the weight to my feet. I took my shirt and pants from the nearby chair and put them on in the hallway.

Downstairs, I turned on the light and, on a couch in the living room, spotted my mother's poem, which she had written in pencil. I had seen but not yet read it. "*For Gerry*," she had penciled across the top, above the title. I sat down, feeling that Claire herself, or whoever had taken possession of her, was insisting. "Darkness," Mother wrote, "is more certain than the light. When winter comes, it settles in. There are no sunny corners of the night! I sense the silent chimes of prayer, more piercing than the sun, dispelling echoes of despair, from this lone suppliant." Why for me? Why this poem, for *me*?

It was warm. I walked outside, across the night's wet grass, cool underfoot. I stood at the top of the steps leading down to the beach. The echoes of Claire's words were still there, now sounding in rhythm with the harbor's waves below as I looked beyond their phosphorus patterns to the land lights across the bay. *stop practicing law, stop, stop, stop, arrêter, arrêter, arrêter* How can I do that? I serve my clients—and yet, and yet—I don't hear them—I figure out what they say. Is that enough—for my clients? Is it enough for me? *you mustn't let your life become a lyrical* And what did Claire herself say that night I woke up to her voice? That I was paid to hear clients—but with my brain and heart—and some day one of them was going to—*exploser*. Melanson's warning was different: "Don't be afraid to break your own heart." Is that the only choice? To be broken or to burst?

I do have my Woolseyphone. But then again, the mikes are crap, and I know it. And my *oiseaux lyres* bring me sounds on a quiet day, the water, the birds, the music, and it's wonderful—but they don't bring me the words. They don't bring me the fucking words. Look down at that beach. Look at the beach! We'll manage— somehow. The waves: imagine the sounds they're making. I could sit there with Claire and Pénélope and the boys, and listen to them close by, on long summer days. And swim with them, too, not *hors de cité*, not an exile from the city but liberated from it. And what did Chang say? "Know thyself." Do I belong in the city, in the world of the hearing? Or in the world of the deaf? Or in both worlds, perhaps, shared with those I love?

When shall I decide? How much time do I have before . . . the winter settles in?

I went back to the house. Claire was still sleeping, her auburn hair now reflecting the pale light of earliest morning. The night's images began to fade into the welcome driftlessness of mind that carries you off to sleep.

We flew from Boston to Paris with the children the next day, Wednesday. We landed Thursday morning, and on Friday I was back in the office. At lunchtime I paid another visit to the American Cathedral just beside us—this time not to pray for the other lawyers and bankers around us or for myself, nor even to converse with my ancient angels and saints, but to light a candle for Mother, who would have loved the notion of a flame alight for her there. The day was slow, and people were thoughtful: "Oh *dorry about or* mother. *Ay zo lay poor sabère." désolé pour ta mère*

At about three I closed the door and took a look at my charts, making the usual comparison with the audiogram, falling like a mountainside, of the deaf ninety-year old whose hearing at virtually every frequency was about 40 decibels better than mine, meaning that most sounds had to contain ten thousand times more energy for me to hear them than for the old gray man. The night before, the French television camera had showed an empty conference room where the G-8 meeting was about to be held, a large room with places for about thirty people around a table. My heart sank. I thought of my promise to Ferrer, a matter of diminishing importance in the light of Melanson's "I believe I am like you," Mother's poem and Claire's words in the dream, which I thought of as her own, though they were just as much my words in Claire's mouth as Cordelia's signs in Gloucester's. It was still the fall, and there was time before the winter settled in.

My phone rang at the end of the day. Jim Kiernan asked whether I might be able to go to Hungary on Monday to help *tired out sub-Hindus Hindus Magyars idduz iron out some issues* that had come up in connection with a construction project in Budapest, a deal in which we were representing the Hungarian Development Authority. I would be briefed when I got there. I agreed and went home early, at about seven o'clock, and we drove out to Mortefontaine with the children. Claire gave me a glass of wine, and I put on some music and thought some more about the charts, Chang, Ferrer, Mother as a lone suppliant, Melanson, lyricals, my heart and pounding head as I unraveled them, the children, the future, the hopelessness. I was determined to work through these issues alone.

On Saturday morning Claire drove down to the stables early and saddled our horse, Atatürk, a retired twenty-year-old racehorse a friend had given her two years before in exchange for our giving Atatürk a happy retirement. Claire's family rented out the stables on the property to an independent manager, but they found a place for Atatürk and lots of room in the open meadows during the day—allowing him a much healthier fate than his namesake, the father of Turkish democracy. I tried to ride Atatürk every weekend I could make it out to Mortefontaine. That morning Claire took him into the forest for about an hour and brought him to me up at the house. As Claire dismounted, I looked into her eyes: happy, not the warning, worried eyes of Claire in the dream. While she held the bridle, smiling, silent (I rode without hearing aids to avoid the clamor of horse and hoofbeat), I put my left foot in the stirrup, lifted myself into the saddle, pulled the reins to the right, and with a *Merci, mon chou*, my dear, trotted off.

As we got to the forest, Atatürk and I moved to a canter, heading south. After five minutes or so, but quite suddenly, he began to gallop, without any signal from me, faster, faster and faster. I tried to pull him up, but you never can when a horse breaks away like that. I had no idea what was spurring him on, or where he wanted to go, but he kept gaining speed, moving now at a dangerous pace for both of us along our two-mile trail leading to the Mortefontaine lake. I looked to my right to see whether I could edge him off the trail, but it was lined with brush and small pine.

When I looked to our left, I saw the source of Atatürk's excitement. A score of deer, led by a large stag, were running beside us, not more than five meters away, an eerily beautiful, silent sight. They were still accelerating, trying to cut across our path to get to the deer path along the shore that led to their usual watering place on the lake's northwestern bank. Each time they did so, Atatürk picked up the pace too, the racer in him refusing to let them get ahead, with no end in sight other than the northeastern shore, now only about two hundred meters away. But at last the stag lowered his antlers and began to cede—to a faltering leg he favored as he lowered his pace. He looked to his right and, raising his head just behind us and still leading the herd, leapt across the bridle path, over the brush, between the trees, and into the woods to take an alternative course, an inland path that led to their destination. Atatürk finally slowed, too, on his own, but only toward the very end, pulling up at the water's edge in a splosh of mud and water as I lunged forward and out of the saddle, managing to grab his neck. When we came to a full stop, I was facing backwards, my head under his chin, one foot around his neck, the other reversed in its stirrup, and my hands clinging to his mane.

Despite the danger it was all wonderful, floating like that in silence, my locusts quieted, hearing nothing but the beauty of the forest flashing by—the pine, the birch, the beech, and the oak—feeling in my breast the horse's muffled hoofbeats and finally those of the racing deer. It occurred to me, as I rode Atatürk back to the stables at a slow trot, both of us breathing heavily, that perhaps the stag had chosen his ultimate, alternate path to remind me, as the dream and my own reflections had the night before, and as Melanson had in New Orleans, of Chang's prophetic words: "Hard to run a race with an ankle always sprained." It was advice that I had shut out from my conscious, lyrically driven mind for almost twenty years.

That afternoon, Claire and I took a long walk around the lake, past the heron, close by, which I could hear with my *oiseaux lyres*, to the chapel in the forest, then back to the house. I said, "Let me be your life," at one point, thinking it a whisper.

"*Quoi?*"

"I'm sorry?"

"You just said, 'Let me be your life.' What do you mean? You are my life."

"God, you have good ears. I meant *you*."

"'You' . . . are you all right?"

"Fine, just thinking. Can you hear the birds?"

"*Et toi?*"

"Yes. We're in the middle of them now. They're beautiful. How hard it would be to live without them."

ON SUNDAY MORNING I CALLED MY COLLEAGUE ANN Baker at home. "I can't go to Budapest tomorrow. Can you?"

"Sure. Is something wrong?"

"Something has come up. It's important. I'd be—"

"Of course I'll go. Don't give it *at all*." *at tall a thall a thought*

I called Jim Kiernan. "Jim, Ann is going to Budapest instead of me."

"What's the matter. Are you all right?"

"Yes. I'm fine. I'll explain it to you tomorrow. Are you free for lunch?"

"I am *out*."

"You are out?"

"No. I am now."

We drove back to Paris that night. I thought of Claire's happy eyes as I had climbed into the saddle the day before. True, she had told me months earlier that my heart or brain would burst if I continued to work as I had. But I had reassured her. Would she support a decision to stop altogether, as she had urged in the dream? I had enough of my wits about me to remember her plea of years before that I never tell her anything troublesome at night—"*toujours le matin*." We both slept well and had an early breakfast. As I put on my jacket to go, I uttered the ritually frightening French words "*J'ai quelque chose à te dire*"—I have something to tell you. She turned white, and I recalled the story she tells of the husband who steps out to buy cigarettes and never comes back. We sat down in the living room, and I told her that I had decided to stop practicing law.

"*Quoi?*"

I set out the reasons and went through the audiograms I put on the table before us. "But how will we live? *De quoi est-ce qu'on va vivre? Et ta carrière, tu es avocat depuis toujours*—you've always been a lawyer and nothing else," she protested again and again.

"I can't do it. I'm too deaf. As you have said yourself, darling, I can't hear—I can't hear words at fifty miles an hour. I don't hear you unless you are as if a part of my eyes and ears, so close, or unless I'm dreaming. I don't hear bells, the phone, the television, movies without subtitles, people in the street, people at home, people in offices, people anywhere, my own children. I don't hear any of them, or much or most of any of them—it depends—until, just as you have said, I figure out what they say. And I can't do it anymore. I have to stop."

"But I was hoping—secretly hoping—there was another way—that perhaps someone could go to your meetings with you and hear for you—"

"That would never work, darling. I can't be—no one can be—half a lawyer."

"You can't do this, Gérald. It will—it will—"

"If I go on, there will come the day *(Don't kill yourself, my boy. Don't kill yourself. For me. For your mother. For some lucky girl!)* when I won't come home, and you'll have to come find me somewhere, in the hospital or worse, with a heart or brain that's given up—"

"OK. OK. OK!"

"I'm sorry, darling. I'm so sorry. I have to go. Just you and I know. I have to tell the firm. I'm having lunch with Jim." I left her there, looking despondent, frozen when I kissed her.

Jim was to come by my office at twelve thirty. At about eleven, the phone rang. Claire was on the brink of tears. I said, *"Mon amour, je suis désolé—"*

"Non, non," she interrupted. *"Je t'appelle pour te dire*—I'm calling to say—*que nous nous débrouillerons d'une façon ou d'une autre."* We'll get along somehow. Claire said she was wholly for what I was about to do. "Please don't think, Gérald," she said, half in French, half in English, her voice trembling, "that there are any echoes of despair, *d'échos de désespoir*, and there never will be." Today her call reminds me of Berthier's reflection on the paths of the deaf: not so long when traveled by two.

Jim and I went to a restaurant nearby, La Fermette Marbeuf, his favorite (though lunches were a rarity for all of us) but an art-deco, glass, metal, and tile acoustic nightmare. But, I thought, as I looked around at all the noise, it doesn't matter anymore.

"This better be good," he said.

"I'm not sure 'good' is the word, Jim. It's far beyond an explanation, and more important than my being in Budapest today and, for that matter, the need that I not be there."

"Not be there—" The waitress came over, "*Bonjour Monsieur Kiernan,*" and as she stood there, he seemed, all at once, to grasp what was coming. It is extraordinary how much can be said with the eyes and how much moments like this one can make you readily understand—words can't do it—their crucial role in both sign language and lyricals.

"*Vous voulez boire quelque chose?*" asked the waitress.

"Uh, yeah," he answered. "Better make it a bottle." We ordered lunch. When the wine came, I took a gulp, put the glass down, and told him it was impossible for me to continue to practice, not because my hearing had become a little worse, but because, I thought, practicing law for me had always—or virtually always—been more or less—or almost, I don't know—impossible. I didn't think clients had suffered, at least not any grave harm, so I guess it wasn't impossible, but the pressure, with huge sums of money at stake, was too great, and it was neither in their interest, the firm's, nor my own, that I go on any further. Thirty years of hell was enough, and I was tired. Very tired, I thought, as I remembered Chang's words. My decision was final, I said. I took the charts out of my jacket pocket and showed them to him, and although to Jim they were Greek, they looked like a stock market crash—in both ears.

I explained that staying with the firm in Paris or New York and simply doing research or writing would be hard to bear after all I had done, or tried to do, however imperfectly. I needed to do something else; I didn't know what. I kept talking, basking in the ease of understanding myself, as he refilled my glass and his, and we got through our lamb chops. He understood it all, of course. The firm's presiding partner, Barry Bryan, who had once also lived, before my time there, in the old house in Paris where I discovered violins and flutes and "Let No One Sleep" ("Nessun dorma") at window-shaking volumes, came over from New York, and when I broke down *(you have no reason to cry in your coop in your soup)*, he put his arms around me as Raymond Chang had done so many years before. Once again the firm, having saved the lawyer who wished he were dead more than twenty years before by sending him to Paris, released him—on generous terms, to a later life.

CHAPTER 25

A SECOND PEACE

M Y FIRST DAYS OF PRIVATE LIFE WERE MARKED BY simple discoveries. In my early morning-to-midnight professional life, I never had occasion to do such routine things as walk about the street in the daytime, browse through a bookstore, or go shopping. Indeed it felt peculiar—I felt guilty—not to be in the office when the sun was out or not long since set. My freedom had been confined to the dead of half-spent nights.

But it was my new encounters in the daylight that proved to be unsettling. When doing errands I would quickly become lost in common exchanges with a grocer, a pharmacist, a dry cleaner. After a while they would see me coming, stiffen a bit while preparing to make exaggerated lip movements, and assure themselves that a pen and notepad lay at hand. When I took a defective printer to a shop for replacement and couldn't make out what the salesman was saying, my son Alexander, age thirteen, finally acted as an icy intermediary, furious with the man when he began to ridicule my failure to understand him. "It's a *U-Back*."

uback you-back two stack a "A 'U-Back'?" "Wrong. A Hewlett Packard—ever heard of them?"

Banks became a risky game when I confused questions about credits and debits, dollars and euros. That exercise was soon performed largely with handwritten notes. In bookstores, the staff go directly to a book they want to suggest and take it off the shelf or table in order to use it as a kind of prop for confirmation and reference. "I was referring to *Cold Mountain*. We still have it. Here it is, right here!" These exchanges were a bit humbling, for I had had no idea how clumsy I could be at the tasks of everyday life. But the real source of my disquiet on such occasions was my mind's racing back to my professional life—my concerns for our clients and misgivings about how I could have done an adequate job as a lawyer over the years amid so much confusion.

But it was time to look forward, not backward, and I set out to learn more about myself and others who heard as I did. Eventually I came to know much about the profoundly deaf as well and to become closely acquainted with the leading schools for the deaf in the United States and France, including Bébian's preeminent National Institute for Deaf Children on the rue Saint Jacques in Paris. Known as Saint Jacques, the school is the birthplace of the methods that launched the profoundly deaf into the written language and broad body of knowledge of the hearing world. Originally a Benedictine monastery, it has been the institutional embodiment of great French teaching since the late eighteenth century.

As I approached the Institute's front gate on one of my first visits, I saw about thirty students gathered outside the ancient building, whose exterior has remained virtually unchanged for the past three hundred years. Hands, faces, arms, and shoulders were moving in animated discussion in several groups of four or five. Though I then knew little sign, I was happy to be among them, with no need for lyricals and lips, relishing the freedom to look at their hands and into their eyes. One student rushed toward me, looked at my hearing aids, and dangled a rubber scorpion under my nose, as if to say, "Sign to us; prove that you're one of us." I jumped, and we all laughed, and the student patted me on the back as I rolled my index finger laterally in front of my mouth, the French sign for a hearing (and speaking) person.

I was greeted by Michelle Balle, the Institute's librarian, who had told me over the telephone that it was in the *inservices inservices intercises interstices* of the history of the profoundly deaf that I would find out more about myself and the partially deaf. When I sat down at the table with the two or three volumes she gave me, I took my hearing aids off and put them on the desk to have absolute quiet, save the locusts, and felt at home. I went to work looking for the in-between things for the rest of the day and, as it would turn out, for whole shelves of time thereafter.

That day was to be the first of well over a thousand days I would spend in that library and others in France, England, and the United States. I met with specialists in the fields of hearing, linguistics, history, biology, and physics in Paris, New York, Boston, Washington, London—everywhere my search would take me. In the historical and scientific literature, and in the words of those I met and corresponded with, I would learn about a world that had hitherto been unknown to me. And it proved to be there, not so much between as in the stitches of the history, that I would find missing parts of myself and an awareness of the extent to which our lyricals, as we struggle to discover the thoughts of others, make the partially deaf a loose end in the commerce of souls.

I studied French sign language in Paris and American Sign Language (ASL) at Gallaudet University in Washington. In a sense, Saint Jacques and Gallaudet are a single institution. Thomas Gallaudet was taught sign by Auguste Bébian and others at Saint Jacques in 1817, and he brought Laurent Clerc back with him to the United States. As a result, Bébian's teaching methods became the cornerstone of deaf education in America. Today when I visit Gallaudet, the world's only university for the deaf, usually once or twice a year, I marvel at its accomplishments. Lectures in history, mathematics, English, the sciences, and other subjects are given in sign in large silent halls. Like their hearing peers, deaf professors use written English (or numbers, equations, formulas) on blackboards or computer screens to illustrate or reinforce points or to put them in context with visual aids.

At a history lecture I attended just last year, the subject was *Marbury v. Madison*, the 1803 case in which the Supreme Court first held that it had the power to declare laws unconstitutional and, using that power, nullified a law that gave the Court itself jurisdiction in the case. The controversy also involved some contentious political issues of the day, notably a dispute between Adams and his successor, Jefferson, over the former's lame-duck political appointments.

"What did the Court decide?" signed the profoundly deaf teacher, William Ennis, in ASL, eyebrows raised, making a kind of double conventional "OK" sign of the hearing, with the right hand, index, and thumb forming a circle, emanating from the forehead, meaning "decide."

"Something," signed one student, carving his left hand with the edge of his right.

"Nothing!" signed another, pursing his lips and rapidly opening the fingers of his hand.

"Something and nothing!" signed another, using both expressions.

"Meaning?" signed Ennis.

"Meaning," signed another student, with collaborative smiles from the first two, now nodding by moving their closed hands up and down from the wrist, like Daniel to me at the League, "that the Court held that the law giving it jurisdiction was no good; so it couldn't act at all, thus extracting itself from the political dispute between Adams and Jefferson. Very nice." The answer was explained to me later, although I caught the last sign, a pleasant smile with the flat right hand smoothly sliding over the palm of the left. Very nice.

Even my celebrated classmate Frances Buttons would have been hard pressed to give as concise an answer. *Marbury* is perhaps the most widely cited case in American judicial history—as standing for at least a thousand inconsistent principles. Ennis took his students through the real issues in the case in a lively give-and-take discussion in sign, noting how the Court dodged the political issue and at the same time established the doctrine of judicial review. The session was much like my classes at law school except that, here, using my vague memory of the case, a smattering of sign, and Ennis's occasional pointing to words on his screen, I grasped the issues more rapidly than when I was struggling with *misbetorpant* (*more important*) and *dinteck* (*didn't check*) in the oral discussion of *New York Times v. Sullivan*. I suspect that the faculty and students at Gallaudet, like most of their peers elsewhere, are relatively unaware of where the methods they have learned and teach came from, or, historically, how their forebears came to possess the extraordinary skills they themselves now enjoy. But they are sitting in Bébian's classroom.

When I take sign language courses with other hearing students in Paris, or at Gallaudet, given exclusively in sign by deaf teachers, I feel at home, an equal learning a new language. But in a neighboring Paris café, or in the cafeteria of Gallaudet itself, amid the clatter of dishes, glasses, and silver, the distractions, and the turning heads, interrupted words, and laughter of others, I am not fully a part of their world. Their conversations are not mine. I'm sorry. *Je suis désolé.* What was that? *Comment?* Could you please repeat? *Pourriez-vous vous répéter?* I can hear people nearby if they're looking at me, I explain—it's the distance, the noise, and the lips. And I feel like an exile, even at Gallaudet, not able to turn to a neighboring table of the signing deaf, where, were I able to master their language, I would at these moments immediately have belonged. I am not saddened on these occasions—they are simply a reminder of my belonging to both worlds. But they do elicit a fear that my lot in the dining rooms will be the plight of implanted children born profoundly deaf, not just in noisy environments but in everyday life, far worse off with their devices than I with my *oiseaux lyres*.

"Picture a classroom," as Bébian loved to say, for a picture is worth a thousand words, a thousand signs, a thousand surveys of the deaf. Picture a debate about politics, language, history, science—the subject of your choice. On the right, you have a seated panel of five unimplanted men and women, deaf since birth. On the left, you have five people, born profoundly deaf and fitted with cochlear implants. Behind each is an interpreter, signing what the implanted are saying or saying what the unimplanted deaf are signing. On one side, you will have thorough and lively conversation, laughter, a complete understanding of all the ideas of everyone in the room. On the other, you will see a struggle for the lips of both their fellow panelists and of the interpreters, an effort to make sense of their speech, to capture the rapid and fleeting ideas of everyone as they pass them by.

In such a scene, I would be working with the vowels I can hear to find the consonants and missing vowels, the missing ideas to which my lyricals may ultimately lead me. The signing deaf will go home from this debate ever engaged, aware of what has gone on, what has been said to and around them, happy and complete. The implanted deaf, I fear, will go home tentative, uncertain of what they heard and of the words to come, tonight and tomorrow. I will go home reminded both of my earlier life and of my newfound freedom.

Still, I have found ways to be very much a part of the hearing world. I've been an active draftsman in legal proceedings involving human rights issues that I think are important to all of us. I am president of an American foundation that originally built (almost a century ago) and continues to support a large children's hospital in France. Though I preside at the annual board and members' meetings, others keep the minutes and pass me notes or repeat, close by, the secrets that fly about the room, keeping me in the community of souls in my own language.

As to my life in general, my imperfect windows into the thoughts of others are now unconstrained by the demands of complex negotiations. Partial deafness, lyricals, and hearing aids in the world of law and business are not violent in any physical sense, but the relentless struggle day in, day out, year after year, decade after decade, to undo riddles requires unforgiving constant attention, a kind of forced sleeplessness, a demand that you *know* and that, if you don't, that you *learn* the meaning of endless mysteries.

My entire life has not become a confusion of lyricals, as Melanson had feared, but they remain an indispensable part of it. I also live in a musical world, in composing simple pieces for strings and piano; singing, alone or with others; and playing the piano as I have all my life. And on lazy days, in a life that Claire had finally wished for and has now made a reality, I listen with my *oiseaux lyres*, with the world growing quieter still, to the unambiguous lyrical messages of the natural world around us in the company of those I love, of those who have become my mornings, afternoons, and evenings and who have transformed my lyricals at last into music, a song of a second peace.

ACKNOWLEDGMENTS

I EXTEND MY PROFOUND THANKS AND APPRECIATION TO THE following individuals and institutions: to Antonia Fraser, Louis Begley, and Andrew Solomon, for reading portions of the manuscript and providing their enthusiastic encouragement and support; to Professor Harlan Lane for reading the entire manuscript and providing invaluable guidance, from the very beginning, on the history of the deaf and other critical issues; to Professor Stephen R. Anderson of Yale University for reviewing the manuscript and for his insight and advice on linguistics, and for identifying the world of lyricals as one that will engender new research into our theories of language; to Laure de Gramont for her thoughtful and generous advice on how to bring the book to fruition.

To Michelle Balle, Chief Librarian at the *Institut National de Jeunes Sourds* in Paris, for her constant guidance throughout the period of my research; to the faculty, students, and library staff at Gallaudet University, including Professor William T. Ennis, Dennis Berrigan of Gallaudet's Kendall School, and Robert McConnell, President emeritus of Gallaudet's student government; as well as, for their patience with and tolerance of a poor student, to my sign language teachers at Gallaudet and at the school of the International Visual Theatre in Paris.

To Dr. A. James Hudspeth of Rockefeller University for improving and correcting my layman's account of the physiology of the ear and the cochlea; to Dr. Richard H. Masland, Dr. Donald K. Eddington, Dr. Joseph B. Nadol, and other members of the staff of the Massachusetts Eye and Ear Infirmary for their generous time in interviews relating to hearing, the ear, and cochlear implants; to Bertrand Duplantier of the Institute of Theoretical Physics (Saclay) and to Dr. Nicholas C. Spitzer of the University of California at San Diego for their advice on issues concerning the physics of sound, and, for his generous advice on questions of physics from the outset, to Dr. John M. Evans. The inevitable errors in the book are and remain, of course, mine alone.

Thanks are due as well to my illustrious teachers and mentors over the years for their personal guidance and support, including Joshua L. Miner III, Robert W. Sides, Dudley Fitts, and Thomas L. Hankins at Phillips Academy, Andover; Professors Jacques Guicharnaud, Victor Brombert, and Franklin L. Baumer at Yale; and Professors Julius Goebel Jr., John N. Hazard, Telford Taylor, and Curtis J. Berger at Columbia Law School. In a number of instances in the book, names of individuals and of corporate and other entities, and transactional and other facts and circumstances, have been changed to protect relationships and client confidentiality.

I offer my profound thanks to my many hearing doctors over the years, notably to my physician for the past twenty-five years, Dr. Gérald Fain in Paris, and to my colleagues at the bar and in the corporate world, particularly for their support and encouragement at difficult times, including George N. Lindsay, Oscar M. Ruebhausen, Harold H. Healy Jr., Edward A. Perell, Barry R. Bryan, Andrew L. Sommer, J. Edward Fowler, H. Francis Shattuck Jr., and, in particular for their warmth and continuing friendship in later years as well, William B. Matteson, Robert B. von Mehren, Meredith M. Brown, and C. Lawson Willard III, all of the New York bar; and, with particular affection, to Lucio A. Noto for his unfailing guidance to and constructive remonstrance and tolerance of his struggling advisor and coadjutor.

I am especially grateful to Merloyd Lawrence, my editor and publisher, for the extraordinary talent she has brought to bear in shaping the book and improving the quality of writing; and to my literary agent, Michael Strong, for his confidence and guidance, practical and editorial, from the very beginning, as well as to his talented colleagues, Markus Hoffmann and Joe Regal.

Foremost and finally, I express my deepest thanks to and affection for my wife, Claire, for her selfless love and support under every circumstance, not limited to her enduring my endless hours late at night and into the early mornings at the office—or away in distant hotel rooms—translating my lawyer's lyricals of the day and preparing for those of days to come, and for her suffering, in later years, my long labors over the book itself; and, for their unremitting filial affection, I express my deepest thanks to and affection for our sons, Sebastian and Alexander, and my stepdaughter, Pénélope. My warmest thanks to her husband, Theo Steward-Stand, as well as to Perseus Books, for their able work on the graphic design of the book. My thanks as well to Jonathan Sainsbury for his imaginative design of the book cover. My debt to many other individuals is expressed, of course, in the text of *Song without Words* itself. I am unable to thank in this small space allotted the many others who have contributed to the making of the book, so I thank each of you here collectively, with my apologies and a promise to express my appreciation another day.

FURTHER READING

WHETHER WE HEAR WELL OR NOT, TO READ OF THE DEAF is to read about ourselves. We are all engaged in a search for language, whether as listeners, speakers, signers, or writers. In the introductory bibliography below I have included a few works that might serve as an introduction to the subjects explored in *Song without Words*.

A perceptive and moving book on the partially deaf is Vikram Seth's novel, *An Equal Music*. His heroine, a pianist losing her hearing, lives increasingly in what Seth calls the mixed world of heard, misheard, and imagined sound—my world of lyricals. David Lodge's *Deaf Sentence* is an enlightening, often amusing account of a teacher's coping with his partial deafness. On lipreading, the first half of David Wright's *Deafness* offers a vivid portrait of his struggles with misheard (mostly unheard) words. On the technical aspects of lipreading, Ruth Campbell's *Hearing by Eye* is a place to begin.

Much can be found on the web on a variety of hearing and language issues addressed in *Song without Words*, and I have not enumerated them here. I have included a few helpful works on the physiology of the ear. The place to start is *Promenade 'round the Cochlea* at www.cochlea.org, which takes the reader on a virtual tour of the outer, middle, and inner ear. William A. Yost's *Fundamentals of Hearing* is an excellent study of sound, the ear, hearing, perception, and our central auditory nervous

system. An important but technical book on the problems of the inner ear is *Cochlear Hearing Loss* by Brian C. J. Moore of the University of Cambridge. Bill Habets's *The Tinnitus Handbook* is a useful book on the problem of this common affliction of the deaf.

A reader interested in exploring the world of the profoundly deaf and sign language should begin with Harlan Lane's history, *When the Mind Hears*, which traces their struggle from the Middle Ages to the beginning of the twentieth century. I have also listed below for both readers and scholars a few leading works on deaf education at the time and place of its origin: Paris in the early nineteenth century. Auguste Bébian was perhaps history's greatest teacher of the deaf and an extraordinarily talented writer as well. Although most of his work has not yet been translated, Harlan Lane extensively discusses his work in his history and has included extracts of Bébian's writing, as well as that of the great contemporary deaf teacher, Ferdinand Berthier, and others in Lane's *The Deaf Experience*.

The bibliography includes the well-known works on or by Helen Keller, and also Thomas Cutsforth's provocative *The Blind in School and Society*, which provides a devastating portrait of Helen's loss of her language and identity. A few interesting papers on Helen may be found in the library of the Perkins School for the Blind in Watertown, Massachusetts, though many of the records concerning her relationship with the school and with Anne Sullivan appear to have been lost or destroyed.

For an understanding of the structure of sign language, William Stokoe's 1960 paper, *Sign Language Structure*, is the seminal work of the twentieth century, though many of his ideas are based on the writings of Bébian. Stokoe's prose is inartful at times, but his important paper in effect revived the use of sign language at deaf teaching institutions after its virtual disappearance for almost a century. *The Signs of Language* by Edward Klima and Ursula Bellugi is easier going, and Oliver Sacks's *Seeing Voices* is a pleasure to read. Laura Ann Petitto, et al., in "Speech-Like Cerebral Activity in Profoundly Deaf People Processing Signed Languages," provide a fascinating account of how the brain functions in virtually identical fashion when hearing and partially deaf people listen and speak, and profoundly deaf people analyze and express sign language. The work of Klima and Bellugi has been groundbreaking in this area as well (see Gregory Hickok, Ursula Bellugi, and Edward S. Klima, "Sign Language in the Brain").

The debates between Edward Gallaudet and Alexander Graham Bell, held before a British Royal Commission in the 1880s, constitute the most extensive account, during the century-old conflict I call the Hundred Years War, of the opposing ideas of the advocates of oral education and the proponents of sign language. More modern advocates of oral education include Bonnie Tucker, David Wright, Michael Chorost, and others, all included below. For a moving, persuasive, and eloquently written exposition on the importance of sign language to a deaf child, see Emmanuelle Laborit's memoir, *The Cry of the Gull*.

Noam Chomsky's *Syntactic Structures* is a leading work on the human language faculty. Chomsky is complex, and to gain a broader understanding of linguistics first, the reader might try Bruce M. Rowe and Diane P. Levine, *A Concise Introduction to Linguistics*. For an intriguing exchange between Chomsky and William Stokoe on the language faculty, see Jane Maher's *Seeing Language in Sign*.

There is an extensive and often contentious literature on cochlear implants, a not inconsiderable amount of which is financed by the manufacturers themselves. For a partially deaf writer who sees in implants the virtual death knell of sign language, see Michael Chorost, *Rebuilt*. Marc Marschark presents a broader and more considered view in his *Raising and Educating a Deaf Child*.

The Partially Deaf

Gemma A. Calvert, et al., "Activation of Auditory Cortex during Silent Lipreading," *Science* 276, no. 5312 (April 1997): 593–596.

Ruth Campbell, ed., et al., *Hearing by Eye II: Advances in the Psychology of Speechreading and Auditory-Visual Speech* (Hove, England: Psychology Press Ltd., 1998).

Bill Habets, *The Tinnitus Handbook* (Encinitas, CA: United Research Publishers, 2002).

Henry Kisor, *What's That Pig Outdoors* (New York: Penguin Books, 1990; First University of Illinois Press Paperback, 2010).

David Lodge, *Deaf Sentence* (London: Random House, 2008).

Brian C. J. Moore, *Cochlear Hearing Loss: Physiological, Psychological and Technical Issues*, 2nd ed. (Chichester, England: John Wiley & Sons Ltd., 2007).

———. *An Introduction to the Psychology of Hearing*, 5th ed. (London: Elsevier Academic Press, 2004).

Vikram Seth, *An Equal Music* (London: Phoenix House, 1999).

Maynard Solomon, *Beethoven* (New York: Schirmer Trade Books, 2001).

Barbara Stenross, *Missed Connections* (Philadelphia: Temple University Press, 1999).

Josh Swiller, *The Unheard* (New York: Henry Holt, 2007).

David Wright, *Deafness* (London: Faber and Faber, 1969, 1990).

Physiology (Ear, Cochlea, Brain)

Promenade 'round the Cochlea, www.cochlea.org.

Georg von Bekesy, *Experiments in Hearing* (New York: McGraw-Hill, 1960).

Hans Engstrom, Harlow W. Ades, and Anton Andersson, *Structural Pattern of the Organ of Corti* (Stockholm: Almqvist & Wiksell, 1966).

C. Daniel Geisler, *From Sound to Synapse* (New York: Oxford University Press, 1998).

Gregory Hickok, Ursula Bellugi, and Edward S. Klima, "Sign Language in the Brain," *Scientific American* (June 2001).

James M. Hillenbrand, *Auditory Physiology* (unpublished manuscript; Kalamazoo: Western Michigan University, 2009).

A. James Hudspeth, "How the Ear's Works Work," *Nature* (October 1989): 397–404.

Laura Ann Petitto, et al., "Speech-like Cerebral Activity in Profoundly Deaf People Processing Signed Languages: Implications for the Neural Basis of Human Language," *PNAS* 97, no. 25 (December 5, 2000): 13961–13966.

William A. Yost, *Fundamentals of Hearing: An Introduction*, 5th ed. (London: Elsevier Academic Press, 2007).

Deaf History

Douglas C. Baynton, *Forbidden Signs* (Chicago: University of Chicago Press, 1996).

Roch-Ambroise Auguste Bébian, *Essai sur les sourds-muets et sur le langage naturel, ou introduction à une classification naturelle des idées avec leurs signes propres (An Essay on the Deaf and Their Natural Language, or An Introduction to the Natural Relationship between Ideas and the Signs That Express Them)* (Paris: Dentu, 1817).

———. *Manuel d'enseignement pratique des sourds-muets (A Practical Manual for Teaching the Deaf)* (Paris: Mequignon l'aine, 1827).

Ferdinand Berthier, *Les sourds-muets avant et depuis l'abbé de l'Épée (The Deaf Before and Since the Abbé de l'Épée)* (Paris: Ledoyen, 1840).

Harlan Lane, *When the Mind Hears* (New York: Vintage Books, 1989).
———, ed., *The Deaf Experience* (Cambridge: Harvard University Press, 1984; Washington, DC: Gallaudet University Press, 2006).

Helen Keller

Thomas D. Cutsforth, *The Blind in School and Society* (New York: American Foundation for the Blind, 1951, 1972).
David Hall (attrib.), *Miss Sullivan's Methods* (unpublished manuscript; Perkins School for the Blind Library, 1905[?]).
Dorothy Herrmann, *Helen Keller: A Life* (Chicago: University of Chicago Press, 1998, 1999, 2007).
Helen Keller, *The Story of My Life (with supplementary accounts by Anne Sullivan, her teacher, and John Albert Macy)* (New York: W. W. Norton, 1903, 2003, 2004).
Joseph P. Lash, *Helen and Teacher* (Reading, MA: Addison-Wesley/Merloyd Lawrence, 1980).

Sign Language

Leah Hager Cohen, *Train Go Sorry* (New York: Houghton Mifflin, 1994).
Margalit Fox, *Talking Hands* (New York: Simon & Schuster, 2007).
Edward S. Klima and Ursula Bellugi, *The Signs of Language* (Cambridge: Harvard University Press, 1979).
Jane Maher, *Seeing Language in Sign: The Work of William C. Stokoe* (Washington, DC: Gallaudet University Press, 1996).
Oliver Sacks, *Seeing Voices* (Berkeley: University of California Press, 1989; New York: Harper Perennial, 1990; New York: Vintage Books, 2000).
William C. Stokoe, *Sign Language Structure: An Outline of the Visual Communication Systems of the American Deaf*, University of Buffalo, Studies in Linguistics, Occasional Papers No. 8, 1960, available at www.oxfordjournals.org.

Sign Language vs. Oral Education

Alexander Graham Bell, *The Question of Sign-Language and the Utility of Signs in the Instruction of the Deaf* (Washington, DC: Sanders Printing Office, 1898).
———. "Upon the Formation of a Deaf Variety of the Human Race," unpublished paper presented to the National Academy of Sciences in New Haven, Connecticut, on November 13, 1883.

Emmanuelle Laborit, *Le Cri de la Mouette* (Paris: Robert Laffont, 1993); translated by P. R. Côté and C. M. Mitchell and published in English as *The Cry of the Gull* (Washington, DC: Gallaudet University Press, 1989, 1999).

Harlan Lane, *The Mask of Benevolence* (New York: Alfred A. Knopf, 1992; Vintage Books, 1993).

Royal Commission of the United Kingdom on the Condition of the Blind, the Deaf and Dumb, etc., Washington, DC: Volta Bureau, 1892.

Bonnie P. Tucker, *The Feel of Silence* (Philadelphia: Temple University Press, 1995).

Linguistics

Noam Chomsky, *Syntactic Structures*, 2nd ed. (Berlin: Mouton de Gruyter, 1957, 2002).

Bruce M. Rowe and Diane P. Levine, *A Concise Introduction to Linguistics*, 3rd ed. (Upper Saddle River, NJ: Prentice Hall, 2012).

Cochlear Implants

Michael Chorost, *Rebuilt* (New York: Mariner, 2006).

Graeme Clark, *Sounds from Silence* (St. Leonards, New South Wales: Allen & Unwin, 2000).

Marc Marschark, *Raising and Educating a Deaf Child* (New York: Oxford University Press, 2007).

B. C. Papsin and K. A. Gordon, "Cochlear Implants for Children with Severe-to-Profound Hearing Loss," *New England Journal of Medicine* 357 (2007): 2380–2387.

Arlene Romoff, *Hear Again* (New York: League for the Hard of Hearing Publications, 1999).

INDEX

ABOUT THE AUTHOR

GERALD SHEA has lived most of his life in New York and in Paris, and practiced law in both cities for many years with Debevoise & Plimpton as a member of the New York and Paris bars. While at Phillips Academy he studied with Dudley Fitts and at Yale with Maynard Mack and Robert Penn Warren. At Columbia Law School he was a Harlan Fiske Stone Scholar, was awarded the Jerome Michael Scholarship for Academic Excellence, and clerked for Professor Julius Goebel Jr., the preeminent legal historian of our time. He has published internationally in legal and financial journals but this is his first work for a general audience. He and his wife, Claire de Gramont, live in Paris and Morte-fontaine, France, and spend summers on the North Shore of Massachusetts.